CLIMATE SENSE

Changing the Way We Think & Feel About Our Planetary Crisis

by Zhiwa Woodbury, M.A., J.D.

(c) 2016

D1414023

TABLE OF CONTENTS

PROLOGUE

"Personal transformation can and does have global effects. As we go, so goes the world, for the world is us. The revolution that will save the world is ultimately a personal one."

~ Marianne Williamson

This book is a *Clarion Call to Awakening,* reaching out to all the hearts and minds of all the people who are rightly concerned about the future of life on Planet Earth. The time has come for us to rise up in response to the existential challenge we are facing - for our children's and their children's sake, and for the sake of all sentient beings living in the world today.

The premise of this book is quite simple. The Climate Crisis we face is not an environmental problem, and there is no environmental solution. It is not a political issue, and there will be no *timely* political solutions forthcoming. It is certainly a moral issue, as recognized by Pope Francis, and every religion should treat it as such. But given the deep psychological roots of our behavior, moralizing about climate change is also not the solution. No, this is a crisis of spirit, a crisis in relationship, raising the question who we humans really are. We can think of it as a kind of collective identity crisis - one that will only be resolved when a critical mass of human beings heal the split between our Psyche, or collective soul, and nature, the soul of the world.

Fortunately for us, though it's tendrils sink deep into the fields of human endeavor, this split is still of relatively recent origin. As you will see in these pages, it can actually be traced back to the splitting of the atom in 1945, which involved humans taking over the reigns of nature and which triggered a seismic shift in the human psyche itself - a splitting apart that we have yet to fully acknowledge and come to grips with. This disruption in our Psyche manifested as a new way of life, the so-called "modern" (or atomic) age, and coincided with the emergence of the nuclear family inhabiting a materialistic, hyper-consumer culture that was seductively labeled *The American Dream…*

In gaining mastery over nature, asserting unimaginable control over the very forces of creation and destruction, we seem to have severed our connection to nature *at its very root*, objectifying the Earth and each other, commodifying our lives, designing artificial living environments called suburbs, and creating an entirely new, virtual reality to soothe our aching souls. In the process, we unintentionally isolated ourselves from our own true nature as earthlings - *creatures of the Earth.* We created a social and cultural matrix of isolation, and then we proceeded to act out this story of separation, objectification, commodification, and alienation in increasingly harmful ways, until now we are unraveling the very fabric of life and assaulting the global ecosystem that has nourished and supported us, and all beings, since beginningless time.

Why have we subconsciously externalized this fundamental split between Psyche and nature in such alarming ways? Because it is an untenable situation. Because we as a species cannot exist apart from our mother for very long. This is called *'Ecopsychology'* - the psychology of placing humans back in their natural "being" state, as earthlings. Ecopsychology is a shared social and cultural undertaking that humanizes psychology by recognizing that we, too, are part of nature and - just as critically - nature is a part of us. They cannot be split up and analyzed separately. That has been the fundamental error of Western psychology. Ecopsychology is the necessary corrective for our climate in crisis, the final piece of the puzzle that can lead us back to a natural state of wholeness and balance.

Make no mistake - this crisis is calling us home. It is nature's way of awakening us from this deluded dream - so that we may reintegrate our *selves* with our world, our human nature.

From the perspective of Americans of European descent, we who have dominated this culture for so long and have largely defined the dominant global culture of subjugation and consumption, this split from the natural world and from our own human nature was admittedly the end of a long and inglorious path. I do not mean to naively suggest that we only recently left 'the Garden.' Far from it! We had already long been on this crazy path of manifest destiny, of man *against* nature rather than *in* or *with* nature, before we successfully split the atom. What was 'achieved' in the Trinity Test over the white sands of New Mexico was the *culmination* of that wayward path.

This unhealthy split actually goes all the way back to Rene Descartes - "I think, therefore I am" - and it only kept picking up steam throughout the feverish pursuit of riches in this, the 'new world.' That locomotive force of ignorance and greed rolled right over and through the ancient inhabitants of this new world, and quickly laid waste to the natural abundance that they had been caretakers of for millennia. Certainly it would be difficult to imagine a more traumatic war against nature than the genocide that Europeans visited on the Earth-based cultures of the indigenous tribes of Turtle Island, or a more heart-breaking ecocide than reducing the dominant species here when we landed, the majestic and socially developed American Buffalo, *bison bison*, from 60 million to fewer than 6000 today - a thousand-fold reduction via slaughter.

Nevertheless, this book is by design ethno- and Euro-centric, because the fact of the matter is that it is our culture that has become the planet's problem, a chronic dis-ease that has spread across the globe, gobbling up species and habitat at an alarming rate. And it is this culture that now demands a cure before it lays waste to the entire biosphere. Since the traumatic culmination of this long path away from nature, with all its terrible consequences, happened in very recent memory, it can still be called up in our collective consciousness and healed.

As the Pulitzer prize winning poet James Agee noted in TIME magazine at the end of WWII, splitting the atom brought us "inescapably into a new age in which all thoughts and things were split." While we see the result in the extreme polarization of society, this split is not irreparable, we humans are not irredeemable, and the truth and reconciliation process that needs to happen is not all that complicated. To become whole again, to restore the *natural* part of 'human nature,' requires only that we hear the deafening call of the natural world, and recognize that something is terribly amiss within, as well - as reflected without. Only then can we actively engage in a concerted, conscientious effort to heal the psychic wound we can all still feel in our hearts whenever we stop numbing ourselves to the dreadful pain inherent in our present predicament.

This book is an attempt to facilitate the *individual* process that needs to be undertaken for each of us to heal, and for all of us to awaken to our incredible human potential, in direct response to the greatest crisis we have ever faced. *Because that is what we do.* That is what makes us human. We rise to the occasion no matter how long the odds. We never give up.

While it would be lovely if we would all awaken together, the truth of the matter is that we can only do this one mind at a time. No one will lead us out of this crisis to some new promised land. We will only emerge from the climate crisis by taking responsibility for it upon ourselves -- by assuming authority for our own psychological state of well being, and by reconnecting to this amazing planet through our own very personal connections to the natural world - no matter where we live - and to our collective psyche, which will look different for each one of us.

That's how it will work. And it must work. We will make it work.

Just before his passing in 1975, noted British historian Arnold Toynbee cautioned us that the "present threat to mankind's survival can be removed *only by a revolutionary change of heart in individual human beings*" - a sentiment now echoed by Pope Francis, and before him by our wise American elder, the psychotherapist, mythologist, and teacher Ralph Metzner:

> *It is in the hearts and minds of human beings that the causes and cures of the ecocatastrophe are to be found.*

There is a school of thought that the true religion of America today is self-help psychology, and that all mythology is individual now. I think there is some real merit to these ideas. I have great faith in our ability to heal through our relations. Mainstream psychology has largely failed us, however, by creating an industry that is too wedded to scientific materialism and Western medicine (and thus the pharmaceutical industry), perpetuating our problems by profitably treating their symptoms without ever getting to the root dis-ease of our culture.

In response to this institutional inertia, Ecopsychology seeks not just to reform psychology, but to displace it. We do this by acknowledging and elevating a natural phenomenon that is both ancient and radically subversive to consumer culture - the *spiritual* connection between human beings and the living planet. In the recent past, such talk has been subject to ridicule. But what is perhaps most notable about this natural phenomenon in the modern context is that it has now been effectively proven by the equally subversive modern science - quantum physics - *precisely* at the time when we of the dominant culture are most in need of recovering that inner-dependent and inter-penetrating connection.

We are 'one flesh,' as the influential Ecopsychologist Andy Fisher puts it, by our very nature inseparable from nature. And so we also are all afflicted by the same mental illness, like a viral strain of deluded awareness. It does little good to mask the symptoms with spirit-numbing drugs, the dehumanizing approach of modern medicine. The aim of Ecopsychology is not to isolate individuals and treat them as identical with their pathology, but rather to awaken us to our true nature and transform society in the process - thus averting (un)natural catastrophe to whatever extent we can. In other words, it is a form of *psychosocial activism* on behalf of the natural world; or, as Dr. Fisher puts it, "psychology in the service of life." That is actually considered radical!

After a lifetime of advocating for wildlife and wild places in courtrooms, I am now forced by circumstance to advocate for mother nature herself in the court of public opinion and social media, as part of an epic struggle many are waging over the heart and soul of humanity - a battle in which my country and my culture happens to be ground zero. The American Dream has become the natural world's worst nightmare. We must rouse ourselves from this suicidal slumber…

As one of my long-time teachers likes to say, "the workshop is the mind." This book is intended to be a catalyst for psychological catharsis that takes place in the reader's mind. Catharsis refers to "*a psychological technique used to relieve tension and anxiety by bringing repressed feelings and fears to consciousness.*" That is my promise to you. The process of reading this book is itself intended to induce a kind of "climate catharsis," leading to a heightened climate sense. I myself experienced this in the writing of the paper that led to this book, and have since confirmed that the ideas set forth here can readily have this same psychological impact on you.

Over the course of our lives, we have all repressed natural feelings of grief over our lost connection to nature herself, our true nature, and we all harbor deep fears as a result. When we get in touch with these feelings and fears, there is a tremendous release of tension, anxiety, and depression. If we have an appropriate spiritual container for processing this natural grief, then we will be transformed by the expression of our repressed grief. We will have greater joy. So…

Do not be afraid.

By acknowledging the losses we have experienced in relation to nature, by embracing our fears and seeing them as intelligent guides along our spiritual path, we have nothing more to lose, really, and everything in the world to gain. Awakening from the nightmare that has been mis-labeled the American Dream does not happen in everyone all at once by some miracle. And yet, *it is already happening* -- one by one. After you read this book, you will no longer be heard to ask meekly "What can I as one person do about the climate crisis?" In fact, you will be able to answer others when they ask this same question.

Who knows, maybe you will be the one whose awakening brings about critical mass, at which point we'll call it a social awakening. But it doesn't really matter whose awakening brings us to critical mass, because once awakened the illusion of separation itself fades. Then we know what to do without being asked, without being led. So, as the Christian Goddess *Pistis Sophia* herself urges us in the psalm "Thunder, Perfect Mind":

Awaken and remember…

CHAPTER 1

The Banality of Climate Change

"The problem with most people is that they cannot believe something will happen until it already has. It's not stupidity or weakness -- its just human nature."

~ from the movie *World War Z*

You are not *to blame...*

Allow that to sink in for just a moment. It is imperative that we begin right here.

In spite of everything that you have heard, I can assure you by the very fact that you have picked up this book, the climate... crisis... is... not... your... fault.

Nor is it "their" fault. As difficult as it is for me, a life-long eco-activist, not to lay blame at the feet of the politicians for this travesty - this desecration of all that we hold sacred - in the final analysis there can be no "other" when it comes to how we choose to see this most unfortunate turn of events on planet Earth.

Make no mistake -- *how we as individuals and as a society choose to view this existential crisis is what will determine and help shape its outcome.*

Which is why this may well end up being the most important book you will ever read. Knowing how that might sound, allow me to explain. There are plenty of good books out there on the psychology of the climate crisis, and it isn't my intention to diminish their importance. The difference with this book is that it is specifically written not just to address how we think about the climate crisis, or why we think the way we do, but also as active therapy. Each chapter of this book is a session on the couch, so that by the end you will be transformed not just in how you think about the climate crisis, but in how you feel about it and about others, and how you relate to the planet. In other words, reading this book is 'eco-therapy.'

I want to assure you at the outset that I am not a charlatan, not in this for money or fame. So please, as soon as you finish this book, pass it on to someone just outside of your circle of influence. If enough of us hear and absorb the messages that I have gathered together between these covers, and more critically, if enough of us do the psychological processing that this book is designed to induce, together we *will* transform this immense adversity into the greatest story that will ever be told. That is my promise to you, to your children, and to their children.

All that is required of you is all that is required of any of us at this transformative time in the history of the planet we have come to dominate -- *to face and embrace your fears.* And not just any fears, either. Your *worst* fears.

(Oh, is *that* all...)

It is the only way to conquer fear. Even better, though, we will convert our worst fears into our most important allies. As you have no doubt experienced at one time or another in your life, there is a tremendous power potential that can be unleashed by fear. Our political leaders have been preying on our fears for too long now, and it is time for us to take ownership of this internal fortress, to liberate ourselves from their nefarious rule by harnessing and mastering this reservoir of untapped potential energy.

Our path to planetary rebirth is paved with fear. It underlies all our denial - and we are *all* in denial when it comes to climate change. The very term embodies that denial. *Change? Really?? Like the weather changes?* These unacknowledged fears feed our depression, and if allowed to fester in our unconscious mind, they will eventually drown us in a sea of despair. But there is a great secret in all this that makes it a lot less intimidating. Like the darkness which is now consuming our world, *fear cannot withstand the light*. In this case, that bright light shines forth in the form of simple awareness. In politics, information is power. But when it comes to the climate crisis, awareness is where our power lies. Please do not underestimate it.

Consider that the only power fear has is in its unacknowledged state. As psychologists have appreciated for sometime now, our actions are largely controlled by our shadow selves, and our shadow selves are shaped by our unacknowledged fears. By acknowledging, confronting, and processing these fears, through awareness we emerge from the self-imposed darkness, into the light, and in the warm glow of that light, we human beings can do anything we put our minds to. Thus, in every emergency, there is the potential for *emergence* into some transformed state of being. That is the latent, unlimited power of awareness.

But paralyzed by fear, we will surely perish.

So listen...

It wasn't so much great evil that perpetrated the Holocaust as it was great fear. That was the startling revelation Hannah Arendt made in covering Adolph Eichman's war crimes trial - what she famously called "the banality of evil." There is much we can learn from Arendt today as we begin to face up to what promises to be one of the greatest "evils" ever perpetrated on our planet.

I use the adjective "evil" here in the sense of being 'characterized or accompanied by misfortune or suffering; unfortunate; disastrous.' Whereas Hitler's gas chambers were targeted at certain people and confined to horrific concentration camps, we are now *inhabiting* a (greenhouse) gas chamber of our own making, and its early victims are being determined largely by geography (e.g., Africa), class (mobility), and species (50-200 going extinct every day, versus a natural extinction rate of one every few days or weeks).

Long term, this unnatural phenomena will end up causing the deaths of many more humans than were lost in the Holocaust. We are likely talking *hundreds* of holocausts here, and likely within the span of a single lifetime. Already, the World Health Organization estimates more than a holocaust's worth of people (7 million) die every couple of years from fossil fuel combustion across this planet. How's THAT for a censured story?!

One of the leading political thinkers of the twentieth century, and author of the seminal work *The Origins of Totalitarianism* (1951), Hannah Arendt became infamous for her controversial coverage of the 1961 trial of Eichman - 'the man in the glass cage.' Arendt, a German Jew forced to flee Nazis twice herself, was aghast at how someone as mediocre as Eichman could be responsible for something as monstrous as shipping Jews by boxcar to concentration camps for swift elimination. In commenting on Eichman's apparent inability to think critically about what he was doing, Arendt speaks forcefully to us from her grave about our own complicity in the climate crisis:

> Clichés, stock phrases, adherence to conventional, standardized codes of expression and conduct have the socially recognized function of *protecting us against reality,* that is, against the claim on our thinking attention that all events and facts make by virtue of their existence.[1]

What could be more standardized in America today, more '*American*' really, than driving sport utility vehicles and oversized trucks, maximizing our income, shopping at strip malls and box stores, eating meat and processed foods, often from fast-food restaurants, drinking bottled water, and frittering away whatever discretionary time we have left with relatively meaningless distractions like reality (voyeuristic) tv, *YouTube, Twitter* and *Facebook*?

When challenged to consider the *consequences* of our chosen lifestyles, to think critically for ourselves, we typically respond with socially acceptable clichés and stock phrases, along the lines of "I'm just one person," "you only live once ('YOLO')," "just trying to get by," the ever-popular "lighten up, dude" or "whatEVer," and perhaps the most cynical and empty of all cliches, "it is what it is." After all, if everyone is equally responsible, as myopically appears to be the case with climate change, then *nobody* is really culpable - practically a textbook definition of 'banality' (e.g., 'commonplace'). This deplorable situation cries out for compassion and understanding, not condemnation and cynicism. Nobody **wants** this!

I used to subscribe to the blame game myself, but rather than affixing it to any one individual I'd tend to blame entire segments of society. I was dumbfounded by this inexplicable phenomenon: individually, every human I have ever gotten to know at more than a superficial level has a good heart and means well; but collectively, we are capable of the most heinous actions, such as electing dangerous demagogues or poisoning the entire planet. Then one time I was on a spiritual retreat, and our teacher asked us to think about blame. After some silent contemplation, we got into small groups, and I shared my puzzlement, citing the horror of Nazi Germany as *Exhibit A*. There happened to be a Buddhist monk in my discussion group whose parents emigrated from Germany, and who had themselves been children in the years leading up to WWII. What this monk said changed forever the way I think about blame.

After WWI, we the victors exercised our prerogative to impose draconian economic sanctions on Germany. That was bad enough, but when the Great Depression pulled the bottom out from

---

[1] Hannah Arendt, *The Life of Mind - Thinking - Willing* (New York-London: Ed. Harvest/HJB Book, 1978), p. 04

under the developing world economy, the situation in Germany became even more intolerable. Parents were simply not able to put food on the table. *Children were starving*. To make a long story short, when Hitler came to power, decades of deplorable economic conditions changed, and for the first time for many of these parents, they were able to have normal family lives structured around normal dinner tables.

As my monastic friend said, "People will overlook a lot of government ills when that government has made it possible for them to feed their children." And don't forget, Hitler himself was not inherently evil, but rather a human being, an artistic one even, whose body was deformed sexually, and whose mind was literally poisoned and permanently traumatized by the insane and unconscionable trench warfare of WWI. Yes, without question, he was a monster - but arguably a monster of our own making. Think 'Godzilla' here.

In today's world, rather than paternalistic governments and maniacal despots, we are governed by paternalistic corporations and sociopathic CEOs. They have given us a standard of living that, while perhaps not the healthiest, is nonetheless unprecedented in the history of civilization. The level of comfort, convenience, and entertainment which we have become accustomed to is mind-boggling when you put it into historical context. But the ends do not justify the means. And rather after the fact, following decades of settling into this cushy lifestyle and in the midst of raising families, we are only now slowly learning that it is this very lifestyle which is causing species extinction, dying oceans, and accelerating climate change -- threatening the very fabric of life on planet Earth. "Come again?"

Is there really any place for personal blame in all of this?

Consider this carefully. When Henry Ford invented the means for mass producing automobiles, was his intention to improve people's lives or to destroy the planet? How about Thomas Edison? Did he imagine coal-fired power plants poisoning the climate when he invented the electric lightbulb? Can there be blame without intent? As a former lawyer, I can tell you that it is not possible to convict someone of a crime without proving intent for this very reason. Similarly, when we drive our children to a soccer match or drop them off at the mall to meet their friends, or simply drive to work or hop on a plane, are we thinking about the number of species going extinct today? How about a mother feeding her kids at McDonalds? Is it her intention to contribute to deforestation of the Amazon, or the cruel, concentration-camp conditions of factory farms and slaughterhouses? Or is she just trying to manage on a limited budget while giving her kids something to be excited about? Who among us is to blame for the population explosion?

Here's what Hannah Arendt had to say about this phenomenon:

> It is indeed my opinion now that evil is never 'radical', that it is only extreme, and that it possesses neither depth nor any demonic dimension. *It can overgrow and lay waste the whole world precisely because it spreads like a fungus on the surface.* It is *'thought-defying'*, as I said, because thought tries to reach some depth, to go to

roots, and the moment it concerns itself with evil, it is frustrated because there is nothing. That is its 'banality'. *Only the good has depth and can be radical.*[2]

'Banality' means that collective evils can be perpetrated without corresponding individual motives: "The sad truth is that most evil is done by people who never make up their minds to be good or evil... the phenomenon of evil deeds, committed on a gigantic scale, [can] not be traced to any particularity of wickedness, pathology, or ideological conviction in the doer, whose only personal distinction was a perhaps extraordinary shallowness."[3] (Ouch!)

In much the same way, climate change has been called "a perfect and undetectable crime everyone contributes to but for which no one has a motive."[4] To say we are *all* to blame for the climate crisis is to say that *none* of us are to blame in any moral sense of the word. And for sure, shaming people about their contributions to carbon in the atmosphere is counterproductive in the same way that shaming an obese person about their eating will not motivate them to adopt a healthy diet and run to the gym. And yet, to say that the climate crisis is a collective problem on a massive scale is *not* to say that the solution does not lie with you and me. It surely does.

This is why I have become convinced that climate change is not a political problem, and there is no political solution in the traditional top-down 'command and control' sense of that word. It is a collective moral issue first - a moral issue of the highest order - because this is about the world we are leaving to our children, this is about our relationship with all of creation, and all future generations will be impacted by the decisions we will make in the next few decades. But it is not an issue of *immorality.* That is a crucial distinction to make in our shame-conditioned minds.

To put it more succinctly, a collective moral issue is not about individual immorality. That's the kind of thinking that has always gotten us into trouble, from the Salem witch trials to prohibition and the drug war or even the war on terrorism. When we become self-righteous over systemic moral issues, we end up relentlessly attacking the symptoms while ignoring the disease and its causes. Then the disease eventually overtakes us. We cannot afford to repeat that kind of mistaken thinking when the disease in question is threatening our life support system.

A significant majority of Americans (>70%) view the climate crisis through this moral lens. That's good news. But underlying the moral issue, underlying *our own collective paralysis*, we will find that this is a deeply psychological issue. Not an overly complicated psychological issue, mind you. But rather a problem with our *collective* psyche, which is nothing more than a reflection of, and is reflected in, our own individual psyches. This is why I can tell you that you

---

[2] Hannah, Arendt, *The Jew as Pariah - Jewish Identity and Politics in the Modern Age.* (New York: Grove Press, 1978), p. 251.

[3] Hannah Arendt, "Thinking and Moral Considerations: A Lecture," *Social Research*, no. 38/3 (Fall 1970), p. 417.

[4] Marshall, G. 2014. "Why our brains are wired to ignore climate change and what to do about it." *The Guardian* 9.23.14).

hold the solution in your hand right now. This is a self-help book of the highest order. It is intended and designed to bring about complete social transformation concerning the way we think about, feel about, and relate to the issue of climate change.

Without guilt. Without blame. Without recriminations. One mind at a time. Just the way a forest burns one tree at a time, fueled by tiny sparks carried on the wind.

Plowing Adversity Into the Path

Here is something else Hannah Arendt understood. If evil "can overgrow and lay waste the whole world precisely because it spreads like a fungus on the surface," then it can also be defeated by the power of a simple, thoughtful idea that *similarly* takes root and spreads quickly across the entire world, eradicating the problem fungus in the same way light eradicates darkness.

It follows, then, that *if we can just get to the psychological root of our climate crisis,* we will have the solution in hand.

As Arendt points out, the moral and ethical standards based on habits and customs can be changed by a new set of rules of behavior dictated by the current society "with no more trouble than it would take to change the table manners of a whole people."[5] Just like Thoreau before her, Arendt had a deep appreciation for the power of ideas:

> *The manifestation of the wind of thought is not knowledge; it is the ability to tell right from wrong, beautiful from ugly. And this, at the rare moments when [all] the stakes are on the table, may indeed prevent catastrophes...*[6]

William Burroughs was onto something when he posited that "language is a virus." Think of the ideas in this book as a highly contagious virus. When they are carried by the wind from one mind to the next, there will be a seismic shift in our collective consciousness, reflected in the subtle but profound shift in your own psyche, a growing awareness that you will feel in reading through these pages. In a surprisingly short time, like same-sex marriage or the fall of the Soviet Union, we will all begin responding appropriately to the climate crisis in everything we say, think, and do - all without any approval from a single politician - and the trajectory of the world will be forever altered.

This is a people movement. It takes a global village...

This is what real democracy looks like. In fact, this is exactly what gave birth to democracy in America. It all began with a simple pamphlet from Thomas Paine humbly titled *Common Sense*.

---

[5] *Personal Responsibility under Dictatorship, published in The Listener*, London, BBC (August 6 1964).

[6] *The Life of Mind - Thinking - Willing* (New York-London: Ed. Harvest/HJB Book, 1978), p. 193.

Which seems relevant again. Paine began his tome with logic Arendt would've appreciated:

> Perhaps the sentiments contained in the following pages, are not YET sufficiently fashionable to procure them general favour; a long habit of not thinking a thing WRONG, gives it a superficial appearance of being RIGHT, and raises at first a formidable outcry in defense of custom. But the tumult soon subsides. Time makes more converts than reason.

And as he subsequently, and quite famously captured the sentiments of our revolutionary birth in *American Crisis,* sentiments that equally apply to the rebirth we must now induce from our *Global Climate Crisis*:

> THESE are the times that try men's souls. The summer soldier and the sunshine patriot will, in this crisis, shrink from the service of their country; but he that stands by it now, deserves the love and thanks of man and woman. Tyranny, like hell, is not easily conquered; yet we have this consolation with us, that the harder the conflict, the more glorious the triumph.

Let us all rise to this momentous occasion with a spirit of glory in the anticipation of our eventual triumph. For this is a struggle we cannot afford to lose. We can now become the kind of planetary patriots that future generations will give thanks for and love to read about, in much the same way as we've all read of the exploits of Paul Revere, Thomas Paine, and Patrick Henry.

It will not be easy. We have to stop fooling ourselves. But nothing could be more worthwhile, no triumph more glorious, than this endeavor.

For a future to be possible…

CHAPTER 2

Climate Mayhem:
The End of Life As We Know It

And The Beginning of The Anthropocene

It is the experience of dying and being reborn that effects the cure.
If we were convinced that death is indeed followed by rebirth,
this might go a long way toward curing nothing less than our lives.
For fear is life's disease.

~ Huston Smith

Okay, brace yourself. This is the part where we begin to face our worst fears. But, as Pema Chödrön says, "Fear is a natural reaction to moving closer to the truth." It is simply not possible to address the psychological dimensions of the climate crisis, or to propose realistic reparations, without first confronting the scope and extent of the problems we are facing. This is especially true when those problems by their very nature must grow worse before they can be adequately addressed, which happens to be the case with a systemic, *time-release* problem like accelerated, abrupt climate change.

We would never enter into hospice without first experiencing the shock of a terminal diagnosis, would we? In the same way, we are not going to experience the kind of fundamental shift in our psyche that is called for by this existential global crisis without first becoming fully aware of the absolute *necessity* of the profound reorientation and transformation - transmutation, even - that the human species is now being called upon to go through.

In other words, dear reader, you are not allowed to skip this chapter!

SOME BIG PICTURE PERSPECTIVE

Climate Change? Global Warming??

The Climate movement has had a public relations problem from the start. A 'greenhouse' hardly sounds like a house of horrors. 'Global warming' sounds like an issue with the weather - global 'heating' would've been much better. 'Climate change' is even worse - a scientifically neutral term that is almost entirely empty of any emotional content. None of these terms conveys the seriousness of what we are up against. It's like some sociopath breaks into your house with an axe, and your partner announces "Dear, we have company."

For the rest of this book, I am going to use instead the term *Climate Mayhem* - or, to avoid sounding like a drone, the terms that scientists tend to use now: climate chaos or climate disruption. Keep that in the back of your mind as you read through this chapter. But just for context, let me explain how I arrived at my favored terminology.

According to my go-to dictionary, the *American Heritage Dictionary of the English Language*, mayhem involves "the infliction of violent injury upon a person or thing; wanton destruction" or "a state of violent disorder or riotous confusion; havoc." It is rooted in the word for "maiming." I don't know about you, but vast oceanic graveyards and clear-cut rain forests sounds quite like maiming the planet to me. The word "wanton," in turn, means "immoral... maliciously cruel; merciless... freely extravagant" and "excessive." That all rings true as well, an apt description for those who would *knowingly* let it come to this (Exxon and those craven scientists on its payroll, by way of example). And just speaking emotionally, mayhem is a word that has always sent chills up my spine - as does a world without elephants, tigers, rhinos, polar bears, orangutans...

Mayhem also happens to be a criminal law term, referring to the infliction of grievous bodily injury. That is precisely what we are doing to the planet. We've detonated over 2000 nuclear weapons (*crazy*, no? after having seen what just *one* did??); we've removed mountain tops and filled rivers to extract coal for burning; we're sacrificing precious underground water supplies to 'fracking' (the process for extracting natural gas by fracturing geologic layers and inserting chemical soups); we're destroying boreal forests that would otherwise absorb excess carbon from the atmosphere to extract dirty tar sand oil; we're leveling rain forests in South America to grow soybeans for cows that get eaten in North America; we're burning rain forests in Indonesia to make way for plantations that produce palm oil for our food; we're continuing with dangerous deep sea drilling, even after the Gulf disaster; and, we're poisoning the ocean with daily doses of plutonium, strontium and cesium from a place ominously called Fukushima - which is still out of control and at serious risk of an even *worse* nuclear catastrophe with the next earthquake in that unstable high-risk zone.

This crisis is not about warm weather, and it's not about change - it's about grievous injury, wanton destruction, and mass extinction.

It is mayhem.

And so, now that we have that little truth-in-labeling issue out of the way...

Welcome to the **ANTHROPOCENE**

Can we even *begin* to appreciate what that 'welcome' mat really entails?!

We humans have been inhabiting the Holocene Age for about 11,700 years. At the beginning of that age, with glaciers that marked the previous ice age retreating, species like wooly mammoths, saber-toothed tigers, mastodons, giant sloths, and even some camels were losing out to natural changes in climate in North America. Copper-skinned humans were but another inhabitant on the landscape, blending in over time and becoming one with their ecological biosphere, adapting to the seasonal rhythms of nature and enjoying their symbiotic relationships with bison and salmon and wolves. All of that changed about 600 years ago, when Europeans arrived rather abruptly on the scene and, as soon as they gained a foothold, proceeded to intentionally exterminate entire species (e.g., 60 million bison, the 'keystone' species in most plains areas) and cultures of people that had developed over the previous 11,000 years.

Quickly, we exerted our 'manifest destiny' over nature - which must have seemed like a limitless abundance of resources as we headed west - damning great rivers that had flowed unimpeded for millions of years, toppling giant redwoods that had stood majestically for several centuries prior to our arrival, converting great prairies into agricultural bread-baskets (and dust bowls), and establishing new cities on well-situated shorelines. While it would be impossible for those 'hardy pioneers' to imagine, it was not long at all before we had not simply settled the whole new world, but had increased our population to over 500 million. It is estimated there were just under a million natives when Columbus landed.

In just a few generations.

It's rather difficult to get any perspective on human growth, and how it is that we have come to dominate the planet to such an extent that scientists have now been forced to admit we have re-made the entire planet in our image. The reason it's difficult for us to grasp this kind of growth is that we are wired to think in linear terms, whereas population growth has been exponential at least since the advent of the Industrial Age. So consider this: It took us about 10,000 years to create the modern city that has come to define our civilization. The first cities with a million people were Rome and Alexandria, around the time of Christ. London became just the fifth city of one million people about *1800 years later*, the beginning of the Industrial Age. So up to that point in time, we were averaging about one new major city every 360 years. But these were followed in rapid succession - about every *five* years, in fact - by Paris, Beijing, Guangzhou, Berlin, and number ten on the list, Manhattan (1874). That's where the exponential curve really begins to kick in.

It also took us about 11,500 years to reach a population of one billion humans on planet Earth - which if you've ever tried to think about it, is an almost unimaginably large number. If you started counting right now, it would take you about 127 years to reach one billion. And then we *doubled* that in about a century. Then from 2 billion in 1927 - three years after my father was born - we hit 3 billion three years after I was born (1957) - a billion more in just thirty years! Try to wrap your mind around this - over eleven centuries for the first billion, and only thirty years for the third. During my brief life, we have thus far added *another 4 billion*.

And get this -- there are now about **336** cities in the world with populations over one million people. Ten major cities in just under 1900 years, then another 226 in just over 100 years!

That is what exponential growth looks like. For some reason, we humans have a hard time grasping this notion. Which is kind of strange, actually, considering we start out as 2 little cells and nine months later come out a fully formed human being with about ten trillion cells! But it is because of this exponential growth over the past couple of centuries, after eleven millennia of mostly linear growth and adaption to a variety of different climates and ecosystems all over the world, that we have now managed to forever alter the very climate we inhabit, and that this alteration keeps accelerating faster than our scientific models predict. We've filled the skies with satellites and airplanes (and lit up the night skies), we've roaded and cleared most of the Earth, making room not just for ourselves but also for a billion or so genetically modified cows, *we've even changed the chemistry of the oceans.* Think about *that* for just a minute. If someone had told me this was possible even twenty years ago, I would've thought them mad. And yes, regrettably, we have become the first species ever to trigger a 'great extinction' of hundreds of thousands of species, forever altering the biological diversity that we co-evolved with - or, if you prefer, that we were gifted by our creator.

The last of the five great extinctions happened 66 million years ago.

If you really think deeply about all this, it is no wonder Nietzsche prophetically asserted that God was dead.[7] Let's be honest here -- we have become like gods. Just as He is said to have created us in His image, we have now taken it upon ourselves to re-shape *His* creation in *our* image.

It should come as no surprise, then, that more than 500 scientific studies published in 2014 refer to the time we are living in today as the Anthropocene, or the "age of humans."[8] The term "anthropocentric" has always been considered rather pejorative, in the sense of our hubris at placing ourselves in the center of the universe and assigning value to all according to its utility to us, and there are still many who object to the labeling of this age as the Anthropocene for that very reason. But it is too late for such objections. The genie is out of the bottle, and we have to own it. This is now effectively, if not literally, our own creation, and the worst thing we could possibly do is not take responsibility for it.

EARLY WOUNDING OF OUR COLLECTIVE PSYCHE

THE SPLITTING OF THE ATOM HAS CHANGED EVERYTHING [EXCEPT] OUR MODE OF THINKING, AND THUS WE DRIFT TOWARD UNPARALLELED CATASTROPHE.

~ Albert Einstein

Most people in our culture have some idea of what it means to have a 'wounded inner child.' It is this early developmental wound that sets many of our relational patterns in life - accounting for the mistakes we make over and over in our relationships - and that surfaces repeatedly in the form of 'emotional reactivity' whenever our buttons get pushed. We get so acclimated to these reactive patterns that we begin to identify them to the point we think they are just 'who we are' and there is nothing to be done about it - it's just up to others to accept us this way.

This is one of the worst mistakes we can make in life. We don't have to continually get sucked into that emotional vortex of suffering. When we are able instead to recognize and acknowledge this deep emotional wound, to honor and work with it, when we can appreciate the extent to which it has made our relationships more difficult than they need to be, and caused more

---

[7] "What was holiest and mightiest of all that the world has yet owned has bled to death under our knives: who will wipe this blood off us? What water is there for us to clean ourselves? What festivals of atonement, what sacred games shall we have to invent? Is not the greatness of this deed too great for us? Must we ourselves not become gods simply to appear worthy of it?" Nietzsche, *The Gay Science*, Section 125 (1882).

[8] AP, *Welcome to the Anthropocene* (Gulf News, Oct. 14, 2014).

suffering than we can really bear, then we are ready to process it and begin the healing process that opens us up to so much more in life.

That's called taking control of our life. It isn't easy work, but it's very worthwhile - as anyone who has been fortunate enough to do this kind of personal work will tell you. In many ways, it's when life really begins. Once we're in control of our emotional life, rather than being controlled by it, the difference is like inhabiting a technicolor 3D futuristic movie, whereas up until that time we were living in an old two-dimensional black-and-white television show. It also teaches us how suffering is as much a part of our human nature as love is. In fact, while it is possible to suffer without love, which is the tragic fate of so many who are emotionally shut down, it is not possible to love without suffering. It's a package deal, and we'll go deeper into this idea in the chapter on grieving and loving.

This psychological concept of being held as an emotional hostage to our mostly unremembered wounding from childhood is called *developmental trauma*. It occurs along a wide spectrum, as everyone is sensitive to it in different ways. None of us, however, are exempt from these painful experiences growing up, even if we imagine that we had an idyllic childhood, and the more serious the trauma - such as when our trust is violated in the most atrocious ways imaginable - the more we tend to close off our hearts, shut down our emotions, and struggle with social adjustment as we grow up. The greater the trauma, in other words, the deeper the wound and the more difficult it becomes to access it for the purposes of healing. And the more sensitive we are, the more we compensate by shutting down.

If this concept resonates with you, and you suspect you haven't done the work you need to, there are plenty of other resources available to get you started. If you have done the work, then I'm not telling you anything you don't already know. So why then *am* I telling you this? Because it happens to be true both individually and at the collective level. And *that* turns out to be the key to understanding, and solving, the climate crisis.

Collective Developmental Trauma

Through culture and society, we are all interconnected psychologically. Sometimes it takes a tragic event like 9/11 to really bring this home to us. An even more poignant, and still relatively recent, example of deep collective wounding shared by a culture is the effect the Holocaust has had on the Jewish people. One of the reasons this example is so compelling is that so many Jews have been so heroic in the ways that they have acknowledged this wound, continuing to process it in healing ways from one generation to the next. A monstrous wound like that is not easily treated, and takes a long time to heal, and certainly we see evidence of how fresh that trauma remains in the way Israel deals with the Palestinian people. With severe trauma, the victim is always at risk of morphing into the perpetrator, as George Orwell's *Animal Farm* so beautifully illustrates for us.

A less successful example of processing a grievous collective wound lives among us as a constant reminder of the cruelty of our own European forebears -- the American Indians, still suffering from the cultural PTSD that is so sadly manifest in their collective struggle with alcoholism and high suicide rates (though they are slowly but definitely starting to recover through cultural resuscitation). And, of course, while we all have vivid imagery in our minds of the concentration camps operated by the Third Reich, our own history happens to include about *two centuries* of concentration camps that housed Africans kidnapped from their homeland - a collective wounding we now have some experience with trying to repair, and from which we are learning just how difficult such reparations can be.

Studies of historical traumas like these reveal that when trauma is not dealt with by those who are most directly affected, it ends up having to be dealt with by their children or grandchildren, as this form of 'inter-generational trauma' is cumulative, and actually becomes *more* intense, not less, with each generation until it is finally adequately dealt with. Recently, this kind of hereditary trauma was actually proven through genetic studies of survivors of the Holocaust, vividly proving the mind/body connection.[9] According to one of the leading researchers, cultural trauma "persists and lingers considerably longer than other kinds of trauma, sometimes over several generations, preserved in collective memory or hibernating in [our] collective subconsciousness…"[10]

So from a sociology standpoint, from the standpoint of the evening news you might say, we already have some idea just how real this kind of collective cultural, developmental trauma is. And we have a sense, as well, that it is not limited to just the victims and their children's children, but falls as well on the perpetrators of the trauma - or rather, their descendants. As a white European, I feel this acutely when I listen to a recording of the haunting song *Strange Fruit,* when I watch a movie like *12 Years a Slave* or *The Butler*, or when I read about the atrocities my ancestors (I'm a Mayflower child) visited upon Indian Americans. These traumas perpetuate themselves, reverberating cyclically with cultural echoes often involving senseless gun violence, and to the extent that they are not adequately addressed, the echoes are cumulative as well - they become more complex and difficult to root out with each succeeding generation.

But as significant as these cultural traumas are, especially in the context of our increasingly violent culture, they are not the traumas that precipitated the climate crisis, and they are quite beyond the scope of this book in the same way that your more personal history is. No, there is a different kind of developmental trauma that needs to be addressed if we are going to address climate mayhem. Because as we've already touched upon, the moment everything changed psychologically and ecologically -- for Americans in particular, and the human race more generally -- was when we tampered with the most basic building blocks of nature by splitting a

---

9 Yehuda et al. (2015), Holocaust Exposure Induced Intergenerational Effects on *FKBP5* Methylation. *J. of Psych. Neuroscience & Therapeutics.*

10 Sztompka (2000).

single atom, and then figuring out how to set off a chain reaction of splitting atoms, unleashing the full Promethean fury of the sun's infernal energy on Earth.[11]

This Anthropocentric Age was presaged by the term 'Atomic Age' - whose advent was witnessed by a few scientists in the deserts of New Mexico about 70 years ago:

> Trinity's witnesses responded just as those to Apollo 11 would, as J. Robert Oppenheimer remembered: "*We knew the world would not be the same.* A few people laughed, a few people cried, most people were silent." Oppenheimer later said the he beheld his radiant blooming cloud and thought of Hindu scripture: *"Now I am become Death, the destroyer of worlds."*[12]
> ***

> "Suddenly, there was an enormous flash of light, the brightest light I have ever seen or that I think anyone has ever seen. It blasted; it pounced; it bored its way into you. *It was a vision which was seen with more than the eye.* It was seen to last forever. You would wish it would stop; altogether it lasted about two seconds."[13]

Most of us have probably heard the Oppenheimer quote before, though this may be the first time you've considered it in the context of the unfolding climate crisis. It's certainly worth pondering, along with the quote from Einstein highlighted at the beginning of this section. But the more obscure quote from Isidor Isaac Rabi is quite profound. It is as if he is speaking for all humanity, not just the scientists. As if he is intuitively sensing the trauma of this eternal moment out of time as it bored its way inexorably into our collective psyche with such relentless ferocity that nothing *could* ever be the same again.

By now we've all seen images of nuclear explosions with their searing white light, fearsome grey mushroom clouds of ash, and nuclear winds blowing everything not incinerated horizontal. It really is a visceral vision that we see "with more than the eye," is it not? What we've learned from the psychology of developmental trauma relates directly to the experience of Trinity. According to the psychiatrist Mark Epstein, trauma *"takes us out of time."*[14] Epstein quotes Robert Stolorow to drive this point home:

> **"Experiences of trauma become freeze-framed into an *eternal present* in which one remains forever trapped..."**

---

[11] Prometheus is the Titan in Greek mythology who brought fire down from the heavens to Earth, greatly angering the gods in the process. Mythological stories are revelatory, in that we encode eternal truths in them. The term "psyche" itself is a mythological term, and thus myths become a source of valuable insight when addressing deep psychological problems.

[12] Craig Nelson, *Rocket Men: The Epic Story of the First Men on the Moon*

[13] Isidor Isaac Rabi

[14] *The Trauma of Everyday Life* (2013), p. 148.

As when a two-second flash of light is seen to last forever with more than just the eye, even though you wish it would stop.

Another myth we are all familiar with is *Pandora's Box*, which you might not know is closely related to the myth of Prometheus. It was considered by the ancient Greeks to be one of the most descriptive myths of human behavior, an explanation of the relationship between human weakness and the several misfortunes plaguing the human race. Pandora's box was secretly sent to Earth, disguised as a wedding present for Pandora and Prometheus' younger brother, as a punishment for stealing the fire of the gods. The swarm of evil spirits released inadvertently by Pandora (whose name means "giver of all"), acting simply upon her curiosity, were said by the Greeks to torment humankind from that point forward. The religiously-named 'Trinity Test' can similarly be viewed as a kind of trigger point we were tricked into under duress, one in which we exercised our highest sense of curiosity and inadvertently opened the way for a parade of ecological horribles to be unleashed on our planet.

In fact, as Einstein and Oppenheimer foretold, *everything really did change unalterably* in that eternal moment out of time we blasphemously named Trinity. Geologists now measure the beginning of the Anthropocene Age from that first atomic explosion in White Sands, N.M.

But that is just at the level of physical reality. Even more dramatic was the change wrought by that rupture in our *psychological* makeup. We went from being *a part of* nature, as we had been (more or less) for about 300,000 years, or 35,000 generations, to being *apart from* nature. It is as if we suddenly and quite unexpectedly stepped out of the matrix, having finally divined the algorithm underlying its program. And we have yet to come to grips with this profoundly unnatural - we could even say, *anti*-natural - mutation of our own species. From the start it was systematically repressed. In the wake of Hiroshima and Nagasaki, news outlets were not allowed by the War Department to relay reports of human suffering caused by the bombs to Americans. Then it was basically lost in the tremendous relief at the war being over, and the long-awaited return of our troops from overseas.

This combination of a rupture in our fundamental relationship to nature with the suppression of accurate reporting of its impacts cast a huge shadow over our culture - and once our culture was imported globally, over the planet itself. This fundamental fissure, this tearing at the fabric of reality that ended a geologic age which had lasted nearly 12,000 years, an age that birthed civilization and defined what it means to be human, is the psychological coagulant that lies at the congested heart of our climate crisis today. In order to finally resolve this crisis, we must begin the process of healing the deep emotional wound that is impairing our collective psyche. Only then will we be able to stop repeating this dysfunctional pattern in our relationship to the natural world, and come back into balance with our own true nature.

While it often seems like the modern world proceeds at a breakneck pace, the truth of the matter is that we humans are kind of slow to adapt our thinking to that (also unnatural) pace of life. In the same way that we are just now beginning to integrate a view of the world that is congruent with discoveries in quantum physics from the middle of the last century, so we are now just beginning to grasp the full significance of our sudden split from nature and our natural, nurturing mother. 'Mater' is the Greek word meaning 'mother' and from which 'matter' is derived. Thus, speaking metaphorically, our psyche split off from our mother, Earth, the moment we split the atom in two, as if cutting the very umbilical cord which had always sustained us in our relationship to her.

It is at least conceivable, I suppose, that the scientific achievement of splitting what had up to that time seemed inviolate - the atom which is the fundamental building block of all matter - could under different circumstances have had a different affect on us psychologically. We will never really know. Because the very first thing we did with this new god-like power over the fundamental forces of nature was to create hell on Earth, converting the Land of the Rising Sun into Dante's Inferno - where even the rivers people dove into while trying to escape the searing heat of the atmospheric fire turned out to be molten cauldrons in which they were boiled alive. Such a world seems unimaginable to us. And while the trauma experienced by those Japanese mothers and children (the men being mostly away at war) and elders can never be overestimated - hundreds of thousands killed (only 150 members of the military) - some leaving behind only shadows on pavement, and hundreds of thousands survived - it was *our use of that force in that way* which buried the trauma deep within our own collective psyche, forever altering American culture and our cultural identity.

Listen to what the future Pulitzer Prize winning poet James Agee wrote on the back page of TIME magazine's August 20, 1945 issue, and you will get some deep feeling for the complex psychological impact associated with our perpetrating the single-most devastating acts of destruction (yes, 'terrorism') in the history of mankind:

> The greatest and most terrible of wars ended, this week, in the echoes of an enormous event - *an event so much more enormous that, relative to it, the war itself shrank to minor significance.* The knowledge of victory was as charged with sorrow and doubt as with joy and gratitude. More fearful responsibilities, more crucial liabilities rested on the victors even than on the vanquished.

> In what they said and did, men were still, *as in the aftershock of a great wound,* bemused and only semi-articulate, whether they were soldiers or scientists, or great statesmen, or the simplest of men. *But in the dark depths of their minds and hearts, huge forms moved and silently arrayed themselves:* Titans, arranging out of the chaos an age in which victory was already only the shout of a child in the street.

> *With the controlled splitting of the atom, humanity, already profoundly perplexed and disunified, was brought inescapably into a new age in which all thoughts and*

things were split - and far from controlled. As most men realized, the first atomic bomb was a merely pregnant threat, a merely infinitesimal promise.

All thoughts and things were split. The sudden achievement of victory was a mercy, to the Japanese no less than to the United Nations; but mercy born of a ruthless force beyond anything in human chronicle. The race had been won, the weapon had been used by those on whom civilization could best hope to depend; *but the demonstration of power against living creatures instead of dead matter created a **bottomless wound** in the living conscience of the race.* The rational mind had won the most Promethean of its conquests over nature, and had put into the hands of common man the fire and force of the sun itself.

Was man equal to the challenge? In an instant, without warning, the present had become the unthinkable future. Was there hope in that future, and if so, where did hope lie?

"All thoughts and things were split" with the opening of "a bottomless wound in the living conscience of the race…"[15] Just as with Rabi's more-than-just-the-eye witness account of the Trinity Test, here we see truth emerging from the depths of our collective unconscious.

We will come back to this almost infinitely potent theme again, for within it lies not just the means of our destruction but also the key to our salvation. For now we are just laying down this radioactive marker to emphasize how dramatic this departure was from all that had come before, in the hope that we can begin to sense the true scope of the physical, spiritual (metaphysical), and psychological repercussions that are emanating *still* from that pivot in space-time which marked the end of one world (and the last world war) and the beginning of something entirely new that we are only now beginning to acknowledge and grasp - the Anthropocene.

What seems important right now, however, before exploring in much more depth just how it is we got from there to here, is to gain a full and honest appreciation of just where it is that this nascent, newly emerging human age has landed us. From a collective psychological standpoint, this is the equivalent of beginning our session with the opener: "So, tell me about your mother."

---

[15] Forty years later, in a TIME magazine retrospective, essayist Roger Rosenblatt would observe that, since the splitting of the atom, *"there seems to have been a general divorce of human life from other natural phenomena."*

CHAPTER 3

The State of Planet Earth

"The World Hangs by a thin thread,
and this is the Psyche of Man."
C.J. Jung

What *is* the state of our mother, Earth? *What hath man wrought*??[16]

PSYCHOLOGICAL DISARMAMENT

Before we consider the 'State of the Earth,' a word or two about our psychological immuno-defense system is in order, as it is quite natural and understandable to experience some emotional reactivity in reading about our current predicament, and we can't really afford to shut down and close ourselves off to this unsettling kind of information. Throughout this book, we are going to be actively dealing with the 3-D's: **D**enial, **D**epression, and **D**espair. All of these are *fear-based*, rooted in our own (individual) wounded nature, and there are antidotes that you will be provided for each of these in turn. You will be glad to learn that, by processing through this book, your marks will improve from D's to A's! The 3 Antidotes are: **A**cknowledgment, **A**cceptance, and **A**wakening. All of these are *awareness-based*. When your 3 D's have been eclipsed by the 3 A's, by replacing fear with awareness, you will become a fully qualified "planetary caregiver."

Already there is hope!

Before we turn to a careful, but concise, consideration of climate science, we need to deal briefly with just the first of the 3 D's, perhaps the most insidious one.

Denial

We're all in denial when it comes to climate mayhem. Yes, you heard that right. Unfortunately, due to the toxic influences of duality-obsessed media and politics, we tend to make the mistake of thinking there are "climate deniers" -- and then there are the *rest* of us. Of course, that is a short-hand reference to those ninnies who deny the inescapable scientific conclusion that we have fundamentally altered the natural world, in spite of the fact that there is now a consensus rate globally of 99% of all scientists who have considered the evidence. Science doesn't get much more certain than that, other than perhaps for the proposition that the Earth is round and the moon is not, after all, made of cheese. Fortunately, the world of climate "denialists" is shrinking faster than the ice shelf, down to about 10% of us according to one recent poll. But climate science is hardly an *exact* science, either. It occurs along a spectrum. At one end of that

---

[16] Just as with Oppenheimer's quotation from Hindu scripture, it is interesting to consider that the first message ever communicated over the transmission lines that would come to define the modern age, sent by Samuel Morse, was "What hath God wrought?"

spectrum, for example, we have the simple physics of pumping unnatural levels of carbon into the atmosphere. At the other, more speculative end, we have things like 'feedback loops' and changes in ocean currents.

Denial, too, occurs along a spectrum. I don't know too many people, including myself, who accept the minority view held by some climate scientists that is often referred to as "near term human extinction" - or NTHE. I see my own view of NTHE as a form of emotionally reactive denial in myself, and so I tend to search out evidence undermining those who maintain NTHE is 'inevitable' (it's *not*!).

So rather than dividing ourselves into two camps - which is how wars start after all - we'd be far better off simply acknowledging that we are all in denial to some extent about climate chaos, and that it is *okay* to allow ourselves to be in denial at least part of the time - to '*manage*' our denial. This fits in with the core idea from the book *States of Denial* (Cohen, S. 2001): denial is a kind of simultaneous knowing and not-knowing that is rooted in our need to maintain some state of innocence (not knowing) about a disturbing situation (knowing). This is a kind of passive denial with which we shield ourselves from the vicissitudes of reality.

A good example of 'healthy denial' is when we lose a loved one. To pretend we haven't suffered a grievous loss would be a real problem, an unhealthy denial. But at some point, it becomes necessary for us to function in the wake of our loss. This requires that we put our loss out of our mind - 'repress' it, if you will - for short spells in order to get on with living our lives. So we go back and forth between our grieving and our living, and gradually the waves of grief become more bearable and less frequent. That's a healthy kind of denial we label 'adjustment.' The more we learn about climate chaos, the more we adopt this model of pacifying denial - for the sake of our own mental health, because we know that obsessing over it would only lead to burn-out.

We humans are complex psychological beings. Because of the way we have evolved, we have certain built-in psychological defense mechanisms. There is nothing wrong with this at all, so long as we are aware of how these defense mechanisms operate - and how they can create problems in our lives. As with fear itself, denial only becomes a problem when we remain unaware of it, and when we refuse to acknowledge it. According to a 2014 Gallup poll, almost a third of Americans believe "climate change" is real but simply choose not worry about it, believing that it is not that big of a deal. I'm sure they don't think of themselves as in denial. While we can live with one in ten people denying reality, a far bigger problem is posed by those who see climate chaos unfolding but choose to go on whistling past the global graveyard.

What we really need to understand when it comes to climate denial is how the psychological phenomenon of "cognitive dissonance" works, and guard ourselves against it. That's a tricky problem once we've given ourselves permission to manage our denial. We don't want to slip into apathy when the continued existence of the human species may demand individual action. So let's take a closer look at this curious psychological phenomenon.

'Cognitive dissonance' is a fancy term for a simple psychological defense mechanism for dealing with conflicts between thoughts, feelings and behaviors. What it distills down to is this: we all have a particular world view comprised of beliefs about the way things exist and the stories we tell ourselves *about* ourselves, our life, and our world. A rather common and simple example is that there is a creator god. Because this is basically our psychological operating system, when someone or some event presents us with a piece of information or some circumstance that conflicts with our world view, we contract and defend it.

An example of the kind of story that gives rise to cognitive dissonance would be "I'm basically a good person, and God watches out for good people." So when bad things happen to good people, such as losing a child, things begin to get more than a little complicated. "God works in mysterious ways," we might say, or "our reward lies in the great hereafter."

While there are many ways we resolve these inner conflicts, the easiest is simply to ignore the offending bit of information. For example, moving from religion to something more (ahem) personal for just a moment, if I tell you that studies have shown that eating bacon more than once a week will likely take twenty years off your life, but you *really* love bacon, then you might just laugh this off, tell yourself it's not true - or at least not true for you. You might think "my grandfather ate bacon every day of his life and lived to a ripe old age." And you go right on eating bacon, though in all likelihood you now have some anxiety associated with that habit based on your healthy fear of dying prematurely.

A more potent example would be a core belief, like the belief in the literal truth of the Bible based on faith in God. So when scientists discover fossils that are 4.5 billion years old, and you 'know' from the Bible that God created the heavens and earth about 10,000 years ago, the hard thing to do would be to change your core belief. The easy thing is to rectify this 'dissonance' between conflicting truths by concluding that God created fossils to test our faith. A more extreme example most of us are familiar with is doomsday cults. When the day of reckoning passes without any horsemen riding across the sky, the faithful do not lose faith - they just assume God is testing them, or even rewarding them for their strong faith.

People in the grip of cognitive dissonance are quick to anger, or else just shut down. They often see themselves as victims, looking to blame others for perceived injustices. Mention the health benefits and global impacts to someone who is overly attached to meat, and they will often respond quite emotionally: "Oh great - now you people are going to tell me what I can eat?!" This is just a convenient and effective way of cutting off any further conversation. People also will tend to over-compensate for insecure beliefs with exaggerated confidence or even arrogance and belligerence. We see this all the time with white supremacists.

As you can hopefully appreciate now, when it comes to climate chaos it is not just the climate science-deniers who are suffering from cognitive dissonance. If you'd like to have some fun by testing this out for yourself, try citing a litany of facts about livestock production being the biggest cause of climate mayhem and species extinction to a rancher or meat-eater who readily acknowledges the climate crisis. The response is likely to fall into one of three categories: nervous laughter and dismissive or insensitive humor ("Oh *puh-leez!* You're telling me *cow farts* cause climate change?"); some tortured rationalization ("we evolved with a paleolithic diet"); or, outright denial ("that's propaganda from PETA!"). Of course, we're not examining alien beings here - we've all employed these tactics at one time or another, if not in relation to climate chaos, then in some other context. I personally have a lot of cognitive dissonance arise when I try to justify my addiction to certain spectator sports to the uninitiated.

Now there are a lot of fancy psychological theories about how to address the dysfunction that arises from cognitive dissonance, but they all boil down to placing more value on truth, an open mind, and a desire to see reality as it really exists, than we place on any of our cherished beliefs and closely held stories. That's a mindset, not a belief system. As we will see in the chapters that follow, in no way does this mean that the climate loses out to religion. Life is sacred, and protecting 'God's creation' is sacrosanct, so someone who cares about the Earth can still be deeply religious, and someone who is deeply religious must care about the Earth.[17] The greater difficulties actually arise in defending our long-standing lifestyle choices and engrained habits, as the meat-eater example illustrates.

In the context of climate chaos, and all the science out there concerning the future, what is also important to acknowledge right up front is that we humans crave *certainty* - especially where our future prospects are concerned. There is no shame in that. But we happen to be facing more uncertainty at this particular time in our history than at any previous time. Most of those polled by Gallup who don't worry about climate mayhem wield uncertainty as a shield. Somehow, we have to learn to embrace that uncertainty, to turn it to our advantage in this race against time.

As I said earlier, climate science is far from being an exact science. It's not unlike predicting the weather, really. We can know with certainty what the weather is right now, we can be fairly certain what it is going to be like tomorrow -- but we become a little less certain what next week holds. And when it comes to predicting the weather a year from now, it takes a kind of hubris to think we might be able to do that with any degree of confidence. One member of the U.N.'s International Panel of climate scientists admits that "uncertainty is present in all phases of climate change research." So when it comes to consideration of the science underlying climate chaos, it is really important to remain humble, to be skeptical to some degree, and to acknowledge the fact up front that what we are learning about our impacts on the climate is likely to conflict with what we have come to believe about ourselves and our lives in the world.

At the same time, we should avoid jumping to any conclusions by reminding ourselves of the conflict between the inherent uncertainty of climate science and our own fundamental need for certainty about the future. In hospice, this is sometimes referred to as cultivating a "don't know mind," a term borrowed from Buddhism. When sitting with someone in hospice, there is a strong

---

[17] Pope Francis is a shining example of this.

tendency to draw a bright line between ourselves as caregivers and the dying person being attended to. But in truth, we don't really know who is going to die first.

In working through our climate grief, there are certain precepts we can follow that will prevent us from sliding into the tar pits of despair. The very first precept is to practice 'don't know mind' -- to consider what we know and what we do *not* know, to be clear about the difference, and to hold what we *think* open to a vast realm of changing possibilities and compassionate responses. As the wise Indian American John Trudeau put it when he was alive, we need to learn to believe less and think more. When we find ourselves jumping to conclusions, rejecting evidence that seems to be based on facts, or just reacting emotionally to what we are hearing, we need to acknowledge that there is fear there, even fear-based beliefs.

When we get better at acknowledging our fears rather than contracting around them, then our fears actually become good teachers. That is the proper role of fear. Consider how our fear of heights keeps us from being reckless near cliffs, or how our fear of death keeps us alert when driving on a busy highway in the rain or snow. *Unacknowledged* fear, by contrast, causes us to act in ways and say things that we invariably regret, or to become prisoners to unwelcome moods and feelings like anxiety, dread, and depression -- or even to harm ourselves and others without really intending to.

Learn to see unacknowledged fear as your real enemy.

So that's the psychological backdrop to our consideration of the State of the Earth. If we want to do the right thing, to be responsible for our part in shaping the future for all who are to come, then we need to allow both the evidence and our own fears to inform our actions. As noted, we will return in more depth to the psychology of climate mayhem in the coming chapters. But in order to inform our discussions, approach, and strategies, let us now turn to a summation of what we know now, or at least as I'm writing this, what we think we know. I promise to leave out anything that we really don't know. Try to be sensitive to feelings and emotions that reflexively arise as you are reading this next section. After this consideration, we will then turn our attention to processing these feelings and emotions in a healthy way that will help the planet itself.

THE *UNNATURAL STATE* OF PLANET EARTH

According to no less an authority than the National Geographic Society, the Great Anthropocentric Extinction is upon us.[18] It is important for us to begin here, to serve as a counterweight to our natural 'anthropocentric' tendency to see climate change only in human terms, when the reality is that every day it is estimated we are losing between 50 and 250

---

[18] See: http://newswatch.nationalgeographic.com/2012/03/28/the-sixth-great-extinction-a-silent-extermination/ Retrieved 11.8.2013.

species. To put that figure in perspective, a *natural* rate of extinction would see the demise of one species every few days at most, maybe one a week on average.

The current rate of extinction is thus about 1,000 times greater than natural, clearly making it "anthropocentric" (human-caused). Even increasing the extinction rate by one hundred-fold would be of far-reaching consequence, especially it was not seen as some kind of temporary anomaly.

As an ecopsychologist, I often ponder what it means to be 'human' now that we have entered this new age of our own creation. We are but a referent point for all other species. Indigenous peoples have always known this. The Sioux tribe called themselves the "Buffalo people" because their lives and very identity were so intertwined with bison. When all the bison were wiped out by European settlers, the Sioux entered a long-term identity crisis that they have still not worked out. While not as obvious, perhaps, those of us who are of European descent have a similar need to identify with so-called "charismatic mega-fauna" - like Bears and Lions and Tigers - as evidenced by the names of our sports teams, our infatuation with zoos, and our fascination with nature films - not to mention our need to preserve and actually go out into the wilds to hunt, fish, or just hike in close proximity to animals we know are higher up than us on the food chain. Anyone who has ever backpacked in grizzly country can attest to their importance to our identity.

What would it mean to be 'human' *without* elephants, rhinos, lions, tigers, grizzly and polar bears, snow leopards, blue whales, gorillas, and orangutans? All of these species are on life-support now, just as the mastodons, wooly mammoths, saber-toothed tigers and giant sloths disappeared at the start of the Holocene Age. A recent Washington Post article carried the title:

Horribly bleak study sees 'empty landscape' as large herbivores vanish at startling rate

(May 4, 2015). Herbivores, or vegetarian mammals, include elephants, hippos, rhinos and gorillas, and the referenced study, from the American Association for the Advancement of Science, envisioned "empty landscapes across much of the planet Earth" in the near future, since once the big herbivores disappear, the large carnivores (lions, tigers, bears, etc.) lose their main food sources. In the U.S., once the bison disappeared (there are only a few thousand left, confined primarily to Yellowstone NP), grizzlies turned to salmon as their main source of protein. Once the rivers were damned, and salmon disappeared, they turned to pine nuts from White Bark Pine trees. Now, with climate mayhem, White Bark Pines are succumbing to blister rust (a fungus) and bark beetles. It is not uncommon now for grizzlies to get hit by trains because they are scavenging grain that falls off of grain cars.

Will we still be 'human' in the wake of all these wild animals disappearing? Will we still be defined by our 'humanity' -- "the quality of being humane; benevolence; kindness; mercy" -- if we are so callous as to allow these majestic creatures to needlessly vanish?

(In contemplating this question for yourself, I would encourage you to spend some time with images of these species you can easily call up on-line (or spend some quiet time absorbing the artwork at the extinctionwitness.org *web site). Really try to imagine a world without them. How would you try explain their absence to your grandchildren?)*

Or would we instead become, by definition, 'barbarians' -- fierce, brutal, cruel people, insensitive and uncultured. We actually have a word for that in our own culture: *survivalists*.

Is that what we are devolving into?

However you feel about these questions, which are really up to each of us to answer for ourselves, sober consideration of the current, cascading scientific evidence leads to this inescapable conclusion: *life as we have come to know it is, quite simply, at an end.*

That is a fact. The Intergovernmental Panel on Climate Change says in its most recent report that "continued emission of greenhouse gases will cause further warming and long-lasting changes in all components of the climate system, increasing the likelihood of severe, pervasive and irreversible impacts for people and ecosystems." According to Dale Jamieson, a professor of environmental studies and philosophy at New York University, "[t]his is a polite way of saying that we're in for species extinctions, political and social instability, millions of avoidable deaths, and the loss of the world as we know it."

While I myself am convinced that we will survive as a species, and that long term it will even serve to make us a more caring and considerate species, that does not alter one bit the fact that life as we know it is now ending on planet Earth. Can you *feel* that? Are you able to contain it? Try holding on to these questions for now…

Watery Graveyards?

Let us consider the less obvious impacts of climate change now, the ones we don't hear enough about for some reason. While rising surface temperatures are largely associated with atmospheric (climate) impacts of carbon dioxide, the fact of the matter is that the oceans have absorbed between *one-third and one-half* of all CO_2 released into the atmosphere since the beginning of the Industrial Age 250 years ago. In addition to serving as a sink for the greenhouse gases themselves, the oceans also absorb 90% of the excess heat caused by global warming. Heat is essentially a measure of increased entropy, or disorder (chaos), and the cumulative impacts of this continuous thermal pollution of the seas, together with the obscene destruction of the ocean floor ecosystems from centuries of trawling,[19] the recent creation of huge dead zones from agricultural runoff (e.g., from the Mississippi) as part of the so-called "Green Revolution" (a.k.a., chemical agribusiness), and even more recently, grossly irresponsible, 'deep water' (high risk) drilling operations, have resulted in dramatic changes in ocean water chemistry -- increasing the acidity of the sea water by *26%* -- and severe degradation of the marine biological diversity that represents the very sanctity of life from which we emerged and upon which we still depend for our life (approximately *half* of our oxygen is produced by marine life).

About a third of the *critical* marine environments — such as sea grasses, mangroves and coral reefs — have already been destroyed, and chemical runoff from agribusiness is creating vast areas of coastal waters that are almost devoid of oxygen.[20] When we think of the seas, we tend to think of great marlins being wrestled out of the water by sport fishermen, shark attacks, or Captain Ahab chasing Moby Dick. However, while we obsess over the weather impacts and extreme events associated with the advent of the climate crisis, we remain mostly oblivious to the fact that, thanks to ruthlessly efficient industrialized ocean harvesting operations, we have managed to deplete large fish populations in the oceans *by 90% in the last 50 years!*

Please stop and think about that for a minute. As Carl Jung observed, the oceans are rather like the physical embodiment of our subconscious minds. Because all marine life exists beneath the surface, we suffer from the "out of sight, out of mind" syndrome, easily suppressing any notion that there could be a problem in these seemingly endless seas. Just as it takes some conscious effort to plumb the depths of our own subconscious minds in order to resolve psychological problems that manifest themselves in harmful habits in our daily lives, or destructive patterns in our relationships, so we need to appreciate that 2/3 of the world's ecological problems are submerged in a way that continually escapes our attention.

If the human population had declined 90% in the last 50 years, say by some terrible plague or escalating warfare, do you know how many of us would be left in the world? *250 million.* That's about how many people there were on planet Earth at the time of Christ. How would we view such a turn of events?

I grew up watching Jacque Cousteau specials on public television. Cousteau was the inventor of the self-contained underwater breathing apparatus, or scuba tanks, that permitted us to begin exploring the oceans in earnest. One woman who was inspired by Cousteau to become an oceanographer and explorer at a time when those occupations were still male-dominated was Sylvia Earle, who grew up on the Gulf of Mexico and went on to become so accomplished that TIME magazine named her the *"first hero of the planet."* It's rather curious that everyone has

---

[19] The practice of using a large, wide-mouthed fishing net dragged by a vessel along the ocean bottom, effectively clear-cutting the affected ecosystem. "As a result of these processes, a vast array of species are threatened around the world...The net effect of fishing practices on global coral reef populations is suggested by many scientists to be alarmingly high." Wikipedia ("trawling").

[20] http://www.un.org/News/Press/docs//2012/sgsm14287.doc.htm (Retrieved 11.10.13).

heard of Jacque Cousteau, and yet so few of us know the name of our native daughter and planetary hero, Sylvia Earle. Maybe it's because she has spent more time underwater than any living human. She once served as Chief Scientist for the National Oceanic and Atmospheric Agency. Today, she devotes all her time and energy to traveling the globe (on land) trying to alert us to the fact that, as she bluntly puts it, *the oceans are dying.*"

Oh… let that sink in for a moment. This is not the kind of statement a scientist would tend to make without a lot of careful forethought.

The oceans are victims of humanity's triple threat: 1) the aforementioned insanely efficient killing machines of industrial fishing, perpetrating a marine holocaust supported by every person who eats tuna fish, shark fin soup, sushi, or factory farmed chickens (chicken feed comes from the ocean); 2) greenhouse gases that are killing the coral reefs, source of so much of the ocean's rich biodiversity, by increasing the acidity of the water to the point that crustaceans may no longer be able to form shells in the very near future; and, 3) over-population – there are just too damn many of us with too much fish in our diets (and our pets' diets).

Please watch the brilliant documentary about Sylvia Earle, *Mission Blue*. It will make you to fall in love with her and her life story, in the same way we love Cousteau, and it presents a very positive role model of appropriate emotional engagement with the climate crisis from someone who probably cares more deeply about the ocean than any other human being on the planet. At the same time, you will be informed about the state of our watery planet at the level of feeling, not just intellect. It is much more important that we feel into these unfolding stories rather than just think them through.

Boris Worm, PhD, of Dalhousie University in Halifax, Nova Scotia recently headed up a study by an international team of ecologists and economists, and published the results of their research in the journal *Science*.[21] Their conclusion? At current rates of depletion, and accounting for the thresholds beyond which fisheries collapse, we can expect our oceans to be *devoid of fish by 2048!*

Oceans without fish!! In our lifetime!!!

As Sylvia Earle puts it in *Mission Blue*, "a world without living oceans is a world without us." And as Dr. Worm (no jokes, please - this is no laughing matter!) stated in a press release accompanying publication of the study, "I was shocked and disturbed by how consistent these trends are -- beyond anything we suspected."

The jolt felt by Dr. Worm from the results of his study was reflected at a more heartfelt level on a recent trans-Pacific voyage by Ivan Macfadyen, the kind of big pond crossing this accomplished maritime sailor had completed many times before. After his most recent trip he distressingly

---

[21] Worm, B. *Science*, Nov. 3, 2006; vol 314: pp 787-790.

recounted his "shock and horror" at the near absence of any life compared to his prior passages: "It felt as if the ocean itself was dead."[22]

From my perspective as an ecopsychologist, so-called 'climate change' is just the tip of the iceberg visible to the human eye, while just beneath the surface of our collective awareness this far greater 'oceanic' crisis is playing out. Viewed from up here on dry land, we tend to limit our perception of climate chaos to the dramatic changes in weather patterns that are just starting to wreak havoc on concentrated human populations - especially those on islands or along coastal areas. But look just beneath the surface, as Sylvia Earle says even she has a hard time doing anymore, and one finds a watery graveyard with ominous portents for our own great dying.

This happens to be what scares me the most right now. If the oceans really do pass a tipping point and die, then we really are not going to make it. Distressingly, according to the 2014 State of the Climate Report, which is based upon research assimilated from 413 scientists in 58 countries, we have already reached a point where it will not be possible to stop the warming of the oceans, which means of course that sea ice will continue to melt for the foreseeable future. Remember, the oceans happen to be immense reservoirs. As Greg Johnson, an oceanographer at NOAA's Pacific Marine Environmental Laboratory explains: "Even if we were to freeze greenhouse gases at current levels, the sea would actually continue to warm for centuries and millennia, and as they continue to warm and expand the sea levels will continue to rise."

It is now a fact that our coastal cities, which happen to be where 40% of us live (think NY, Boston, Miami, Houston, LA, SF, Seattle), are going to be increasingly battered in the coming decades, and will likely have to be evacuated in our children's lifetimes. It is *not* a fact yet, however, that these rising oceans are going to die, which would likely seal our fate as a species. The fact that they are *dying* right now is really all the information we need to resolve to take drastic actions to turn this critical situation around. Out of sight, out of mind will lead to out of luck if we fail to act on what we now know in relation to the deep blue sea.

Meth Heads

Let us now emerge once again from the depths of our global subconscious, and turn our periscopes onto dry land. People may snicker when informed that cows are a bigger problem for our planet than cars. What they fail to appreciate is that with 1.5 billion cows on Earth at any given time, there are 10.5 billion cow stomachs. Due to the nature of the bovine digestive system, cows are constantly emitting methane *through their mouths* (not just their anuses) from those 10.5 billion stomachs - one cow stomach spewing methane in both directions for every man, woman and child. Plus all those nasty cow pies coming out the business end. All tolled, a single cow emits about 30-50 gallons of methane per day, or about 15,000 gallons per year.

---

[22] Ray, G., "The Ocean is Broken," *Newcastle Herald*, Oct. 18, 2013 http://www.theherald.com.au/story/1848433/the-ocean-is-broken/ (Retrieved 11.10.13).

Multiply that by 1.5 billion cows, and we arrive at over 22 *trillion gallons* of methane per year just from cows alone. That's *22,000,000,000,000.*

The problem with methane is that it has about 100 times more heat-trapping potential in the short term than the main greenhouse gas, carbon dioxide, and about 25 times more over the long term (CO2 lasts a lot longer). So when you apply this to 22 trillion gallons of methane, and then you factor in all the CO2 emissions associated with clearing rainforest to graze cows and/or grow soybeans to feed them, and all the transportation costs associated with processing them and getting them to your plate, you begin to appreciate the magnitude of the problem with 'what's for dinner.' FACT: the livestock industry (livestock + byproducts) is responsible cumulatively for over half of all global warming today!

We are eating our McMother alive.

From the viewpoint of many scientists, methane is our biggest concern, and it has nothing to do with cows -- apart from the complicity of the livestock industry in warming the planet. Because once the planet heats up enough to trigger methane releases from permafrost and the ocean floors (frozen methane called clathrates), it is not unlike having a gas leak in your home -- a silent, invisible killer with explosive potential. If you had a gas leak in your home, you wouldn't tend to think "Oh, I'll take care of that when my financial situation improves." You'd act with a sense of life-and-death urgency. Not so, apparently, with a leaky planet threatening all higher life forms.

The worst of the five previous great extinctions, the one that is ominously referred to simply as the "Great Dying," resulted in the loss of 95% of all marine species and 70% of all land and airborne species. The severity of the Great Dying, which required ten million years to recover from, is largely attributed to mass releases of methane -- not from prehistoric cows, mind you, but rather from the oceans and tundras. These releases were triggered by, and had the effect of quickly doubling, a spike in global temperatures of *only about six degrees celsius* (attributed to increased volcanic activity burning off massive coal reserves, which were much closer to the surface at that time).

Baked Alaska

Fact: a 3.5 degree celsius increase in the planet's average temperature *could* render this planet uninhabitable for humans, and at a minimum will make it very difficult for us, due to severing the food chain at the fundamental level of oceanic plankton and prompting temperature swings that would severely limit our ability to sustain crops.[23] Humans have never lived on a planet at 3.5°C above baseline. It might not sound like a dramatic rise, but we're talking about over 6° Fahrenheit for what is a living planet. The best way to think of that is how concerned would you be if your child's temperature was over 104°? Exactly.

---

[23] http://www.truthdig.com/report/page3/are_we_falling_off_the_climate_precipice_20131219

While the Great Dying resulted from a rise of only 6°C (10.8°F), under the current (unenforceable) emission targets embedded into the Paris accords, we are on track for a 4-6°C rise in temperature before the end of this century - this according to no less an authority than the World Bank.[24] And this estimate happens to be on the low end of the probable rise.

A 2011 paper authored by Senior Scientist Jeffrey Kiehl and others from the National Center for Atmospheric Research and published in the peer-reviewed journal *Science* "found that carbon dioxide may have at least *twice* the effect on global temperatures than currently projected by computer models of global climate."[25] Contrary to the IPCC's own worst case scenario of a 6°C rise in average global temperature by 2100, which would in itself result in a virtually uninhabitable planet, *Kiehl et al.* distressingly conclude that our current trajectory may actually result in an unimaginable *16C* rise by the end of the century!

And then there is the problem with the internationally agreed upon threshold of 2°C itself. This, too, turns out to have been a political result, not scientific. It began as a scientific guess, actually, in 1990 of what would be a safe limit. However, the science has developed quite rapidly since then. According to a more defensible study by 18 of the world's leading climate experts, led by James Hansen, cumulative emissions associated with the 2°C global warming threshold would spur "slow" feedback loops (e.g., the thawing permafrost alone is projected to add as much as 1.5°F by 2100, and ocean acidification could add another 0.9°F), and these amplified feedbacks would, in turn, lock in another 1-2°C of warming, with "disastrous consequences" (e.g,. a sea level rise of *several meters*). The study concludes that we are already at the danger threshold with 1°C average global temperature rise, and we need to do everything we can to stay in this range, including *reducing* CO2 levels in the atmosphere before they are taken up as changes in our climate.

But don't tell that to our political leaders.

All of this is only compounded by the *real* 'inconvenient truth' - one that is rarely brought up in discussions of climate change, and which I bet 90% or more of Americans either do not know or still do not fully appreciate the significance of:

Fact: there is a *forty year* lag-time between global emissions (what we do) and climate impacts (what we experience).

---

[24] All the extreme weather events we are seeing now, from chronic droughts everywhere, to unprecedented flooding in Pakistan and Thailand, to super-storm Sandy, to the mega-typhoon that just devastated the Philippines, are the result of only a .8C rise to date. http://www.rollingstone.com/politics/news/global-warmings-terrifying-new-math-20120719

[25] http://www.commondreams.org/view/2013/05/18-1 (retrieved 11.11.13), Ahmed, N. (Executive Director of the Institute for Policy Research & Development), "Obama's Arctic Strategy Sets Off a Climate Time Bomb," Guardian, May 18, 2013. The conclusions of this study have more recently confirmed by other scientists writing in the same journal.

In other words, the record average temperatures of the last decade are a consequence of emissions *from the 1960's*, and the acceleration in climate change that we are now witnessing is locked in till at least *2060*.[26] As if this was not itself alarming enough, *there has been as much CO2 emitted since 1970 than during the entire period of the Industrial Age before 1970.*

So as we are already at 1C, as a result of all the CO2 released prior to 1970, and we have emitted that much CO2 again since 1970, Michael Oppenheimer, a professor of geosciences and international affairs at Princeton University and a member of the IPCC, states that a 2°C (3.2°F) rise is already baked in, thanks to the time lag. We are in for some very substantial changes to ecosystems and large scale transformations of the biosphere - such as loss of the coral reefs, which happen to serve as the nursery for the diversity of ocean life. Renowned Arctic expert Prof. Peter Wadhams, head of the Polar ocean physics group at Cambridge University, states bluntly:

> We are already in a 2C world in terms of the heating potential of carbon dioxide that we have already put into the atmosphere. The heating will reach 2C before 2050 and will then go on to 3-4C globally by the end of the century. Even a 2C world involves the probable loss of Arctic sea ice for much of the year (and 4C for most of it), which will ensure maximum methane release from the exposed shallow seas of the continental shelves.

Thus, while politicians continue to pay lip service to the agreed threshold of 2C average temperature rise, their emissaries - the climate negotiators for the Paris accord - were not themselves playing this dangerous public relations game. According to a report in the New York Times:[27]

> *The objective now, negotiators say, is to stave off atmospheric temperature increases of 4 to 10 degrees by the end of the century; at that point, they say, the planet could become increasingly uninhabitable.*

Say *what*?! Do you see the extent of the disconnect here?

While the science has developed from a largely unsupported assumption in 1990 that 2°C might be a safe threshold, the politics has developed to the point of shooting for somewhere *between* 2°C and 4°C! This is tantamount to the axis powers negotiating with Hitler in 1942 to limit deaths in his concentration camps to somewhere between 3-5 million.

This kind of political myopia is *symptomatic* of our disease, not a place to look to for a *cure!*

---

[26] Source: skepticalscience.com : climate change and the 40-year delay between cause and effect.

[27] Davenport, C., "Optimism Faces Grave Realities At Climate Talks" (Nov. 30, 2014).

So we know that things are almost assured of getting *at least* twice as bad as they are right now in the near term, given the political landscape, and it is looking like they are going to get a lot worse than that in our children's lifetimes. But living here in America, or elsewhere in the developed world, you might think to yourself "things don't really seem all that bad right now - apart from a freak storm now and then and unusual heat waves and cold snaps." I suspect that is the most prevalent form of cognitive dissonance in my homeland. So before going any further with this rather grim assessment of the state of the planet, let us ask ourselves: just what *is* the impact of climate change in the world right now - on *humans*.

Is This the Beginning of the End?

Let us consider more closely the bewildering disconnect between science, on one hand, and politics, media, and public sentiment, on the other. In an alarming *2007* report from the IPCC, these normally staid scientists warned that world governments had *eight years* to take 'drastic actions' in order to avoid catastrophic climate change. Three years later, the U.S. torpedoed any chance of taking *any* effective action globally, let alone 'drastic' action, before 2020 - thus locking in accelerating climate chaos now until at least 2060.[28]

That same year (2011), the International Energy Agency, an autonomous intergovernmental organization established in 1974 as an information source to its member states on international oil and energy markets, released a report warning world leaders that "unprecedented climate change has Earth *hurtling down a path of catastrophic proportions.*" This is not the kind of language usually employed by policy wonks and scientists. They went on to predict "giant waves of migration and mass mortality" in the absence of drastic actions.

Sure enough, it was not long before Europe was being overwhelmed by giant waves of migration out of Africa due to war and strife that is closely associated with climate-related extreme draught. And as already noted, the World Health Organization estimates that 3.5 *million* human beings die every year as a result of fossil fuel emissions. Here is another report you will not have seen in the corporate media: according to *The Global Burden of Disease Study* published in 2010 in the British medical journal *The Lancet*, there has been a *523% increase* in mortality due to "exposure to forces of nature" since 1970, making it the fastest growing cause of death of the 235 categories monitored.

A stark example of this kind of *un*natural disaster occurred, ironically enough, during the climate talks at Doha, Qatar in 2012, when a devastating typhoon swamped the Philippines, killing more than 500 and leaving more than a quarter-million people without homes. Yeb Saño, a member of the Philippines Climate Change Commission, broke down while addressing the Doha assembly:

---

[28] When the U.S. won agreement at the climate summit in Durban, S.A. in 2011 to kick the can down the road, many of the activists in Africa protested vigorously, and with credible science backing them us, that this amounted to a death sentence for as many as *20 million* Africans! None of the American corporate media outlets covered this story. Not one. Can you say 'institutional racism'? And America's most virulent climate denier, who shall remain nameless on these pages, exclaimed that Obama was, in his eyes, much 'better' than Bush on the climate.

"We have never had a typhoon like Bopha, which has wreaked havoc in a part of the country that has never seen a storm like this in half a century. And heartbreaking tragedies like this are not unique to the Philippines, because the whole world, especially developing countries struggling to address poverty and achieve social and human development, confront these same realities. Please... let 2012 be remembered as the year the world found the courage to take responsibility for the future we want. I ask of all of us here, if not us, then who? If not now, then when? If not here, then where?"

The next climate talks to take place, in Warsaw, Poland, coincided with yet *another* devastating typhoon in the Philippines, 'Super Typhoon' Haiyan - said to be *the strongest tropical cyclone ever to make landfall in recorded history*, and the deadliest ever to hit the Philippines, killing over 6300 people - and once again Mr. Saño addressed the delegates, this time as the head of the Philippine delegation:

"What my country is going through as a result of this extreme climate event is *madness*. The climate crisis is madness. *We can stop this madness*. Right here in Warsaw. Typhoons such as Haiyan and its impacts represent a sobering reminder to the international community that we cannot afford to procrastinate on climate action... We have entered a new era that demands global solidarity in order to fight climate change and ensure that pursuit of sustainable human development remains at the fore of the global community's efforts... *Can humanity rise to the occasion?* I still believe we can."

The response from the world community was to ensure that Mr. Saño would not be invited to the next round of climate talks, in Lima, Peru in 2014 - apparently a result of pressure being brought to bear on the Philippine government by the U.S. When the Lima talks were taking place in 2015, without Mr. Saño's participation, *Super Typhoon Hagupit hit the Philippines!* Good thing the U.S. negotiators were not confronted with that inconvenient coincidence, as it might have made them more uncomfortable in gutting the process previously established for compensating small countries like the Philippines for bearing the brunt of our irresponsible affluence.

First climate chaos claimed Africans - but I was not African, so I ignored it. Then climate mayhem was felt by the Philippines - but I was not a Philippine, so I paid it no mind... (Does this sound familiar?)

Here are the words from Mr. Saño that made the delegates so uncomfortable in Warsaw, which effectively make the point that even those who are charged with addressing the climate crisis by the 190 participating countries in the climate talks are in deep denial:

To anyone who continues to deny the reality that is climate change, I dare you to get off your ivory tower and away from the comfort of you armchair. I dare you to go to the islands of the Pacific, the islands of the Caribbean and the islands of the Indian ocean and see the impacts of rising sea levels; to the mountainous regions of the Himalayas and the Andes to see communities confronting glacial floods, to the Arctic where communities grapple with the fast dwindling polar ice caps, to the large deltas of the Mekong, the Ganges, the Amazon, and the Nile where lives and livelihoods are drowned, to the hills of Central America that confronts similar monstrous hurricanes, to the vast savannas of Africa where climate change has likewise become a matter of life and death as food and water becomes scarce. Not to forget the massive hurricanes in the Gulf of Mexico and the eastern seaboard of North America. And if that is not enough, you may want to pay a visit to the Philippines right now.

That is called speaking truth to power.

Here is a very apt summation of the fact that the European refugees from Africa are, in fact, climate refugees, from a rather unlikely source (an evangelical Christian blogger, bless his soul):[29]

The catastrophic 2011-12 droughts in the Russian, Australian and American breadbaskets drove global spikes in grain prices that resulted in intense food riots in North Africa, later known as the Arab Spring. The multi-year drought in Syria drove a tide of small farmers off their land into urban slums, intensifying pressures that led to the bloody civil war that still rages there. The Darfur genocide of the last decade has been widely called the first climate change war, as Muslim pastoralists fleeing persistent drought clashed with Christian agrarian villagers.

Yes, that's right - the civil war that has torn Syria apart was precipitated by mass migrations associated with climate-related extreme drought and food shortages.[30] In fact, the first shots were fired by government forces at displaced farmers who were attempting to dig wells without a permit near the capitol.

Finally, a June 2014 report from the United Nations University's Institute for Environment and Human Security acknowledges the fact that *"hundreds of thousands of people are already migrating because of climate change..."*[31] In fact, there are millions already who have fled Syria

---

[29] Beloved Planet (belovedplanet.com), "Hearing the gospel's call to care for an injured world." I say unlikely because of my perception that there is a strong tendency with Christian Evangelicals to quickly resort to end-times Biblical prophecy, which assumes of course that God, and not humans, is in control of the situation. It is really encouraging to see something constructive like this, instead.

[30] See, e.g.: Fallows, J., "Why Climate Change May Be Responsible for the Horrors in Syria," *Alternet* (Sept. 2, 2013).

[31] Brown, P., "Help Needed Now For Climate Refugees," *Climate News Network* (June 11, 2014).

alone, so the report conservatively excluded that 'giant wave' as a result of war, not climate chaos. According to the report, rising oceans, extreme weather events, and more gradual natural disasters such as the kinds of chronic droughts we are already seeing (at 1C above baseline) will continue to cause unplanned mass population movements which will continue leading to armed conflicts and lack of basic security. And according to former U.N. Secretary Kofi Annan's non-profit group, we can expect another 60 million refugees out of Africa - before 2020!

Climate Insecurity & Scientific Uncertainty

There are perfectly reputable, rational scientists today that have concluded from the body of evidence referenced above that near term human extinction is inevitable. To me, as an Ecopsychologist, that is not just an untenable projection - I suspect it actually represents a subtle kind of despair dressed up in scientific garb. To some extent, it even seems to be based on the same kind of scientific hubris that made us think we could control and manipulate our environment in the first place (i.e., the predictability of complex living systems). When it comes to proving that climate chaos is being caused by humans and our obsession with digging up fossils and burning them, science is very reliable. But when it comes to predicting the future, climate scientists have been notoriously unreliable.

This unreliability now occurs along a spectrum. At one end of that spectrum is the IPCC and its assertion, until very recently, that we still have time to curb emissions and avoid a two degree celsius rise above baseline. That wishful thinking was mostly the product of political spin, and represents a kind of scientific assuredness that is at odds with the simple fact that climate change has outpaced and surprised climate scientists at every turn.

At the other end of the spectrum, we have climate scientists who are obsessively focused on the worst news, and their predictions regarding the inevitability of near term human extinction is a kind of scientific pessimism that is not qualitatively different than the hubris of the IPCC. Is near term human extinction a significant risk? *Of course it is.* Is it inevitable, or even probable? It is still impossible to say, even in the long term.

One reputable scientist who happens to agree with me on this point is Lee Klinger, an independent scientist who worked for many years at the National Center for Atmospheric Research, a leading institution in the study of climate. Mr. Klinger points out that most of the science we read about on the climate presumes that the Earth is not a living organism itself, and thus does not present a big variable in their equations. Because of this, he cautions:

> Regarding the science of climate change, it is my observation that many scientists on both sides of the debate are expressing a much higher level of confidence in their findings than is warranted by the data.[32]

---

[32] "Climate Change and the Living Gaia," *The Ecologist* (1.10.15)

Based upon a lifetime of experience in environmental science at many of the major institutions around the world, Mr. Klinger has come to the conclusion that the Earth is, in fact, a living organism. This scientific world view, known as the 'Gaia theory' first put forth by the UK scientist James Lovelock, considers the many biological and ecological couplings with air, land, and ocean that are involved in the self-regulation of a living planet, and concludes that something as complex as the climate is not reducible to tidy little mathematical formulas, which Klinger characterizes as the prevalent 'standard Earth theory.'

It is critical that concerned laypersons like ourselves keep this distinction in mind when we consider the scientific conclusions of those who would pretend to know what is going to happen decades from now. Not that we should ever *dismiss* any credible views. Just that we need to consider them in an appropriate context and put them in perspective, rather than becoming overwhelmed when we find ourselves reacting emotionally.

What more do we really *need* to know than what we can see happening right now before our collective eyes?
• A great extinction unfolding unlike anything that has occurred in the last 65 million years!
• Nearly *half of all wildlife* has been wiped out during the short time in which our global population has doubled.
• The oceans are in deep trouble.
• There is a 40 year time lag between carbon emissions and climate change, and we have emitted as much in the last 40 years as was emitted in the entire industrial age leading up to that point in time.

It is abundantly clear, therefore, that life as we have come to know it and think of it is ending. And we are just at the *beginning* of this process. There is no reason to go any further in our consideration of the science. As it definitely represents a terminal condition for many vitally important species, like elephants and polar bears, and as it implies a tremendous amount of human suffering, we would be well advised to begin preparing to alleviate all this suffering as much as possible right now.

About That Population Explosion...

Elizabeth Kolbert, a wonderful scientific reporter who was the first in the mainstream to sound the alarm on what is happening to our oceans (in a New Yorker series), and is author of *The Sixth Great Extinction*, lamented to an audience in Missoula once that she was in despair over the lack of any change in attitudes, let alone action, following her award-winning series. She enlisted a marketing firm to help her understand this, and discovered that the average consumer believes that if things were really that serious, surely our government would do something about it. This was near the turn of the millennium, and my sense is that we have since learned just how broken and deeply dysfunctional our government has become -and how beholden it is to large multinational corporations.

Our government is not going to lead us out of this mess. Instead, they are going to follow us. It is up to us. This is why I am writing this book. To let you know that. We are our only hope.

Here's something else we know from the science of biology. The kind of exponential population growth that we have been experiencing since the advent of the industrial age is not sustainable. Species are limited by the constraints of their ecosystem, which for 7 billion+ humans now happens to be the planet itself. When species gain an advantage over other species and have no other limits on their ability to reproduce, their population grows according to the law of the Malthusian curve, which looks like this:

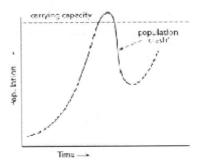

Climate chaos is the clearest indication that the collective emissions of ourselves, our machinery, and our cows have now surpassed the planet's ability to absorb those emissions. And so it appears to me, and this is my own personal conclusion (not a fact), that we humans are now perched *atop* the Malthusian population curve, poised to peak somewhere near 9 billion, and then as climate mayhem *really* kicks in, as droughts become pandemic, diseases like ebola (maybe not ebola itself, but like that) spread, or antibiotics stop working thanks to their overuse by factory farms, as resource wars heat up and economies collapse (likely to happen *long* before the population peak), as natural disasters become the rule, and not the exception, perhaps when ocean currents shift - a big game-changer that is no longer unlikely - and extreme weather also becomes the norm (which it kind of is already, but even more so), we are bound to experience a *precipitous* drop in our population. Probably back down to 3 billion much quicker than we doubled it, and quite possibly even below a billion before the climate has a chance to stabilize.

Can We Have a Happy Ending?

So, not a pretty picture. I hope I'm wrong, of course, but I'm afraid my intuitions are not far off the mark here. I am convinced, however, that we will survive. And believe it or not, I'm an optimist! What do I mean by that? Fair question.

I actually believe that adversity brings out the best in human beings -- and this is going to be the greatest adversity that we have ever faced. Therefore, it is going to bring out something better in us than we have ever known we are capable of. Remember, the Great Depression and Hitler's Holocaust produced what many justifiably call "the greatest generation." The so-called 'millennials' - the first generation to grow up in this brave new world, knowing from an early age that the future of life on planet Earth was no longer a given - may well turn out to be even greater than the greatest. I have a lot deeper regard for kids today than I do for my own peers or the Gen-X crowd. It looks like all these wise old souls are coming on line at this most critical of times.

A pessimist would say dropping off the Malthusian curve is going to bring out the worst in us, and I agree that the survivalist mentality of those who would react emotionally by isolating themselves in sheltered enclaves with plenty of ammo is going to be a problem. But I suspect that they will end up effectively forming circular firing squads. From my perspective, we humans embody eternal truths in our mythologies, not our histories. The stories we tell ourselves about ourselves reveal essential information in times like these. We can look to our collective myths for answers about both the past and the future. Just watch the *Lord of the Rings* trilogy sometime if you want to see what I'm talking about here, or even *The Matrix*. These kinds of resonant myths surface from our subconscious during times like these for a reason. There is great utility and wisdom in our determination to plow any and all adversity we encounter into our path with great compassion, dignity, and love. In the end, the hobbits return to the Shire. Zion survives because of Neo's great love and sacrifice. Humans are actually pretty cool.

So it is quite enough, thank you very much, to simply recognize and acknowledge what is unfolding all around us, to consider the very real suffering associated with these cascading developments, to begin fortifying ourselves for the future, and to recognize the prevalent absence of adequate psychological tools for dealing with all of this calamity in our present health care structure. I'm really unclear on what the point is in speculating about the odds of the human species surviving or going extinct. The mere risk of human extinction should certainly be motivation enough for us to fully engage with the crisis we face. In fact, the mere fact of unnatural rates of extinction for other species should be enough in itself.

After all, people, we already know that we're all going to die, don't we? Every human being who has ever lived has died - except those of us alive today. And a tomorrow will surely come that does not include me or you. Sometimes I wonder if those who are jumping to the conclusion that we are doomed as a species are not projecting their own fear of mortality onto the entire human species. But that is mere speculation on my part. I'm not here to judge others' fear.

Regarding future outcomes, then, we can see the great wisdom in the practice of "don't know mind" when it comes to the climate crisis. This does not mean that we don't acknowledge the whole range of unattractive possibilities. Our fear of those various possible outcomes can intelligently inform our actions. Instead, it means we should avoid unnecessary *fatalism* regarding future outcomes, and deal instead with witnessing and accommodating what is unfolding in the present moment as best we can. There is great wisdom in that.

Together, I know we can get through this. But we have to get our story straight first.

Let us find common ground upon which to begin building a better future for all who are to come, human and non-human. In other words, let us take responsibility for our own future, rather than leaving it to chance or to a global political establishment that has proven itself incompetent, immoral, and unable to lead.

This is what we are being called to do.

<u>CHAPTER 4</u>

RADICAL INTERDEPENDENCE:
The Rise of a New World View

"No longer simply a religion of individuals and of heaven, but a religion of humankind and the earth---that is what we are looking for at this moment, as the oxygen without which we cannot breathe."

~ Pierre Teilhard de Chardin, Activation of Energy

War of the Worldviews

From an environmental perspective, the climate crisis began with the Industrial Revolution about 250 years ago. Some would go further, all the way back to the time when we developed agriculture on the banks of the Tigris and Euphrates rivers, clearing the way for the development of cities and states from what had up to that point in time been a nomadic, hunter/gatherer, nature-based culture. While there is definitely truth in that big picture observation, for our purposes it would be difficult to maintain that humanity lost its intimate connection to nature the day we started cultivating the Earth.

Agriculture was not about turning away from the natural world. Instead, quite simply, it was just a new and exciting way of coming into relationship with the natural world - to work *with* it to cyclically produce food with the seasons, instead of what must have felt up until that time like always being at the natural world's mercy, almost like working *against* it (e.g., by needing to kill prey in order to survive, and in turn being preyed upon by other carnivores). Depending on the Earth for sustenance and survival in some ways made us even more intimate with her, and for millennia we would pray to the heavens and Earth for her fertility, and we even developed a wide variety of rituals honoring that near complete - but relatively satisfactory - dependence.

For the most part, we remained in intimate relationship with, and cultivated a healthy respect for, our Mother Earth throughout the agricultural age and the advent of modern civilization - connecting with her daily through our mouths and stomachs, in addition to our daily and seasonal rituals. The nurturing relationship with our mothers that we enjoyed at birth, nursing for our sustenance from her bosom, was quite naturally transposed onto the Earth itself, deriving a lifetime's sustenance from her rich, dark fertility by the banks of great, surging rivers and in the light of the waxing sun and full moon. Until we inadvertently poisoned this relationship with lethal, toxic, and even radioactive chemical substances, it was a pretty good deal! It worked for over eleven hundred centuries.

But this is still all rather academic, because the climate crisis is not, as we have been led to believe, an environmental problem. To say that the climate crisis is rooted in a split between psyche and nature is not the same as saying it is a *psychological* problem, either. The psychology of the climate crisis, which involves the suppression and repression of grief over the loss of this natural, immemorial connectivity, is crucial to resolving the crisis, as we will see. But *the split itself* - the split *qua* split, or unconscious schism - is rooted in something even deeper than our psychological response to the dust bowls of the Great Depression, when nature appeared to turn on us, and the horrific conclusion of the Holocaust, when we as a people under assault assumed real dominion over nature and total control over the forces of creation and destruction. No, the *deep* taproot of this existential crisis we are now facing, reflected and forcefully manifested in runaway climate chaos and 'abrupt climate change,' is ultimately a *spiritual* problem.

As Naomi Klein rightly points out in her book *This Changes Everything:*

**Any attempt to rise to the climate challenge will be fruitless unless
it is understood as part of a much broader *battle of worldviews*…**

Our worldview is no longer harmonious with the world itself. We have fallen out of balance with
nature, we are increasingly falling out of any rational relationship with time… and it seems like
we cannot get up. But if we do not recover our balance with nature, if we do not harmonize and
synchronize our worldview with the natural world and cyclic time, then every attempt to solve
the climate crisis will just lead to unintended consequences, serving only to perpetuate the crisis
in different ways. That has been the history of the environmental era. For every problem we
"solve," three new unintended problems are created. We see this carried to extremes with so-
called technical fixes like fracking, advanced as some kind of 'bridge' to a cleaner future.

The reason for this dysfunction is that we are forever addressing physical symptoms, acting as if
the world is our laboratory instead of seeing ourselves as an extension of the world. We never
seem to get around to acknowledging, let alone treating, the underlying spiritual dis-ease that has
us at such odds with the natural world. This is what a career in environmental law and wildlife
advocacy spanning three decades taught me. When the symptoms progressed from local to
bioregional to global, from illness to cancer to terminal dis-ease, I had to walk away from the
conflict/political arena and explore the spiritual and psychological dimensions of the crisis we
have created through our collective hubris.

I am one who compulsively traces things to their roots, as well as one who can not seem to
tolerate complications. I long ago took Thoreau's injunctive to heart: "Simplify, simplify,
simplify." At the risk of over-simplifying this issue here, I am reminded of a song from the
influential "space rock" band of the early 70s (my wastrel high school years), Hawkwind:

> *Think about the things that we should have done before*
> *The way things are going the end is about to fall.*
> *We took the wrong step years ago*
> *We took the wrong step years ago*
> *We took the wrong step years ago*

The last refrain always haunted me, because it seemed like they were expressing a deep intuition
shared by many of us who were "experienced," as Jimi put it. There was something rotten at the
core of our culture that we sensed but could not quite put our finger on - though it seemed to taint
everything about the society we were raised to believe in. My mind may be slow, but I am able to
compensate for not being really quick on the uptake by being doggedly *thorough*. So it may have
taken many years, but I finally have learned what that wrong step we took many years ago was.

51

Splitting the atom may have effectively severed our connection to nature at its physical root, but this split was conceived in our guiding philosophy centuries ago, with the revolutionary, pervasive influence of a French philosopher famous for not trusting his own senses. Whether or not you know him by name, you definitely know him by his words:

"I think, therefore I am."

Speaking of great bands of my youth, I always appreciated *The Moody Blues* addendum to Descartes' famous dictum: *"I think, therefore I am... I think."* The wrong step that Rene Descartes (pron. "day cart") took, and in so taking led all of humankind down the primrose path, is today referred to as 'Cartesian Dualism' - another fancy term that is not that complicated. Simply put, it is the monstrous idea that there is me, *in here*, and all of nature *out there*. This is the divisive seed that mushroomed three centuries later in a cloud of poisoned fire over the White Sands Proving Ground, and then over Hiroshima, and then Nagasaki, the Bikini atolls...

This absurd notion that humankind somehow stands apart from nature!

It seems rather inevitable from that starting point that we would eventually want to *control* nature, to assert dominion and become gods over all that we surveyed. Sure does explain the European expansion into "new worlds" - doesn't it? It reached its height with the westward expansion and settlement of America, where we eliminated not only indigenous peoples, but replaced native bison with European cows and changed the courses of mighty rivers to suit our whims. *If only Descartes had spent a few months hiking solo in the wilderness!*

As Christ, Buddha, and Mohammed all did. Rene's corrosive, 'citified' idea of our separation from nature is still fundamental to the way we think, the way we see ourselves, and the way we view 'our' world (i.e., as *ours*!).

And it is killing us…

Cartesian dualism is all about the 'reification' of subject and object. Reification is a really important term to keep close to mind if we want to reduce suffering in our life. To reify something means to take a concept and concretize it, making it synonymous with reality in a way that does not permit competition from alternative views. For example, to say that Jesus Christ is God, or the reification of 'ego' by Western psychologists. To reify subject and object, therefore, means that - from Descartes on - we take *ourselves* to be the subjects, supremely real because God created us in His image (yes, Descartes was very much a theologian), and we *objectified - or made impersonal objects out of - everything else.*

This is reflected in the way we talk at almost every level. "It's raining outside." *What* is raining outside, exactly?

This is the basis for viewing/treating animals as unfeeling objects with no souls (since bodies, even our own, are just meat machines in Descartes way of thinking, with the soul being the 'ghost in the machine' that is unique to humans - *uggh!*). Thus it is the basis for experimenting on animals and subjecting them to factory farms, among other inhumane atrocities. It happens to be the basis as well for the very kind of scientific experimentation that eventually led to splitting the atom and creating hell on Earth. And it goes without saying that it fits hand-in-glove with the idea of manifest destiny, by which wilderness is to be 'tamed,' savages are to be exterminated, 'primitive' (godless) people enslaved, and nature itself becomes something God put here for us white Anglo-Saxon people to exploit for our own ends, without regard to any unintended consequences - such as displacing other living creatures from their natural ecosystems, or the 'collateral damage' suffered by natives and slaves.

God has a 'plan,' after all - which apparently included industrial ovens and gas chambers for 6 million Jews, *also* a product of the Cartesian world view. Jews were 'other,' unfeeling swine, and vastly inferior to the god-like Germans, in much the same objectified way that blacks and Indians were inferior to we Europeans and not deserving of our sympathies.

In other words, the very idea of a *consumer society*, which is based on objectifying animals as "commodities" and exploiting natural resources to the point of exhaustion, would not have been feasible without this world view of Cartesian duality. Calling it 'religious' does not make it so. We would not be perpetrating the world's 6th Great Extinction, and we would not be confronted with this existential climate crisis, if we still (by way of example) happened to share the world view of the Aboriginal people of Australia, or the non-dualistic perspectives of any of the remaining nature-based peoples of the world who would never *think* of seeing nature as something to be possessed, dominated, spoiled, and disposed of.

Therefore, the very first step each of us must take in assuming personal responsibility for our shared climate is to ask the simple, but profound, spiritual question:

Was Descartes right?

Ironically, the very institution of modern science which Descartes gave birth to eventually proved that the world view he enshrined, and which became the basis of European world domination - and, yes, our very own American Dream - was fatally wrong.

Oops!

The Emerging Quantum World View

The most famous scientist to reject the validity of Cartesian dualism was Albert Einstein. Einstein's methodology was famously subjective, using his own big brain (and chalkboard) to conduct his experiments while leaving it to others to prove his theories through more traditional ('objective') scientific means. But his subjectivity went much deeper than simply disdaining laboratories. Consider *his own* world view, as related in a letter to the N.Y. Times towards the end of his life, in 1950:

> A human being is part of a whole, called by us the 'Universe,' a part limited in time and space. He experiences himself, his thoughts and feelings, as something separated from the rest--a kind of optical delusion of his consciousness. This delusion is a kind of prison for us, restricting us to our personal desires and to affection for a few persons nearest us. *Our task must be to free ourselves from this prison by widening our circles of compassion to embrace all living creatures and the whole of nature in its beauty.*

Einstein wasn't alone in his non-dualism. A whole new world view began to emerge from science around the middle of the twentieth century. During what clearly was the darkest time in our civilized history, a new light began to emerge in the form of a 'new' world view that just happens to rather accurately reflect the much older wisdom still cradled by the indigenous cultures we have consistently dismissed with ignorant labels like 'primitive' or 'backward.'

But before illuminating this world view from its sprouting in quantum physics to its subsequent flowering in Ecopsychology, let us consider why it is that the Cartesian world view still dominates our culture, and why we have yet to make the necessary course corrections. The answer to this question is revealed by examining just how it is such systemic shifts in our collective consciousness come about. If we are going to be part of such a shift now, it helps to understand how it is that, as the bumper sticker says, *SHIFT HAPPENS*.

A 'paradigm' is a shared framework of ideas, assumptions, and examples that all flow from, and serve to illustrate, the core theme or discovery - from which they emanate out like spokes from the hub of a wheel. Not unlike a world view, though perhaps not quite as pervasive. For example, when Copernicus discovered that the Earth revolves around the sun, the paradigm that placed humans at the center of the universe began to shift to the more participatory paradigm that underpins our modern world view today. Suddenly, we were just one of many planets revolving around the sun. One can imagine, over time, how this might effect religious thinking, and lead eventually to the existential angst of the Earth being just a solitary speck adrift in a vast, impersonal universe. Even politically, we can see how undermining the idea of a perfectly ordered universe, with God above and Earth at the center, might lead people to begin questioning a monarch's divine right of rule, in which all his or her subjects revolve around the ruler as the naturally ordained representative of God. All previous assumptions slowly came into question as people learned that the natural order they had always been assured was 'fixed' was, in truth, not the way things existed at all. This is an example of a paradigm shift in world views.

Stanislav Grof offers the most insightful and concise description of how paradigms change in Western science in his book *Beyond the Brain* (1985). "A really new and radical theory is never just an addition or increment to the existing knowledge," Grof points out. Instead, it "changes basic rules, requires drastic revision or reformulation of the fundamental assumptions of prior theory, and involves re-evaluation of the existing facts and observations."

No field has really seen the kind of cataclysmic paradigm shifts that physics has over the last century. For the longest time, two centuries in fact, science developed in a kind of linear, orderly fashion from the paradigm shift ushered in by Copernicus and Newton, culminating with Einstein's theories of relativity. But then, before it even had a chance to realign itself in accordance with Einstein's theories, with all the strangeness they entail - such as bent space and non-linear time - along came **quantum mechanics** and all *its* mind-altering discoveries, which even baffled Einstein himself! While he is famous for refuting the central theories of quantum mechanics with the dismissive assertion that "God doesn't play dice," in truth, after he had died, it was proven that God really *does* play dice. Einstein's characterization of non-locality as "spooky action at a distance" has also been shown to be real, no matter how spooky he found it.

We can even transport particles instantly across space and time now! Did you know that? Just like *Star Trek*! How many people are even aware of that fact? Or how many people realize that when they go in for a CT scan, they are benefitting from anti-matter traveling *backward in time* to meet matter? While technology may race ahead at breakneck speed, from the Wright brothers finally getting a plane off the ground in 1902 to landing the 'Eagle' on the moon just six decades later, it actually takes a lot longer for our world view to change. We're only now beginning to develop a quantum world view.

According to discoveries in quantum physics, we now know without any question that the objectivity of Descartes was an illusion - there is no reality *apart from* the participation of an observer to perceive that reality. In other words, no objective reality exists apart from the subjective observer. In fact, the reality perceived depends in part on the *expectations* of the observer! Many see this as the most startling discovery of the 20th Century, and given that science was developed entirely on the foundation of Cartesian dualism, the subject/object split and the idea that anything could be viewed in isolation from us, we can perhaps understand in retrospect why this scientific reality from quantum physics seemed so hard to accept. For many of us non-scientists, it still is.

Take the classic example of the electron. As a preliminary matter, an electron only exists as a cloud of potential, or probabilities as to where it might be at any given point in time, and it is only when we seek to *measure* the electron that this cloud of probability, called a wave function, collapses into the appearance of an electron, as if it is 'permitting' us to observe it in some measurable way. Stranger still, when we set up a laboratory test to prove that an electron is a discrete particle traveling through space, as we have always imagined it to be, it behaves as such - piercing a permeable barrier in one discrete place. But if we set up the same apparatus instead to prove that the electron is a wave, not a particle, it behaves as a wave - penetrating the barrier in multiple, interval places at the same time! Suddenly the laws of classical physics themselves collapse! How can an electron be in two places at once?! Thus, an electron is now referred to as a particle-wave that exists as a probability cloud until we observe it.[33]

This may sound like so much theory, or even science fiction, until you stop to consider that it is electrons that determine how atoms behave and form elements, and that we ourselves are comprised of atoms and elements. Electrons are basically the animating (electrically charged) force of life, and they are everywhere. They are not just "out there" somewhere to be observed by our mind. It is as if they are *conjured up* by our mind! Nor is our mind just "in here" as if encapsulated and insulated from the world, taking it all in as if enjoying a movie on a screen. The states of our mind, our moods and thoughts, themselves co-emerge with nature in dependence upon electrons in the atmosphere that are entering into our brains through our blood via the breath in our lungs.

For example, the reason that we feel better when in nature, especially at higher elevations ("Rocky Mountain high"), while we feel cranky in a big city, especially a polluted city on a hot day, is because the air we are breathing into our lungs and blood in the mountains is *charged* with negative ions - atoms that have an extra ('free') electron - while the air in a big city is charged with positive ions - atoms that are missing an electron. So in this case, a negative state of mind is good! In Los Angeles, when the Santa Anna winds - unusual winds massively charged with positive ions - seasonally blow in off the western slopes of the Santa Anna mountains, the police go on high alert and even add staff because they know that violent and domestic crime rates will spike.

As the Nobel Laureate quantum physicist Wolfgang Pauli commented to Carl Jung, "the unconscious is in both man and nature" - in much the same way light is both in the bulb and in the room. Mind and matter are not so distinct.

So one very funda*mental* way we are intimately connected to nature is through the air we breathe. Obviously, the same can be seen from the things we drink and eat. When we get dehydrated, our mind becomes delirious. And we really *are* what we eat - quite literally. Even our *dreams* can be altered by the foods we eat. Eating junk food leads to poisonous thoughts. Have you ever heard of the 'twinkie defense' - the issue in a criminal trial of a sugary diet's contribution to depression, that can in turn contribute to someone snapping and acting out violently? More commonly, every parent knows full well the effect sugar has on children. Another common example is the drugged effect the tryptophan in turkey has on people at Thanksgiving. We'll leave entheogens (e.g., magic mushrooms) out of this discussion!

The point here is that, contrary to Descartes' idea that we are apart from nature, ensouled in bodies like ghosts in a machine, what is just beginning to emerge in our consciousness is a more

---

[33] Just so the reader doesn't make the mistake of thinking this phenomenon is relegated to electrons, it should be pointed out that the largest 'object' so far to have been tested as a wave, and observed to behave in a wavelike manner, is the molecule fullerene, made up of 60 carbon atoms!

quantum world view where there are really *no boundaries* in the world, nothing that separates us from nature - or all 'others' for that matter. 90% of the cells in our bodies have their own DNA! Meaning that we are actually only 10% 'human.'[34] In fact, of the 4.4 million genes in the human body, only 21,000 are human. The other 99.5% of our genes belong to viruses, bacteria, fungi, and other organisms that live in us.

In Ecopsychology, we see the human being as a natural ecosystem in communion with a larger ecosystem. There is the story of the world being supported by a turtle. "What is the turtle resting on?" Another turtle. "And that?!"

Turtles all the way down.

And as almost everyone knows by now, every single atom in our body originated in a star. There isn't even a boundary between our mind and our body. Diet contributes to mental disease, stress is associated with cancer, and thoughts can produce cures.

So slowly, but surely, the dualistic and materialistic views from scientism that have been handed down to us through the ages from Descartes are being replaced by a much more radical and naturalist view of the world that everyone and every 'thing' is interconnected and interdependent.

But guess what? *There are no things!*

When we really get right down to it, splitting the atom up into component parts and trying to measure those, we eventually get to a point where we are measuring mass-less particles, like photons of light. There is no 'there' there! Only referent points. According to physicist Laurent Nottale, the "profound view of the very nature of existence" that emerges from the quantum world is that since "things do not exist in absolute terms, but do nevertheless exist, then their nature must be sought in the relationships that bring them together. *Only these relationships between objects exist, and not the objects themselves.* Objects are relationships..."[35]

Think about THAT in relation to our world view today. *We objectify everything* - and only rarely consider the web of relationships that give rise to the object of our acquisitive desire. Such is the power of cultural conditioning in a consumer society. This is proof that the emergent world view of interdependence is only half-formed at best -- superficial and formative. And our habit of objectifying everything, including nature, including *each other* even, is really a destructive addiction. Try to think of any problem in the world, or in your life for that matter, that is not founded on objectifying some thing. We fight wars over these imaginary ideas that this is Israel, and that is Lebanon, with a line drawn on a map through a desert where sand is blowing from

---

[34] See, e.g.: *10% Human*, Collen, A., p. 8 (2015, Harper books).

[35] Heisenberg, W. 1971. *Physics and Beyond: Encounters and Conversations.* NY: Harper & Rowe. (from Ricard & Thuan, *The Quantum and the Lotus*, p. 88.

one side to the other. Sexual violence and aggression is based on objectifying women and children. Heck, it wasn't that long ago that we considered women and slaves as property.

This objectifying world view is perhaps the greatest human affliction, or mental disease, in our civilization's history. *What if we had a 'relational' world view instead?* One that was actually in accordance with, and not opposed to, the way things actually exist? A 'realistic' world view?

Thanks to globalization and the internet, most people now at least recognize that we're all interconnected, and when we consider climate change, we start to appreciate how interdependent we all really are with everyone and everything else. But when we consider a hamburger, for example, most of us are still reduced to our inner Homer Simpson, still just seeing a hamburger -- *'yumm, tasty!'* -- and not the factory farm where the cow was raised, the thousands of gallons of water that went into that single meat patty, or the complex relationships between ourselves and our environment that are presented to us on that styrofoam plate upon which the burger rests.

We just see a juicy hamburger - "mine" - and we only feel our sensual desire for it. We don't even see all the pervasive conditioning from which that desire emerges. Like social automatons, or the meat machines that Descartes imagined in his schizoid brain. "I'm hungry, therefore I eat." A more relational world view would look like this:

> "I think about where my food came from, therefore I am connected to a healthy planetary system of life."

The Evolution Will Not Be Televised!

Objects are relationships…

What kind of paradigmatic shift is *this* startling scientific discovery starting to arouse? And what kind of cultural revolution will result from integrating this relational perspective into our world view? A *relational* worldview versus an *objective* worldview - how would that look in the world? How does it make you *feel*?

The central point of Grof's book *Beyond the Brain* was that we were, at that time -1985, during Reagan's second term - just beginning to see "a paradigm shift of unprecedented proportions" that would in time change not just our concepts of reality but *of human nature itself.* Even so, as Grof was quick to point out, many theoretical physicists *themselves* refuse to grapple with the unsettling philosophical questions raised by quantum mechanics, a point echoed twenty-five years later by Matthieu Ricard - a brilliant French mathematician in his own right who became a Buddhist monk - in his book of conversations with Vietnamese physicist Trinh Xuan Thuan, *The Quantum and the Lotus.*

So we shouldn't feel bad if we as laypersons have yet to integrate the still-emerging quantum world view into our dietary choices! Change happens along a spectrum - slowly, slowly, one at a time and then all at once.

The point of all this is not that if someone is concerned about the climate crisis and is ready to assume responsibility for their part in it, they need to study quantum physics! No, if you haven't guessed already, the point here is that there is no 'Earth out there' and 'me in here' or even a 'you over there' to begin with.

The Earth is not an object!

No more than you or I are objects. As James Lovelock so brilliantly asserted over forty years ago, and Sir David Attenborough so beautifully illustrated in his popular television series for the BBC and then PBS, the Earth is an organism - *we are part of a living planet*. We are kind of the 'biome' in Mother Earth's gut. When we get so out of balance, she becomes ill.

It necessarily follows, then, that the climate crisis is *a crisis of relationship*. Our relationship to the Earth, to nature. And since we are actually a part of nature, and not apart from it, since the natural world is passing through us 24/7, as water, air, and fuel, this really comes down to how we relate to ourselves -- which depends of course on how we *think* about ourselves. Everything is not only relative - it is relational. And relationally, if we are honest with ourselves, we can see the climate crisis as a *spiritual* crisis playing out in our *psyche*, or soul, and being projected out onto and into the world around us, the see of energy and interpenetrating relationships that we are swimming in, demanding our attention in the same way it is now believed that our psyche's nightmares are a product of continually ignoring a message conveyed in dreams. Do you see how seeing the world relationally ends up erasing the boundaries between psyche and nature?

Which brings us back to our worldview...

The Emergence of the Ecopsychological Worldview

Ecopsychology represents a paradigm shift for Western Psychology, a shift that began when Stanislav Grof first coined the term '*transpersonal* psychology' - referring to a revolution in the way we think of ourselves psychologically - beyond (trans) identification with the ego (personal). The emergence of Ecopsychology from the deep ecology movement was largely made necessary by Western Psychology's failure to contribute in a responsible and meaningful way to the existential crisis we are facing at this pivotal point in human history, together with it's insistence on marginalizing Jung's prophetic insights in favor of Freud's more limited worldview. Freud was dogmatic about the "objectivity" of the analyst in relation to, and apart from, the analysand. Ironically, the reason for this dogmatic failing has much to do with the obsessive need by mainstream psychology to be viewed as 'scientific,' in accordance with the model of Western Medicine - the Cartesian trap - when Albert Einstein himself advised: "Look deep into *nature*, and then you will understand everything better."

One gets the impression from much of Western Psychology that 'human nature' is a contradiction in terms! By contrast, *Ecopsychology* "neatly explodes [the] age-old divide between mind and nature, between the psyche 'in here' and nature 'out there.'"[36]

Grof tells us: "Scientific revolutions are those noncumulative episodes in which an older paradigm is replaced in its entirety, or in part, by a new one that is incompatible with it." As one of the most formative thinkers of Ecopsychology, Andy Fisher, points out, the irreconcilable difference between Ecopsychology and Western Psychology lies in the conflict between their respective world views: Western Psychology from Freud onward, with the few exceptions quickly relegated to the margins, is organized around the dualistic thinking and assumptions of classic science. *It is this dualistic thinking,* which sees human beings as unwitting victims of a mostly hostile environment - Freud's dark worldview - that Ecopsychology aims to overthrow.

One way to think about this paradigm shift: Ecopsychology is to mainstream, *Ego*-psychology what Quantum Physics is to classic (Newtonian) Physics. Our world view is still largely tied to Isaac Newton's mechanistic view of the world, objects in motion or at rest, and our view of our selves, or psyche, is still largely determined by Sigmund Freud's views of ego and id. If you go to a psychiatrist today, he or she treats you like a machine with defective chemistry that can be treated with drugs. Pretty much all psychiatrists do any more is to write prescriptions, rarely spending more than 15 minutes with a 'patient.' If instead you go to a psychologist for help in dealing with problems in your life, he or she may ask you to talk about your relationship with your parents, your work situation, your home situation, or maybe even your extended social circles. You are unlikely ever to be asked "So how do you feel about the climate crisis?" (though this is beginning to change) or "When was the last time you spent some quality time in nature?" or "Do you garden?" or even "How's your diet?" (these, unfortunately, not really changing).

From the worldview of mainstream science, to which mainstream psychology is still captive, we are still apart from nature, not an integral part of nature. Ecopsychology presents a radically different view of humans *naturally* being. One of its founders was Theodore Roszak, who explained in his book *The Voice of the Earth* (1992):

> *Ecopsychology holds that there is a synergistic interplay between planetary and personal well-being.* The term "synergy" is chosen deliberately for its traditional theological connotation, which once taught that the human and divine are cooperatively linked in the quest for salvation. The contemporary ecological translation of the term might be: *the needs of the planet are the needs of the person, the rights of the person are the rights of the planet.*

Or, as contemporary Ecopsychologist Mary Gomes has so eloquently put it:

---

[36] David Abram quote from Fisher, A. 2002. *Radical Ecopsychology: Psychology in the Service of Life,* p. 9 (New York: SUNY).

Ecopsychology has emerged over the past several years as an intellectual and social movement that seeks to understand and heal our relationship with the Earth. It examines the psychological processes that bond us to the natural world or that alienate us from it.... *We need to uncover ways to heal the culture as well as the individuals who live in it.* Ecopsychology is essentially about becoming cultural healers.[37]

But my go-to person for Ecopsychology today is still Andy Fisher and his revelatory 2002 dissertation published under the title *Radical Ecopsychology: Psychology in the Service of Life* (2d Ed., 2013). Fisher pointed the way out of our climate crisis by outlining humanistic principles intended to support us in:

1. finding our place in both human and more-than-human society
2. perceiving a world beyond the boundaries of strictly human reality, and
3. *learning to see our own lives symbolically mirrored and bound up in the flesh of all living things.*

Significantly, poignantly, Fisher recognizes that the egoic way of coping with our modern world, which is actually *reinforced and propped up* by Western Psychology, is so "antagonistic to and split from nature" that Ecopsychology must call us toward a *spiritual* world view, a way of being human that will overthrow the ruinous reign of Ego. Thus, to restore our psyche in the world, we must replace ego with eco - 'egology' (or egoism, as Ayn Rand liked to call it in her me-against-the-world philosophy of selfishness) with ecology; capitalism (ego-based competition) with eco-socialism (nature-based cooperation); and, most urgently, industrialized agriculture (chemical-based) with agro-ecology (soil-based).

One of the central organizing principles of Fisher's naturalistic psychology is the recurrent theme of *one flesh*:

All phenomena interweave as a single cloth or 'common tissue' [that] are mutually informative in their commingling with one another... *because they are of the same elemental stuff.*

We begin to see how this world view is *relational* in its essence, engendering the very kind of compassion that Darwin viewed as innate in us, in stark contrast to our conditioned worldview of objectification (subject and object) that invariably leads to isolation, exploitation and on the global scale, imperialism. Here we begin to see the revolutionary potential of something as simple as a change in worldview. While we tend to think of our own flesh as something that encapsulates us and serves as a barrier from our environment, this itself is a product of scientific dualism. In truth, our flesh is a permeable boundary that *connects* us to our environment in the

---

[37] *ReVision* (Spring 1998).

same way our ears, eyes, lungs, nose, and taste buds connect us with our world. We know this in our hearts, we express it in our intimate relations, but we are conditioned by our culture to erect mental barriers with the 'outside world' we call 'boundaries' - as if they really exist.

Fisher describes 'flesh' here as something more than just our skin tissue. For Fisher, flesh becomes: "the *element of being* itself... a medium more primary than mind and matter, which are differentiations *within* flesh." In other words, he is emphasizing the permeability by which we are constantly in interactive contact with all we consider to be external to us, or "other." The changing worldview is not reducible just to interdependence - there is a more fundamental level at which every relation interpenetrates and is interpenetrated by every other relation.

It's an interesting question we rarely stop to ask. Is the air we breathe not us? When we sip soup, or eat an apple, at what point does it stop being food and become part of our being? The more we consider this, the more we begin to appreciate that we are processes interacting with (and within) processes, not separate bodies moving in the world. In fact, the world moves through us, not the other way around. Even our waste products have a place in the world, though you wouldn't know it by the way we deal with them, just as the air we breathe is the waste product of plants. We swim in an ocean of interpenetrating interdependence, within which we are like energetic waves emerging and submerging, rising and falling with each breath of life.

I remember His Holiness the Dalai Lama once commenting that if we consider ourselves honestly, our bodies are little more than 'poop-making machines.' He asked us in meditation to try to visualize all our solid waste from our life up till now in a big mountainous pile in front of us! Our minds, by contrast, are boundless and timeless - just look how right now your mind and mine are connecting quite intimately without regard to time and place. Where does my mind stop, and your's begin? Are these minds not more like holographic referent points that can expand out indefinitely by cultivating relations with other referent points in time and space? We are not our bodies - why don't we agree to stop obsessing so much over them. That is, after all, the self-identity that is most closely associated with the scientific-materialist worldview that is now proving false and destructive. The worldview of consumerism, make-up, fashion, conflict, prejudice, and image, versus the more natural worldview caregiving, health, simplicity, cooperativeness, compassion and imagination.

Now if you find yourself resisting Fisher's idea of 'one flesh' as too far-fetched, somehow, then compare it to the description of how phenomena exist *in reality* - from the father of Quantum Physics himself, Werner Heisenberg:[38]

---

[38] Awarded the Nobel Prize in Physics for creating the field of quantum mechanics.

> *The world thus appears as a complicated tissue of events, in which*
> *connections of different kinds alternate or overlap or combine, and*
> *thereby determine the texture of the whole.*[39]

Is this new world view beginning to crystallize in your mind now, reader? Remember, 90% of the cells in our body are not really us, as they do not share our DNA. And we, in turn, are like the 90% of Earth tissue that is not really her, though in both cases it is not possible to conceive of one without the other. I, a human being, am composed largely of non-human elements… Seriously! Interconnected, interdependent with all that is other, and *interpenetrating*. Those are the real "I"'s. True identity as a product of what we now know about how the world really exists, not a product of engrained mistakes in our thinking. We begin to see the very ideas of 'self' and 'other' as illusory constructs.

I am a referent point for all that is other. *How amazing!* All the great spiritual prophets grasped this radical reality at a very basic level, and thus quite naturally placed the interests and happiness of all 'others' before their own. In a world where everyone has been conditioned by the delusion of separateness to place their own interests ahead of others, we have devolved into a world of constant war and strife. In a world based on the most accurate view of reality, a 'truly' scientific rather than a scientific-materialist perspective, we would all try to serve and look out for one another, and all others, which would quickly become a world without borders. As my wise teacher likes to point out, all conflict in the world can be reduced to three words: I, my, and mine. My property. My religion. My people. My country. I want! Mine!

Adopting and integrating this revised world view is a critical first step in assuming personal responsibility for climate mayhem and our children's future. It is as if we are being asked by the Earth to evolve just a little bit quicker if we want to survive within her forgiving body. To break the dualistic habits of our conditioned minds takes some real effort - the conscious effort of re-minding ourselves again and again to see things as they really exist, to actively employ our imaginations to see ourselves as referent points in a beautiful web of relations, and to stop the proliferation of thoughts that are based on the many ways we've been conditioned to think of things as objects, to be possessed and consumed. But if we do this enough, we can rewire our brains. As the field of neuroscience is proving, our brains are formed and re-formed by our thoughts anyway - we might as well take control of the process and put them to some good use!

This is the real revolution that needs to occur, that is occurring, and it manifests as a relatively simple evolutionary spark in each of our own minds. Of course, as is probably quite clear, this is very much anti-media. We've each been conditioned by hundreds of thousands of commercial messages in our life that train us to view things (and each other) as objects of desire, as basic commodities, and to see ourselves as incomplete beings forever in need of a fix. This engine of

---

[39] Heisenberg, *Physics and Philosophy,* quote taken from Ricard & Thuan, p. 72. For a more "natural"metaphor, consider physicist Thuan's own description: "The world is like a vast stream of events and dynamic currents that are all interconnected and constantly interacting" (p. 278).

consumption is reinforced by our political leaders. As George Bush most brazenly put it in the wake of the tragic attack on the World Trade Towers in 2001: "Americans must shop."

(OBEY!)

As Fisher sees it, the critical task of Ecopsychology is to place *psyche (soul) back into the world* -- within a non-dualistic (i.e., non-Cartesian) theoretical framework. He thus quite naturally characterizes the implicate order from which all these interpenetrating, interconnected, and interdependent relationships emerge, and in which we ourselves are embedded, as the "*soul of the world*" - known in pre-modern times as *Anima Mundi*. As Fisher points out, what follows from this, again quite naturally, is liberating for both ourselves and the world:

> **Once we externalize psyche or contest the mind/world split,**
> **then reality becomes *psychological* through and through.**

This is the most subversive action we can take in response to the climate crisis.

What does it mean for reality to become *psychological through and through*?

One way of appreciating this is to consider that we have been conditioned to see reality as material and 'out there' - external to our isolated (and incomplete) selves 'in here.' Obviously, from a non-dualistic world view, externalizing our psyche is the equivalent of *internalizing* the 'soul of the world.'

The very word *psyche* after all comes from the Greek Goddess Psyche, and means 'breath' or 'soul' - that which connects us to the world. Isn't it interesting that in exploring how our world view is changing, thanks largely to Quantum Physics, we are finding ourselves returning to our ancient roots as human beings? Just as Hawkwind intoned:

"We took the wrong step years ago…"

CHAPTER 5

CLIMATE PROPHESIES

"Therefore, we may consequently state that: this world is indeed a living being endowed with a soul and intelligence ... a single visible living entity containing all other living entities, which by their nature are all related."

~ Plato

The Christian Prophet Carl Jung & The Resurrected Spirit of St. Francis

If this book is beginning to resonate with you, or you with it's ideas, it's because you are still a *'human-being-nature'* at your core. We *know* this stuff! We've just forgotten it in more recent times, and been led astray by having some unnatural ego-logic injected into our psyche through social engineering. Unlike the pervasive unsatisfactoriness we feel from the objectification of our desires by the consumer culture we are immersed in (imprisoned by?), the connectivity we get in touch with by integrating eco-logic into our worldview, like ecopsychology, *actually satisfies* that sense of lack we've been haunted by every since we were expelled from the relative paradise of our childhood (which, by the way, had its own distinct world view, one that was much more intimate with the natural world).

Not all Western Psychologists made the mistake of turning Freud's ideas into religious dogma. There is Carl Jung, of course, who famously fell out of Freud's favor, and was way ahead of his time. If you want to see an example of how Jung speaks to our day and age, look at this quote:

> All time-saving devices, among which we must count easier means of communication and other conveniences, do not, paradoxically enough, save us time but merely cram our time so full that we have no time for anything. Hence the breathless haste, superficiality, and nervous exhaustion [of the modern world] with all [its] symptoms - craving for stimulation, impatience, irritability... They are deceptive sweetings of existence [that] unpleasantly accelerate the tempo of life and leave us with less time than ever before.[40]

He first said this in 1941! Jung's ideas are only now beginning to have the influence that they deserve. It is certainly no coincidence that he was fascinated by quantum physics. We will come back to Jung shortly, but more recently we have the example of Jungian and Archetypal psychologist James Hillman, who concluded in his ground-breaking book *Re-Visioning Psychology* that "psychology cannot be limited to being one field among others, since psyche itself permeates all fields and things of the world" (1976, p. 130).

What these great thinkers have in common with the Greek philosophers, who laid the foundation for the development of civilization - and all the world's indigenous cultures as well - is this vital, elemental and, as we are now learning, *indispensable belief* that the world itself is animated, alive, *ensouled*, and we are all connected at the deepest *participatory* level of conscious awareness with that world soul - ***anima mundi*** (lit. animating force of the world).

Plato was the first one to recognize this natural phenomenon, and quantum physicists have now proven it beyond almost any reasonable doubt. While it is difficult for we who have been

---

[40] CW 18, para. 1343.

thoroughly conditioned by, and fully indoctrinated into, American culture to wholly embrace the idea that we are connected to, even inextricably entangled with, a living planet - let alone a world soul - we really need to *at least* suspend our disbelief over such an important concept, given the grave situation we are facing. After all, every religion seems to have understood this sacred relationship at one time or another, too, and all religious mystics still do.

Our mother, Earth... *Mater - Gaia...* Mother Nature.

And while we've been conditioned to imagine ourselves superior to indigenous people, they look on in utter disbelief at our foolishness in risking all creation for a lifestyle that only keeps us distracted at best, disconnected at its worst, or in endlessly fouling our own nest - something no other species is foolish enough to do. Our own 'disbelief' in the superiority of nature and natural (versus man-made) processes flows directly from Rene Descartes to us through our factory-like schools, our heartless institutions, and our superficial consumer culture -- all of which have failed us in one way or another.

Where does true wisdom reside in this dichotomy? Rather than perpetuating the ignorance that permeates the pejorative terms 'primitive,' 'backwards,' or 'savage' when referring to indigenous people (or better, 'first peoples') many of the more thoughtful academics now refer to them as "wisdom cultures." It wasn't that long ago that it was legal to sport-hunt Aboriginal people in Australia (as recently as early 20th century!), or indiscriminately kill the indigenous people in America (with bounties provided during the Gold Rush in California) - and then, of course, there is that whole slavery thing. *America? Racist??* Who, *Us*?!

In retrospect, which were really the more "evolved" people? Who was more wise? We of European descent, especially, need to get off our cultural high horses and acknowledge that the wisdom of the heart, which is typical of wisdom cultures, is perhaps more evolved, or 'advanced,' than the wisdom of the head - especially when the latter is cut off from feelings and emotions. I realize this sounds preachy, but it is offered here more in the spirit of *mea culpa* - my forebears having come over on the second voyage of the Mayflower - than in the spirit of righteous indignation, though I confess to some of that as well. I am a child of privilege who has come to learn that the history books they taught me from in school were deeply flawed, as was the paternalistic (Catholic), ethnocentric (American exceptionalism), and anthropocentric (animals have no souls, fish feel no pain, their here for us) world view I grew up with.

While that paternalism is exemplified by the Roman Catholic Church of my youth ('Father' instead of pastor), even Christians have a name for *anima mundi* -- *Pistis Sophia.* Not that I learned this in church, mind you. Nonetheless, early Christians (ca. 200 A.D.) believed her to be present at the creation as a Goddess, but she was edited out (ca. 400 A.D.) of later versions of Genesis for political reasons.[41] The Syrian Gnostics, the oldest known to us, specifically referred

---

[41] She still speaks on her own behalf in Proverbs, especially No. 8, though in some versions of the Bible even her name is edited out in favor of "wisdom" -- which was the meaning of her name.

to her as the '*Mother of all living*' and related to her as the 'world soul.' So saying this climate crisis is a spiritual matter in no way is intended to undermine world religions or personal spiritual beliefs in favor of paganism. There is simply no inconsistency there, and no reason that a Christian country like America cannot accept a belief in a world soul, call it what we will, and see ourselves as intimately embedded in nature, creation, and ecology. That is the crux of an ecopsychological world view. Sacred, holistic, and harmonious balance between human nature and the natural world, between our psyche and the soul of the world.

Blessed Be Mother Earth

It is long past due for modern Christians to resurrect and embrace that same 'soul-of-the-world' Goddess in all her magnificent forms, rather than just tolerating Christian cults like the Black Madonna. And it would seem that, in responding to the root causes of the climate crisis, Pope Francis has done just that.

Pope Francis skillfully casts his climate encyclical, <u>Laudato si'</u> *(Blessed Be)*, as an *"*urgent appeal for a new dialogue about how we are shaping the future of our planet." The Pope begins his long papal letter to all 7 billion earthlings by reminding us that our home planet is like "a *sister* with whom we share our life and a *beautiful mother* who opens her arms to embrace us." He then pleads Her case:

> This sister now cries out to us because of the harm we have inflicted on her by our irresponsible use and abuse of the goods with which God has endowed her. We have come to see ourselves as her lords and masters, entitled to plunder her at will… she 'groans in travail' (Rom 8:22). We have forgotten that we ourselves are dust of the earth (cf. Gen 2:7); our very bodies are made up of her elements, we breathe her air and we receive life and refreshment from her waters.

This is Ecopsychology, too! Infusing the world with a feminine soul. The Pope concludes this powerful opening exaltation with a simple, most profound statement, set apart from the rest for effect:

Nothing in this world is indifferent to us.

The Pope's perspective is obviously in line with the more radical strains of Ecopscychology, though he refers instead more broadly to what he calls 'integral ecology' - a distinction without much difference - I learned Ecopsychology myself at the California Institute of Integral Studies. Both perspectives seek to acknowledge and elevate the symbiotic relationship between psyche and nature. The Pope's views resonate quite harmonically with those expressed by ecopsychologist Bill Plotkin at around the same time:

> In an era when the revealed interdependency of all things is radically reshaping every field of knowledge, what might we recognize or discover about the human

psyche – the totality of our psychological capacities, both conscious and unconscious – when we allow that we, too, are expressions of nature's qualities, patterns, and motifs?

***

In all cultures and on all lands, we're now being summoned by the world itself to make urgent changes to the human project, but most central is a fundamental revisioning and reshaping of ourselves, a shift in consciousness. We must reclaim and embody our original wholeness, our indigenous human nature granted to us by nature itself.[42]

This is the very kind of radical change in world view that Jesus exhorted his followers to adopt two millennia ago (*"metanoite"* - to radically change one's way of thinking, subsequently mistranslated as 'repent' - to change one's ways), and that advocates in the fields of Deep Ecology, Transpersonal Psychology, and Ecopsychology (and permaculture, and others) have been advancing for decades now to catalyze the kind of social transformation needed to avert climate catastrophe. As the popular spiritual teacher and clinical psychologist Tara Brach says:

> The experience of universal belonging is at the heart of all mystical traditions. In realizing non-separation, we come home to our primordial and true nature.

True nature, or human nature, or what Pope Francis refers to quite beautifully as *"the heart of what it is to be human…"*

The *heart* of what it is to be human. In stark divergence from the pessimistic psychology of Sigmund Freud, Carl Jung split away from Freud over Freud's dogmatic refusal to acknowledge the spiritual component of the human psyche, and as a *natural* result had a more redemptive view of human nature. Jung is thus more relevant to the psychological crisis of our age. He developed a close relationship with Nobel physicist Wolfgang Pauli, who was immersed in the discoveries of quantum physics and whose fascination with Jung's idea of synchronicity prompted his life-long dialogue and collaboration with the mystical depth psychologist.

Peering into the depths of consciousness and reality, Pauli and Jung were able to foresee the existential crisis of our time. They understood that resolving this crisis of relation with the natural world would require the resurrection of *anima mundi* in the human psyche. For Jung, the most important religious development of the 20th Century, therefore, was the Catholic Church's 1950 pronouncement of the Assumption of Mary into Heaven, where she assumed her rightful place "crowned" in the presence of God. As the Jesuit psychologist Eugene Kennedy noted in the *Catholic Reporter*, this assumption represented nothing less than "the return of Mother Earth to the Heavens" - what Jung referred to as the "sacred marriage."

---

[42] "Rewilding Psychology," *Ecopsychology journal* (March 2014), 6(1): 2-4.

The significance of this divine feminine principle is never far from Pope Francis' mind in writing *Blessed Be.* He refers to the ascended Mary as "the Mother and Queen of all creation" who "now cares with maternal affection and pain for this wounded world." Pope Francis is speaking to our hearts through our minds. Inasmuch as Mary "now understands the meaning of all things… *we can ask her* to enable us to look at this world with eyes of wisdom [Sophia]." How this ascended virgin-mother, to whom the Pope enjoins us to pray for wisdom, is any different from the Goddess *Pistis Sophia* to whom early Gnostic Christians prayed, and were thereby deemed heretics, is rather difficult to fathom. No matter…

The Holy See goes on to inform us that "She is the Woman, 'clothed in the sun, with the moon under her feet, and on her head a crown of twelve stars' (Rev 12:1)." I hope we are able to appreciate just how radically historic this is coming from the very top of that long-time bastion of patriarchy, the Catholic Church! In a very real sense, what we have here is nothing less than the recovery of the Divine Feminine by the world's largest church at the most critical time in our historical development - just as Carl Jung prophesied would be the result in 1950.

Pope Francis also identifies the 'objectifying' world view of Decartes (and Francis Bacon) as the root of evil in our world today, that which is giving rise to so many social ills, and indirectly to climate mayhem as well. The wisdom of the heart that emerges once we break the habit of objectifying all that is other, which is the habit that isolates and alienates modern people even in crowds, is the wisdom that sees all creation as sacred, to be celebrated and shared - rather than as profane, to be subjugated and possessed.

Catholic priest, cultural historian, and ecotheologian Thomas Berry (1914-2009) forcefully and persuasively maintained that the "ancient human-Earth relationship must be recovered in a new context, in its mystical as well as in its physical functioning." Pope Francis eloquently takes up this challenge: "The universe unfolds in God, who fills it completely. Hence, there is a mystical meaning to be found in a leaf, in a mountain trail, in a dewdrop, in a poor person's face." And it is with these awe-inspired eyes of grace that we are able to intimately connect to, and fall into relationship with, the soul of the world found not only in nature - *but within our own human nature.* Once reconnected with this indwelling, though dormant, humanist nature at the level of society and culture, once we remember what it means to be human, we would no more cause harm to the planet or its inhabitants than we would intentionally strike our mother, our sister, or our infant child. And I believe at its heart, that is what the Pope is trying to convey to us in the most urgent and effective way he can.

One World

Of course, Carl Jung himself was *deeply* Christian - the son of a minister. He took his religion very seriously, as a matter of fact. For Jung, the ultimate question we each must answer is this: are we related to something infinite or not?[43] Just as with the world view of quantum physics, we

---

[43] Jung, *Memories, Dreams, Reflections* (1961), p. 325.

are also just now beginning to catch up with Jung's (r)evolutionary ideas about the sacred spiritual relationship of humans to the world that holds us in its bosom.

And just as Ecopsychology advocates a spiritual prescription for problems rooted in ego, Jung maintained that the greatest limitation of modern society is our limited idea of 'self.' He found an antidote in becoming aware of the vastness of the unconscious realm, which opens us up to experiencing the self as *simultaneously* limited and eternal, as both transcendent and imminent, one *and* other.[44] Listen to this contemporary description of the new world view in science from systems theorist (and concert pianist) Ervin Laszlo:

> At the cutting edge of contemporary science a remarkable insight is surfacing: the universe, with all things in it, is a quasi-living, coherent whole. All things in it are connected... A cosmos that is connected, coherent and whole recalls an ancient notion that was present in the tradition of every civilization: it is an enchanted cosmos... We are part of each other and of nature. We are a conscious part of the world, a being through which the cosmos comes to know itself... We are at home in the universe.

Consistent with this expansive view of human being, Jung saw the psyche as *'pure nature.'*[45] He himself explored an ***in-between realm where psyche and matter are one:***

> That the world inside and outside us rests on a transcendental background is as certain as our own existence, but it is equally certain that the direct perception of the archetypal [symbolically patterned] world inside us is just as doubtfully correct as that of the physical world outside us.[46]

He called this transcendental background *unus mundus,* or 'one world' - a unified field from which we each emerge, to which we each return, and with which we never really lose our connection. Our task, according to Jung, is "to become conscious of the contents that press upward from the unconscious."[47] But for Jung, this 'unconscious' realm is not only personal to me or you, as it was to Freud. Instead, it is shared by all who are conscious, just as we all share the ground provided by Earth and the air provided by plants. As Pauli exclaimed, "the unconscious is in *both man and nature,*" part of the 'one flesh' referred to by Andy Fisher.

---

[44] **Jung (1961), p. 325.**

[45] **Stevens, 1990, p. 47.**

[46] Jung, 1960, Vol. 14, para. 787.

[47] Jung (1961), p. 326.

Is this not exhilirating? Is it not exciting that at the time of our greatest existential crisis, we have someone in the position of Pope Francis bringing this powerful message of spiritual awakening to the world at large, and not just his flock in the Catholic Church?!

In considering this relationship to the whole, and accepting our responsibility towards *unus mundus,* it is important to understand precisely what Jung meant by the 'unconscious.' In his view, it is divided into a personal realm - which includes all the experiences we have had in life but are no longer conscious of, subliminal impressions formed by our conditioning, as well as feelings we repress because of their inconsistency with our attitudes and beliefs - and an *impersonal* realm as well. This was based upon his own experience, but was nonetheless revolutionary, bridging the world of spiritual being and Western psychology. And this scared Freud not because he didn't think it was true, but because it didn't accord with his view of psychology as a scientific discipline.

Jung referred to this impersonal unconsciousness as the 'collective' unconscious realm, whose contents we inherit from all who have gone before, much like instincts that we are born with. Jung experienced and envisioned the impersonal conscious contents that form the background of our minds as 'archetypes' -- "primordial images which have always been the basis of man's thinking - the whole treasure-house of mythological motifs…"[48] Included in this realm were the oldest archetypes of all - God and Mother Earth.

It is at the level of this collective unconscious realm - the very deepest level of awareness that we experience in dreams, in visions, during psychological crises, in deep meditative states, in trance (entrained) states of dance or music, or even in simple reverie - that we are intimately connected to *anima mundi*, the world soul that is our mother, our source of life ('*anima*tion'). We and her together comprise the *unus mundus* - and by 'we' I mean all creatures with consciousness. If as a Christian it helps you to think of *unus mundus* as God, then that is perfectly okay. Jung would approve.

While it may sound mystical, this is exactly the kind of psychology that emerges from a non-dualistic, quantum world view, as opposed to the ego-obsessed, isolating and ultimately alienating psychology that Freud initiated. And it was this spiritual, collective experience that Jung was unable to deny that caused Freud to dissociate himself from the one person who he had previously felt worthy of being his successor. In other words, the student surpassed the teacher. The apprentice became the wizard, if you will - an apt analogy given Jung's fascination with all things alchemical (a fascination he shared with the likes of Pauli, Newton, Da Vinci, and so many other influential thinkers).

While it is beyond the scope of this book, it is nonetheless instructive to point out here that America has become very much a Freudian, and not Jungian, society - again, for political reasons. Freud's nephew was deeply embedded in the highest circles of politics and business in

---

[48] Jung, *The Structure and Dynamics of the Psyche* (1970), pp. 310-11.

America, from the end of WWI forward. And it was Freud's daughter, Anna, who actually conceived of and designed what we now think of as the *American Dream*. How many of us realize just how much we are a product of social engineering in this country?

For those who are interested in the elitist anti-democratic conspiracy that gave rise to our consumer culture, which was expressly intended to distract us from meaningful political engagement, I cannot recommend enough watching the BBC documentary *The Century of the Mind*, freely available on line. If our schools actually taught history, we'd all know this essential background information - and we would not stand for it. Fortunately, so many are now becoming cognizant that our emperors have no clothes, that the empire itself is crumbling beneath our feat.

As should be readily apparent by now, Jung did not 'invent' any of these ideas about the unconscious. His method, after his falling out with Freud over his intuitive convictions, was more to surrender to what was within. Like many of us, he felt Freud was a little obsessed with the whole sexuality thing, more than a little pessimistic about human nature, and that psychology needed to deal more honestly with the spiritual concerns that impart meaning to our lives. Jung paid a heavy price for his integrity. In the process, however, he resurrected the idea of a world soul from Plato.

According to the Platonic worldview, which influenced several systems of thought throughout early world history, this idea of a world soul was not some kind of revolutionary belief, but rather a basic recognition of the underlying connection between all living things on the planet. It is because of Jung's own powerful *experiences* of this intuitive, deep-seated sense of connection that he felt confident in radically affirming Plato's assertion that our world "is indeed a living being endowed with a soul and intelligence... a single visible living entity containing all other living entities, which by their nature are all related."[49]

While this idea is firmly grounded in ancient philosophy, as well as in mystical traditions like Alchemy and Taoism, and in indigenous wisdom - *as well as* early Christian gospels and theologies - Jung had also befriended Albert Einstein early in his career, and subsequently formed the close friendship with Pauli (who Einstein once commented was the only other physicist who really understood his theory of relativity). Jung and Pauli corresponded for over a quarter century, and were convinced that nature reveals herself to us a unity of mind and matter, a unified field of subjective (conscious) and objective reality upon which our lives are projected. Pauli referred to this unity as "a cosmic order of nature beyond our control to which *both* the outward material objects *and* the inward images are subject." He felt that it would be "most satisfactory if physics and psyche could be seen as complementary aspects of the same reality."[50]

Obviously, this was before the advent of Ecopsychology! But there are its seeds.

---

[49] Jung, *Psychology and Alchemy* (1968), p. 12.

[50] Burns, C. (2011), "Wolfgang Pauli, Carl Jung, and the Acausal Connecting Principle: A Case Study in Transdisciplinarity," *Metanexus Journal*.

We can really appreciate from this how modern physics has shed new, revelatory light on the wisdom of ancient and universal spiritual ideas like *anima mundi* and *unus mundus*, and we can perhaps also begin to understand why quantum physicists like Pauli and Heisenberg, among many others, became quite interested in spiritual wisdom traditions. No great leap of faith is required for us to accept the idea that the world is alive, that it has a soul, and that we are and have always been connected to that world soul - regardless of our Western cultural amnesia. Once we accept this profound notion, it shakes up all our beliefs and transforms our worldview.

Just as Pope Francis has taken great pains to inform us, *anima mundi* cries out to us now to reunite with her, as a mother would to her wayward children. As the late, great Jungian psychotherapist James Hillman put it, after concluding that he found the pathology of the world soul reflected in our own pathology:

> *The world, because of its breakdown, is entering a new moment of consciousness: by drawing attention to itself by means of its symptoms, it is becoming aware of itself as a psychic reality.*[51]

Let us put this in more personal terms. *Anima Mundi*, the natural world, because of our split from her, is entering into a new conscious relationship with us. You can find expressions of this new relationship all over the internet, as well as in the papal encyclical. As Thomas Berry pointed out before Pope Francis: "This presence whether experienced as Allah, as Atman, as Sunyata, or as the Buddha-nature or as Bodhisattva; whether as Tao or as the One or as the Divine Feminine, is the atmosphere in which humans breathe deepest and without which they eventually suffocate."

It is our individual experience of the world soul that is imperative, not our beliefs about her. Because by drawing attention to Herself by means of the climate crisis, She is becoming aware of *Herself* (and forcing us to do the same) as a psychic reality through each of her awakening children. In fact, if I am to be totally honest with you, it is She who is writing this book through me. All the rest is just synchronicity.

And… *listen…*

She is calling us home…

Buddhist World View: *Indra's Net*

Zen Master Thich Nhat Hanh, one of the world's leading meditation teachers, certainly echoes the clarion call sounded by Hillman and amplified on the world stage by Pope Francis. When asked what we need to do to save our world from the climate crisis, Hanh responded: "What we most need to do is to hear within us the sound of the earth crying."

---

[51] Hillman, J. (1992) *The Thought of the Heart and the Soul of the World.*

Thay, as he is called by his followers, teaches us that the distress calls from Mother Earth are like mindfulness bells calling us back to our true nature, re-minding us what it means to be of the Earth, to be 'earthlings' - connected in a realm of 'inter-being' as he calls it:

> *If you are a poet, you will see clearly that there is a cloud floating in this sheet of paper. Without a cloud, there will be no rain; without rain, the trees cannot grow: and without trees, we cannot make paper. The cloud is essential for the paper to exist. If the cloud is not here, the sheet of paper cannot be here either. So we can say that the cloud and the paper inter-are.*

> *If we look into this sheet of paper even more deeply, we can see the sunshine in it. If the sunshine is not there, the forest cannot grow. In fact nothing can grow. Even we cannot grow without sunshine. And so, we know that the sunshine is also in this sheet of paper. The paper and the sunshine inter-are. And if we continue to look we can see the logger who cut the tree and brought it to the mill to be transformed into paper. And we see the wheat. We know that the logger cannot exist without his daily bread, and therefore the wheat that became his bread is also in this sheet of paper. And the logger's father and mother are in it too. When we look in this way we see that without all of these things, this sheet of paper cannot exist.*

That is a quantum worldview, the kind of sense we need to bring to the climate crisis. On a surface level, people get this. We yearn for connection, after all, and in some very startling ways we've never been more interconnected. It is no coincidence that at a time when we are being called by the planet to awaken to our interdependence, we have developed a means of interconnecting globally and labeled it the '*world wide web*' or 'internet(work).' It is also no coincidence that Buddhism has been reborn in the West at this particular time, and more and more people are turning to it for perspective on their lives - whether or nor they embrace all of its beliefs (e.g., Buddhism rejects the idea of a creator god).

Unlike the predominant world view of scientific materialism - a product of Cartesian dualism inspired by Christianity - the world view in Eastern cultures never really suffered this same kind of alienation from nature. It is also true that many of Buddha's ideas, which are more about psychology than philosophy or religion, happen to resonate strongly with discoveries in quantum physics. A simple example of this is the essential point of the Heart Sutra that "form is emptiness, and emptiness is form" - the basis of Buddhist non-dualistic philosophy. Over 2500 years later, we now know that what we see as form is *in fact* 99.999% empty space - and when you really look for the other .0001% that gives us the illusion of solidity, you can't find it. There really is no 'there' there. Form really *is* empty. And in what is called a 'quantum vacuum,' defined by the complete absence of any material, matter mysteriously emerges and then disappears again. Emptiness really *is* form.

While we can look to Buddhism for some guidance in this spiritual quest presented to us by the climate crisis, just as we can look to Plato and Jung and Pope Francis and quantum physics, it is important to remember that we do not have to abandon our own religious beliefs in doing so. Jung was insistent on this point, as is His Holiness the Dalai Lama. While I myself am a dedicated Buddhist practitioner, I came to Buddhism out of a deep experience of Christian mysticism, and to this day I still think Buddhism is much more psychological than it is religious. There is even good reason to believe that Jesus may have been influenced by Buddhism during his pre-messianic years. So from a spiritual standpoint, it is quite alright to become a 'Jewish Buddhist,' a 'Christian Buddhist' (as many consider Thomas Merton to have been late in his life), or even a Taoist Christian or Quantum Buddhist Christian!

Please - let's not get hung up on the differences between different spiritual traditions. More than ever, we need to come together over our commonalities, and all the world's great religions are united by their mystical traditions.

According to the renowned Buddhist scholar Garma C.C. Chang, the highest teaching of all the Buddhist schools throughout history actually was represented by a Chinese school from around the 7th Century that no longer even exists, but whose philosophy became the basis for all the Zen schools, as well as the Chan and Pure Land schools of China and Korea. This Buddhist 'Teaching of Totality' from the *Hua Yen*, or 'flower ornament' school, combined all the major lines of Buddhist thinking at that time into a philosophy of *totalistic organism*. It is from *Hua Yen* (pronounced like "Hawaiian") that we received the popular idea of the 'Jewel Net of Indra' - reality as a web of interdependence.[52] You do not have to be a Buddhist to appreciate the inherent wisdom of this school of thought.

Francis H. Cook wrote a book on *Hua Yen* Buddhism in 1977. He referred to it as a kind of *'cosmic ecology.'*[53] Cook saw Indra's net as a "vast web of interdependencies" whose "urgent message" comes to us at this time as an "eternally abiding truth" bursting in our consciousness that we may reassess the manner in which things exist (i.e., as relations, not objects) and adjust our conduct accordingly. The beauty of *Hua Yen* is that it envisions a world of radically interpenetrating interdependence that flat out contradicts the common complaint people have today when talking about the climate crisis: that they are 'only' one person, and thus powerless. According to this ancient teaching on totality, grounded in impeccable logic:

> *Each individual is at once the cause for the whole and is caused by the whole,*
> *and what is called existence is a vast body made up of an infinity of individuals*

---

[52] At every node of the web is a jewel that reflects, and is reflected in, all the other jewels at all the other nodes of the web, stretching out to infinity.

[53] Cook, F.H. (1977).

all sustaining each other and defining each other. The cosmos is, in short, a self-creating, self-maintaining, and self-defining organism.

Just like the idea of *unus mundus*, or perhaps more accurately extending that idea, there is just *one being*, rather than a multitude of isolated beings. Or as the British mystic and teacher Alan Watts might have said, there is *just being*. Because of this, "the part exerts *total power* in the formation of a particular whole." How does that make you feel?

As the contemporary philosopher and Zen Buddhist teacher David Loy puts it, "I am what the whole universe is doing, right here and now." And indeed, if we look at any individual in this culture, we can see the climate crisis playing out in their psyche and in their life. There is not a climate crisis 'out there.' The climate crisis is right 'in here' as a crisis of relations.

Just as with 20th century quantum physics, in this 7th century Buddhist view of totality **"*things do not exist; only events exist momentarily under relative conditions.*"**[54] We inhabit "a universe which is nothing but the complete mutual cooperation of the entities which make it up" - each and every single illusory one of us! This is really radical stuff! And a great antidote to our own mistaken ways of conditioned thinking.

It isn't that I am not an individual, but rather that I am not an *isolated* individual - as there is no such thing in a world where mercurial bubbles at each node on Indra's net reflect all other bubbles, and find their reflection in that is other. We are referent points for all that is other, and all that is other depends on us - to the same extent that we depend on all that is other in referring to our own individuality. Without you or me, it is impossible to conceive of the universe; and, without the universe, it is impossible to conceive of you or me.

When we begin to see the world in this way, when it really starts to sink into and infect our awareness - this is what meditation is for, by the way, as the most tried and true method for breaking down the conditioning of our minds and re-conditioning them to accord with reality - it has a profound effect on the way we think of ourselves in relation to the world. We can never again take an action without some level of awareness concerning the impact it will have on all that is other. Our eco-logical self begins to grow and displace our ego-illogical self.

This is the real meaning of the '*world wide web.*' This is the emergent world view that will resolve the climate crisis of its own moral force, once it firmly takes root in our collective consciousness - which as you now see depends entirely on each of us nurturing it in our own mind stream. We depend on all of nature for our very being, and all of nature depends on us.

---

[54] Chang, G. (1971) *The Buddhist Teaching of Totality*, p. 81.

Is this not the emergent meme of our time? Is it not the salve for our crisis?

It is not possible for me to conclude this chapter on our changing world view without giving a nod to Charles Eisenstein and his amazing book *The More Beautiful World Our Hearts Know is Possible*. While I have devoted just this one chapter to the philosophy that undergirds the existing world view that has given rise to the climate crisis, and the emergent world view that will resolve it, Eisenstein has devoted an entire book to illuminating just this sea change, and I urge everyone I can to read his inspiring book. My book is focused on psychology, as I am an eco-psychologist, while Eisenstein considers himself an eco-philosopher - his book is focused more on philosophy. If you read these books together, along with the re-issue of Joanna Macy & Molly Young Brown's ground-breaking book *Coming Back to Life: Practices to Reconnect Our Lives, Our World*, you will in the process most assuredly become part of the solution to the climate crisis. You will no longer question your actions. And you will sleep like a baby at night no matter what tumult develops in the world around you.

(That is not to say that there are not other amazing and valuable books on point - there are - but these three are all anyone really needs to add their weight to the critical mass that is building for this evolutionary shift in human consciousness.)

So let's conclude this chapter with four resounding, reinforcing quotes: one from *anima mundi's* resident Eco-philosopher, Mr. Eisenstein; one from a scholar of Tibetan Buddhism, relating the lessons from the Tibetan Book of the Dead to our climate in crisis; one from Sufi master Llewellyn Vaughan-Lee; and, the last word will be from the founder of Japanese Zen, Dogen.

> *Whatever the mechanism - greenhouse gases, deforestation, or solar fluctuations - climate change is sending us an important message. We and Earth are one. As above, so below: what we do to each other, even to the smallest animal or plant, we do to all creation.*[55]

We are experiencing the initiation of the human race into a new level of consciousness, and that is a very terrifying experience. It does no good to turn and run from the terror of our darkness into light... We must take our counsel from *The Tibetan Book of the Dead* and realize that these frightening projections of famines, economic disasters, ecological catastrophes, floods, earthquakes, and wars are all only the malevolent aspects of beneficent deities. If we sit and observe them, do not identify with them, but remember our [true] nature,

---

[55] Eisenstein, C. (2013), p. 51.

we will not be dragged down by them into an incarnation of the hell they prefigure. If we run from them, we validate them; we give the projections the very psychic energy they need to overtake us. Then, as Jung has pointed out, the situation will happen outside as fate.[56]

~*~

The world's wounds and imbalance are our wounds and imbalance, and we have within us the knowledge and understanding to realign ourselves and the world.

'I came to realize clearly that mind is no other than mountains and rivers and the great wide earth, the sun and the moon and the stars.'

---

[56] William Irwin Thompson, "Evil and World Order."

<u>CHAPTER 6</u>
CLIMATE CATHARSIS:

GRIEVING THE LOSS
OF OUR NATURAL SELVES

"Each separate being in the world
returns to the common source.
Returning to the source is serenity."
~ Tao Te Ching

Gaining Clarity

Getting clear on our world view is the *easy* part of taking personal responsibility for the climate crisis. As we just saw, all that is necessary is some honest appraisal of our present assumptions, comparing those against what we now *know* to be true, and making the necessary adjustments in our thinking. That is the arena of the philosophy of climate change, or eco-philosophy, and is the kind of intellectual processing we have no problem with so long as we are open-minded. It's actually kind of fun and interesting.

Getting clarity in our own heart, straightening our *feelings* out, and getting to the roots of our own *lifestyle* choices in relation to nature, culture, and society is quite another matter. Now we are entering the realm of Ecopsychology - the psychology of climate change. This is not so easy. It requires honest assessment of our own difficult emotions and compulsive habits. It takes a kind of open-heartedness without regard to the pain an open heart often invites into our psyche. And - *as promised (!)* - bravely confronting our deepest fears and unresolved grief.

Of course, this is what makes us human. This is what makes life meaningful and facilitates growth. And I have some good news for you as well - it is not nearly as complicated or as hard as you might imagine. In fact, the whole point of this book, and this chapter which is the heart of the book in particular, is to empower you to do this on your own, without the need of professional help. This book will end up being the most affordable therapy you've ever received.

I'll even go farther than that. If you have taken the world view of the previous chapter to heart, and are reading all this with an open mind, then this chapter can actually facilitate a kind of *awakening* in you. I realize that's a bold claim. Certainly, you will awaken from the American Dream once you have read and digested this. That's a given. But even more than that. We are witnessing the early stages of a societal awakening, a shift in consciousness from bland egoic consumerism to spiritual (and global) citizenship, that is (as Naomi Klein asserts) *changing everything*. Such an awakening unfolds slowly at first, happening one mind at a time, and then builds momentum until it becomes an undeniable social phenomenon.

Now is *your* time.

I call this ecopsychological phenomenon "climate catharsis," and so we need to begin with some simple definitions. In this context, we are using the term 'climate' in a much broader sense than just the scientific term, one that is intended to highlight the connections between our own psyche, the collective psyche, and the world soul itself; that is, *climate* as used here includes "the prevailing attitudes, standards, or environmental conditions of a group, period, or place."

Catharsis is a psychological term that refers to the release of tension and anxiety for the purpose of providing relief from powerful emotions that we have repressed.[57] Consider this chapter your initiation into the new world that is unfolding before our eyes, right at our feet…

GOOD GRIEF!

> *When we stop distancing ourselves from the pain in the world, our own or others', we create the possibility of a new experience, one that often surprises because of how much joy, connection, or relief it yields. Destruction may continue, but humanity shines through.*

~ Mark Epstein, M.D., from *The Trauma of Everyday Life*

Perhaps the most powerful emotion we experience, at least on a par with love, is grief. In fact, the "Grief Walker" - Stephen Jenkinson - calls grieving 'the other side of loving.' Unlike love, however, we have for some reason in recent times largely forgotten how to grieve, and even learned to fear the grieving process. **Francis Weller, in his book** *Entering the Healing Ground: Grief, Ritual and the Soul of the World,* **points out that "we live in a flat line culture, one that avoids the depths of feeling." We suffer from what Weller calls "premature death, where we turn away from life and walk with ambivalence towards the world, neither in it nor out of it, lacking a commitment to fully say yes to life" (pp. 87, 89).**

Does that description of modern society resonate with you? We can be so uncomfortable with someone lamenting a loss that we will often express this discomfort by telling them (or thinking to ourselves) "get *over* it it," when in truth there is no way over or around grieving. We either go *through* it, or we cut it short by suppressing it, adding it to our personal reservoir of unresolved grief. We might cut people some slack when it is a loved one whose loss they are grieving, but beyond that we have little tolerance for, or acceptance of, the need to grieve loss.

I suspect this had a lot to do with the institutionalization of the dying process - taking dying people out of their homes and putting them in hospitals whose sole function is to 'defeat' death at all costs. It used to be that people just 'passed on' and died 'of natural causes' because it was 'their time' - now we read in one obituary after another how people 'lose the battle' after a 'valiant fight.' Is fighting really how we want to end our life? Is death *really* our enemy?

It was not that long ago that babies were born in the home, and elders died in their 'death beds' at home as well, lying 'in state' for three days while friends, neighbors, and family came to pay their last respects before burial in the earth. Then at some point it became the norm for babies to be born in hospitals, with mothers treated as if they are afflicted by some kind of illness. I myself was born at a time when it was quite routine to sedate mothers on an operating table and surgically remove the baby as if it were a tumorous growth. When we have life-threatening

---

[57] Aristotle coined this term for the process of fully experiencing and releasing repressed emotions, and he felt that the mysteries of death and rebirth provided a powerful spiritual container for this experience.

illness or disease, we are then expected to return to these same sterile, colorless environments to die, behind closed curtains, since to do otherwise would be tantamount to admitting to defeat. Once the battle is lost, the body is unplugged from all its chords and tubes and removed immediately underground to await final disposal. While hospitals still place their morgues in the basement, burial in the ground is no longer favored. Just stick the body in an industrial oven, quickly reduce it to ashes, and THEN maybe we can be returned to our home to be placed on a mantle somewhere.

Strange...

In other words, we've "progressed" from a comforting and natural process of birth and death, which admittedly involved some pain (rites of passage usually do), to a relatively traumatic one (though painless and antiseptic) that is forcefully taken out of the hands of those we are closest to. Does it really come as any surprise to us that this institutionalization and 'medicalization' of birth and death, this sterilization and traumatization of life transitions, might create *some* dysfunction in relation to the grieving process!

Fortunately, we have begun to come to our common senses, and not only is the medical profession itself becoming more humane and sensitive to the importance of these critical transitions, but we've also begun having babies at home again (without drugs), and the hospice movement has emerged to help take the trauma out of the dying process - in part by removing the dying from hospitals in favor of more peaceful environments. It is in this more progressive cultural context that we can now look back and see what the consequences have been from our illusion of 'progress' in our standard of living over the last several decades, a time span that just happens to have coincided with the illusion of the American Dream, and begin at last to recover and process our grief over what has been lost in the name of progress.

Stated in its simplest terms, grief is the feeling we have when we lose something or someone dear to us. It is this natural experience of loss, as well as its anticipation, that opens us up to love and vitality in our life. So if it is true that we have lost touch with our most intimate connection to nature, that we have become alienated from the world soul, if it's true that we have lost touch with our *own* eternally natural selves, our 'true nature' as it were, then we must pose the question: *what has happened to our natural grief over THAT loss?*

And here we may well find the key to the climate crisis. Because the truth is that we were never *allowed* to grieve this lost connection to our true nature, the natural world, and the world soul. Instead, we were bamboozled into thinking it was actually the best thing that ever happened to us! We were sold a bill of goods called *The American Dream.* Collectively, and individually as well, any feelings we quite naturally might have experienced over the years from being separated from nature were repressed because *we were not supposed to have those feelings* ("Do you have any idea how *lucky* you are?!"), and any hints of natural sadness were patched over with more positive (feigned) feelings we were programmed to have toward unnatural things - like shiny metal toys, Barbie dolls, stereos, and cars in the early days of consumerism, and more recently video games, smart phones, and firearms. If these feelings of sadness persisted, we were deemed maladjusted, or even mentally ill. There are pills for that - even if you're a child. That is part of the 'better living through chemistry' sham.

This is the real danger of living in a society that *itself* manifests some kind of neurotic tendencies - healthy people who don't buy into the collective neurosis get labeled 'neurotic' based on an assumption that it is the norm that is healthy. We saw this at an exaggerated level in the 1950s, when perfectly healthy people were subjected to electroshock therapy, and worse yet - prefrontal lobotomies. Because they didn't 'fit in.' Accordingly, the pressure to conform was intense.

Could you imagine someone in 1950s American complaining of grief over our unnatural lifestyle?

But here's the thing about grief, especially grief over the loss of something so fundamental to our mental well being as nature, and something as essential to life as wonder and awe in relation to the soul of an animated world (and cosmos). *It cannot be disposed of.* Not even in a throwaway society. Repressed feelings as potent as these end up surfacing in myriad ways, including mental illness and social disorders. And since we are repressing feelings over our relationship to *nature*, it comes as no surprise that we might act out these powerful repressed feelings in *unnatural* ways, in effect taking our aggression out on Mother Nature herself.[58] Just as might be the case if we were forced to repress our affections for someone we love because of their unwillingness to accept those feelings. In such a case, we might eventually begin to lash out at them in misplaced anger, or lash out at others to avoid lashing out at them. Repressed feelings create chaos because they're looking for an escape valve.

Collectively, we've been lashing out at *anima mundi* at least since the end of WWII, and in progressively destructive ways. Let's take a closer look at how that has been reflected at the cultural level in our society.

Generally speaking, grief itself unfolds in progressive stages. Elizabeth Kubler-Ross was a pioneer in this field of grief psychology, and is famous for identifying 5 stages of grief: *Denial; Anger; Bargaining; Depression;* and, *Acceptance.* Our collective repression of grief over our lost connection with nature has also followed these stages, and at every stage the object of those repressed feelings, the natural world itself, has became progressively more ill, trending ever closer to a terminal state - which, unfortunately, only serves to reinforce our need to repress our collective grief. That's because repression, like cognitive dissonance, is a psychological defense mechanism that protects us from information we are not presently equipped to deal with, and *nothing* in our evolutionary history has equipped us psychologically to deal with this idea that we might be the cause of our own demise and the demise of so many other precious life forms - or what Bill McKibben referred to in the title of his first book as '*the end of nature.*' What a term!

---

[58] As Pope Francis recently put it, "it is man who has slapped nature in the face... I think we have exploited nature too much..."

Which has led us inexorably to our present quandary, and to *anima mundi's* urgent attempts to awaken us to our own existential crisis. In order to resolve this crisis of spirit, in order to unravel the complexity of our own feelings in relation to it, we will now go back to the beginning of this story, dig up the root of the problem, and then build our perspective slowly, proceeding through the steps of our own collective grief repression, which we all share in. In this perspective building process, we will release our feelings through the insights that come from simple awareness. And we'll do this in the same order, but at a very compressed timescale, as we have been acting our repression out culturally over the last several decades.

Think of this as a kind of cultural regression therapy. It will be important to monitor your feelings as we go through this process together. Watch to see where your buttons are activated (strong reactions one way or the other), and where your moments of recognition and recollection come as well. And take your time. Don't speed read this part of the book!

No matter what comes up, remember to have compassion for yourself. What that means is that we really want to liberate ourselves from any suffering that we've experienced in the past as it arises afresh in the present. As humans, we're uniquely equipped to do this by the fact that we are able to take ourselves and our feelings as the object of our own subjective awareness and attention. Please appreciate that it is in the nature of the *power* of this awareness -- of simply sitting with, or attending to, such difficult emotions with an open heart and an abiding love of all life, including ourselves -- to *release* these feelings and emotions as they come unglued from the sticky places inside where they have been stuck all these years.

It's just like shining light into dark places. The instant the light illuminates that place, the darkness disappears.

We should never be afraid of 'falling apart,' in spite of our culture's obsession with keeping our shit together. What's so great about our shit, anyway? The more we compulsively struggle to keep our shit together, the more shit we end up holding onto, right? We should really prefer letting our shit go! To put it in slightly more psychological terms, *disintegration naturally precedes reintegration,* and we certainly need to reintegrate at a societal level now. I've often thought that if we were all more willing as individuals to allow ourselves to fall apart, we might have a much easier time coming together at the levels of community and society. Instead, our fear of vulnerability just makes us ever more vulnerable, and this spiraling vulnerability gets expressed communally and socially as aggressive defensiveness and extreme polarization of views with no middle ground.

Whew... We really need to get over that! Let THAT shit go!

And that's where healthy grieving comes into play. The more we are able to call up repressed feelings of loss, which we carry in our bodies and which manifests in the patterns of our relationships, the more we process through these difficult feelings, the less we find we have to lose, and consequently the more comfortable we become with our vulnerability. A positive feedback loop is created as we begin to see that expressing grief over loss will not kill us, or even diminish us in the eyes of others. We become more courageous in our relationships, and our hearts begin to expand. In truth, we learn that the more vulnerable we are able to be, the more open to loss and aware of its natural inevitability we become, the more open we become to love as well. A broken heart is an open heart, and a love that includes grieving over impermanence is a more complete love, leading us into a more fulfilling life.

It's like the lesson the Thai forest monk Ajahn Chah used to impart to his students by referring to his favorite drinking mug that he kept by his side at teachings. "This glass is *already broken*. Yet when I learn to appreciate this, every minute I spend with it is precious to me."[59] This is such a deep teaching on death and impermanence. Think what your life might be like if all the things you value, including those you hold precious, were to have labels affixed to them as reminders of impermanence: *ALREADY BROKEN!*

This is what Stephen Jenkinson refers to as taking grief onto our path, and you can appreciate how it might deepen the way we love. We in the West tend to implicitly assume the objects of our love and affection will always be there with us. This becomes quite evident when a favorite coffee mug falls off the table, a bike is stolen, a car is wrecked, or a loved one passes. We ourselves go to pieces because we've *deferred* all that grief by living in a story we tell ourselves that just… isn't… true…

Believe it or not, it is this tendency to defer grief and pretend that everything is permanent that has created and perpetuated the existential crisis that is being reflected back to us now by *anima mundi* in the shape and form of our own climate crisis.

Grieving is a means of letting go. Catharsis means release. These are the tools we need to solve the spiritual dimension of the climate crisis. Grieving leads to catharsis, and catharsis lightens our emotional load, freeing us up in relation to the natural world and to others to love and live more deeply than before.

Starting now.

Cutting the Umbilical Cord

Begin again…

When we split the atom, unleashing the awesome creative/destructive power of nature - "all thoughts and things were split." Or, as another poet named Bob Dylan would put it many decades later: "The atom bomb fueled the entire world that came after it."

We had split ourselves psychologically from the world soul - much like severing the natural umbilical cord that connected us collectively to our mother, Earth, opening "a bottomless wound in the living conscience of the race." We assumed the role of creators, taking dominion over

---

[59] As recounted by Epstein in *The Trauma of Everyday Life*.

nature itself, and effectively failed the Trinity Test by unleashing hell on Earth with our new, Promethean power. This induced a kind of collective trauma born of cognitive dissonance in our shared psyche, a 'developmental trauma' that set off a chain reaction in our relationship to the natural world, opening Pandora's box, and leading us inevitably into the present existential crisis we are now confronted by.

It is so interesting, from an Ecopsychological viewpoint, that this just happened to be reflected in the following decades by an unprecedented trend, perpetrated by the medical community, whereby mothers were somehow convinced *to stop nursing their own babies* - in favor of formulas delivered by artificial, technological means.[60] Subconsciously, we were acting out this traumatic disconnection from our mother Earth by aggressively disconnecting mothers themselves from newborns.

What were we thinking?!

Of course, it is not really possible to *completely* cut humans off from human nature. We have always been, and will always be, interdependent with and interconnected (really, 'inner' - connected) to *anima mundi*. It is perhaps more accurate to say that the sudden trauma of splitting the atom and detonating the atom bombs, of suddenly asserting the role of a creator being and using it to subject tens of thousands of mothers and their children (most of the men being away at war) to hellish torment in Hiroshima and Nagasaki, represented an acute 'rupture' in that primordial relationship. This rupture, in turn, induced a kind of collective amnesia in our collective consciousness by which we forgot that the Earth upon which we were unleashing these destructive forces was sacred, something to be regarded with reverence.

A Word or Two About Trauma

It would be helpful here to return to the psychological idea of trauma. We've all heard of examples where someone who was traumatized in childhood suddenly 'recovers' the memory of that trauma many years later, as adults. How is it that an experience that is so painful can somehow be *forgotten* in the first place, with the child going on with their lives as if it hadn't happened, and then decades later quite unexpectedly resurface in memory?

The key to understanding this phenomenon is to appreciate the difference between explicit and implicit memory. Explicit memory is what we normally think of as memory. What happened to us yesterday is there in our memory today, and slowly fades in inverse proportion to its significance. But when we experience trauma, we 'check out' mentally, or 'dissociate' from what is happening to us. It is just as if we are not present *mentally*, not fully conscious of what is happening to us because it is so unbelievable to us, so that no explicit memory is formed. But we are definitely present *physically*, and what most people don't appreciate is that our body stores memory, too. The simplest example of this is that when you get onto a bike, you don't have to

---

[60] By the 1950s, over half the babies born in the U.S. were formula-fed, and the rate peaked at about 75% in the 1970s before women began coming to their senses and re-asserting control over their babies with their bodies!

remember all the steps involved in riding a bike that you learned the hard way as a kid. Your body and muscle memory kicks in. Typing this manuscript is another example. This is what's called 'implicit' memory - a kind of memory we are not consciously aware of until we need it.

So when we are traumatized, we check out mentally and the experience is registered in our unconscious mind and stored in our body. I know of at least one experienced shamanic healer who is able to place a person on a massage table, and while giving them a relaxing massage, she can actually 'read' the stories of the various traumas stored in that person's somatic structure. She does this with great detail, recounting the approximate age of the person when they experienced the trauma, the nature of the trauma, etc. And from all accounts, her readings are always accurate.

Now, once the implicit memory of a traumatic experience is triggered, and brought into conscious awareness *for the first time*, it is as if the person is actually experiencing that trauma in the present moment. That's because they were not consciously present when it was initially experienced. This is a common symptom of PTSD with war veterans. When the repressed implicit memory is triggered, it is not that they suddenly *remember* the battlefield scene; instead, it is as if they are *experiencing* it right then and there. The repressed emotions associated with that acute rupture in our reality can then finally be experienced for the first time, inducing a kind of 'catharsis' in which the person finally is able to release all of that pain they have been storing in their bodies, or what is now called our 'somatic consciousness,' all those years.

Now let's broaden our perspective using this knowledge of how trauma works. If the trauma of the Trinity Test was received in our *collective* unconsciousness, how would the implicit memory of that experience be *stored*? Well, just as our individual conscious mind is associated with our physical body, our collective consciousness is associated with our culture, which is itself an expression of the 'body politic.' Remember, from the perspective of our new, quantum world view, we are not so separate after all. We are relational being-ness, not objectified individual beings. So we can see that no great quantum leap is required from that world view to this idea of collective developmental trauma. Epstein points out that, in the case of the individual, the "emotional reactions of fight or flight associated with a specific trauma *live on* in the bodies of traumatized individuals *as if in an eternal present*. The traumatic reactions are locked into place, ready for a threat the individual has already seen but not explicitly known."

As long as the memory remains implicit in the body, the person will act it out in dysfunctional ways, through patterned behaviors rooted in the unconscious. A simple example would be a child who has been sexually abused by a trusted figure in their life. Later on in life, they may be frigid, they may become promiscuous, or they may simply continue to 'check out' (dissociate) whenever engaged sexually - still trapped in the eternal present of that original, unfathomable experience, and thus unable to enjoy a healthy intimacy. The greater the trauma, the more we seek out relationships which somehow reflect the initial hurtful relationship, as if in a desperate effort to recreate the experience we were *unable* to experience in our emotionally undeveloped state - hoping without even knowing for some kind of redemption.

As someone who was privy to the mental evaluations of imprisoned sexual offenders during a period of my legal career, I can tell you that every sex offender whose evaluations I ever saw (hundreds) was sexually abused as a child, and then perpetuated the cycle under the influence of intoxicants. It's uncanny how pervasive this story is. The alcohol and/or drugs (usually both) are resorted to for the purpose of numbing the psychological pain that plagues victims of childhood sexual abuse, and then has the unfortunate effect of lowering their sexual and psychological inhibitions to the point of wanting to recreate the traumatic circumstance of their own childhood. They then tend to rationalize their behavior with some kind of delusional thinking that it is a 'pure' form of love, or that the circumstances are otherwise exceptional in some way that exempts their behavior from societal norms. It's not that they don't know that their behavior is illegal - it's that they don't *feel* it is morally wrong in the moment.

Can you begin to see how this psychology of developmental trauma might apply to our cultural development since the end of WWII? We've already seen one way we may have been acting out culturally the rupture in our primordial relationship to Mother Earth that resulted from splitting the atom - we severed the most intimate and natural relationship between mothers and infants, replacing the warmth and softness of a mother's bosom with plastic nipples and synthetic milk. But this was just symptomatic of a much larger campaign of acting out subconsciously to 'prove' that we didn't need to be intimately connected with our natural world after all.

Once our boys returned from the battlefields of Europe and the jungles of the South Pacific, Americans engaged in pervasive self-medication in a fruitless effort to stuff the intense grief and pain we were feeling following the twin traumas of the Great Depression and the Great War. Young men just out of their teens - think of it - still haunted by memories of concentration camps populated by human skeletons, and nuclear battlefields full of rubble, charcoal bodies that had been instantly carbonized by the bombs and humans suffering for the first time from radiation sickness, were reunited with their best gals back home, the ones they had spoken of in foxholes to one another, or else quickly found suitable brides. There was no such thing then as "PTSD" - and mental illness was largely stigmatized, much more so than today. So they set about having more babies than any society had ever produced before, the subconsciously named "baby boom" generation, and imbibing copious amounts of hard liquor (along with nicotine), acting out their separation from the natural world by proceeding to build artificial lives in artificially constructed worlds. This is the world we've inherited from that shell-shocked generation.

But before getting into the details of suppression and acting out our repressed grief over losing touch with our 'universal mother,' we need to be very clear on just what the nature of this natural connection is. What exactly are we talking about when we say that we and our mother, *anima mundi*, are one? Is this some kind of new age nonsense? In thruth, this idea of a world sould, once common to all earthlings, has become a foreign concept. So we need to revisit and reconsider the idea before going further in our process here.

Human Nature & Subtle Conscious Being

We touched on this a bit in the previous chapter, but it is worth revisiting briefly. Jung was like some kind of feral, though highly educated, *pscyhonaut* - exploring the depths of his own psyche and finding connections in there to all that had up to then been considered 'other.' Not just *living* others, either. Jung became quite convinced from his experience that the dead are ever-present among us, and speak to us and through us internally, in our psyches. I should note here that we are still in the process of 'discovering' the depth and breadth and meaning of Jung's profound contributions to our understanding of the human condition, as evidenced for example by the recent release of his *Red Book* - a secret journal he composed over the course of his lifetime that many Jung scholars believes casts all his previously known works in a new light, and is prompting some leading scholars to reconsider psychology itself.[61]

While it is a slight over-generalization, the fundamental difference between Freud & Jung, the irreconcilable difference that led to their acrimonious 'divorce' early on, is that Freud had an exceedingly pessimistic view of human nature, convinced that we are in effect prisoners of our most aggressive primal forces (our 'id' or *it*), while Jung had a much more redemptive view of human nature, convinced that the spiritual component of our being was at least as worthy of consideration as the sexual and egoic bits. Thanks to the incessant and nefarious meddling of Freud's nephew (Edward Bernays) in American politics, culture, and business in the decades leading up to and following the WWII, Freud's pessimism carried the day - and our culture has been impoverished spiritually ever since.

While it is not necessary to go into great detail about all this here, it is still important for us to appreciate the extent to which we in the West have been conditioned by Freud (and *long* before him, St. Augustine) to think poorly of human nature. With the resurgence of Jung's influence, however, it is now due time for us to redeem our views of our own nature. Humans are most certainly prone to great mischief, plagued by ignorance and suffering, but we are still basically good. As Ann Frank herself remarked, locked away in a secret attic from the most monstrous of human beings: **"In spite of everything I still believe that people are really good at heart."** If humans by nature were not good, how would we be capable of such great love and compassion, expressed continuously over time in countless small ways and astonishingly great ways as well?

To say we are misguided and even easily manipulated is not the same as saying that we are evil by nature. Sexual offenders are not born that way. Even Hitler was dosed with poisonous gases in the trauma of WWI. If war is more indicative of human nature than love, then why would so many of us be so traumatized by our experiences on the battlefield? Think about it. This is such an important point, and to the extent you find yourself not agreeing with it, please locate a copy of Holocaust survivor Viktor Frankl's book *Man's Search for Meaning*. If people like Anne Frank and Viktor Frankl can retain their faith and conviction in the basic goodness of human nature, then who are we in this privileged time and place to disagree with them?

---

[61] See, e.g., *Lament of the Dead* (2013), Hillman & Shamdasani.

Returning to Jung's experiential findings, and employing the iceberg analogy that Freud himself popularized, only our waking consciousness appears above the surface. Just beneath the surface is our personal unconscious, which dwarfs our waking consciousness in the same way that a large percentage of an iceberg is submerged in the ocean. But what Jung famously discovered was that there was an *even deeper* level of unconscious being that is like the ocean itself, in that it is not personal to us but is rather the environment that all icebergs inhabit. What's more, the boundaries between the personal unconscious and this collective unconscious realm turn out to be quite permeable. It's the place, for instance, where dreams bubble up from.

According to a contemporary Jungian psychotherapist from the U.K. who is also a life-long Buddhist practitioner, Rob Preece, what Jung "discovered" has long been common knowledge in the Eastern cultures of Hinduism and Buddhism. This is no coincidence, as Jung's empirical, experiential approach to the mind and mental states is what gave rise to Eastern ways of knowing in the first place, and in contrast to the relatively recent advent of psychology in Western culture, Buddhist psychology goes back over 2500 years.

In Buddhist psychology, the personal consciousness that is represented by the exposed part of the iceberg is called 'gross consciousness,' while the submerged part is referred to as 'subtle consciousness.'[62] What Jung labeled 'collective unconsciousness' is referred to in Buddhism as 'extremely subtle consciousness' since, as Buddhists and Taoists and Hindu tantric practitioners (as well as indigenous shamans from every part of the world) have been demonstrating for thousands of years, *all* levels of consciousness are accessible to us (and thus they have never labeled any of these realms as *un*-conscious) if we only deepen our mental senses. In the same way that a concert pianist deepens her sense of hearing beyond what we hear, a meditator deepens her sense of mental awareness beyond conceptuality, going deeper and deeper into the substrates of mind and psyche - as Jung himself did.

And at the very bottom of the ocean, when we plunge all the way down to the depths of *unus mundus*, where all boundaries dissolve, there is something Buddhists yogis refer to as the *clear light nature of mind*. This is the mind of highly realized masters, or prophets like Jesus,[63] and moves through the world and our minds as *anima mundi* herself. What we are really talking about here is not consciousness in the way we in the West are accustomed to thinking about it, which has become so heavily colored by the Cartesian world view of rationalism, the identity of consciousness with conceptualization that is encapsulated in the phrase "I think, therefore I am." Instead, it is a kind of conscious *being* we know more directly, or experientially, as *awareness* (or luminosity in Buddhism, which defines mind as luminous and aware).

While highly realized beings live in the light of this kind of awareness, it does not necessarily follow that we ourselves are incapable of experiencing it. Everyone has lucid moments and

---

[62] *The Psychology of Buddhist Tantra* (2006, Snow Lion Publications), p. 91.

[63] Remember, the 'Spirit of Christ' descended on Jesus at the River Jordan, when John baptized him, after which he retreated into the desert for 40 days of deep prayer and meditation.

sudden insights at some point in their life. Being in the presence of someone who lives in such light can induce a direct experience of it as well, since ultimately these boundaries between our minds are mere constructs. And as anyone who has ever had such an experience will attest, *that* is our true nature. That is *human* nature. Maybe there are highly realized dolphins, whales, and snow leopards, and maybe there is no difference between their realized states and ours. But at least many highly realized beings throughout history in the Buddhist traditions have claimed this is not the case. Who knows? Let us stay focused on what we know to be true here.

In early Christian sects, which seem very close to the living church of Christ that Jesus spoke of, this clear light nature of mind was called *gnosis* - which can be translated roughly as 'direct knowing' (i.e., without the intermediary of thought). We experience this awareness as intuition and premonition - 'knowing without knowing.' We don't really have any explanations for these common phenomena, and are always astounded when we experience synchronicity in our lives - such as thinking of someone we are close to, but haven't spoken with in some time, and the phone rings within moments. Or the uncanny ability women possess of knowing the second someone is watching them in a crowded place! We don't have explanations for these common experiences because they don't fit into the orthodox world view we've been conditioned to accept as 'real.' But these experiences *are* part of our reality, and they fit quite nicely into the quantum world view where consciousness is primary, before all other phenomena - and not just a secondary (*epi-*) phenomenon produced by electrical impulses and chemical reactions. We can now call these experiences examples of non-local consciousness, entanglement, morphic resonance,[64] and interdependent arising, or 'inter-being.'

New words for the timeless experience of what it means to be human.

We inhabit an intelligent universe.[65] We are literally swimming in a sea of conscious energy manifesting fluidly in miraculously diverse forms, and we are all connected to one another, to our pets, to the animal kingdom itself, and to the world soul by simple *awareness*. It is at the level of this kind of clear knowing revealed in the clear light nature of our mind where we and Earth are *intimately* interconnected. It is where our true nature shines through within the light of mother nature's warm embrace. We are conditioned to dismiss this kind of thinking/feeling by scientism and rationalism. But we know in our hearts that this is true. It has always been true. It is just a matter of admitting it to ourselves and then opening ourselves up, opening up our hearts and minds, to these subtle realms where we can connect with our true nature - *human* nature.

When I was a full grown man, I spent a year backpacking around the world, seeking out natural experience. As part of this adventure, I spent nearly four months hiking and meditating in the Eden-like splendor that is found on the South Island of New Zealand. I should probably point out

---

[64] Rupert Sheldrake's biological theory that self-organizing systems inherit a memory from previous similar systems, with the mind 'receiving' such information from 'morphic fields' in much the same way radios receive signals from electromagnetic fields.

[65] See any of renowned mathematician and cutting edge evolutionary cosmologist Brian Swimme's fascinating videos on this point, available at: https://storyoftheuniverse.org

for context that I very much considered myself Christian at that time in my life, inspired by Thomas Merton (Trappist monk) and Princeton Divinity Chair Dr. Elaine Pagel's clear and luminous presentations of the Gnostic Gospels. I went into the wild mountains and deep rainforests of Eden with a question that had formed and taken shape through many prior wilderness experiences: who is this 'I' that I am in nature?! I always felt so different after a week in the wilderness, but the difference always faded upon my return to the city - like carrying a snowball from the mountaintop in your pocket, and finding only a wet spot on your return. Now I had given myself *months* to contemplate and meditate on that feeling in one of the most natural places on Earth.

At some point along the trail, probably meditating on a large boulder beside a stream, the answer emerged very clearly from the space of non-conceptual awareness: the 'I' that I am in nature *is* nature! It isn't some alternative 'self' or aspirational being - it was just my true nature, deeply felt. I sincerely wish every human being in the world could have that same opportunity to experience their true selves at length immersed in nature. I have no doubt whatsoever that we'd each come to the same conclusion.

So what happened! What became of our human nature after the Trinity Test? After that brightest light anyone has ever seen 'pounced' and 'bored' its way into our collective psyche, splitting all thoughts and things? After that instant when the self-proclaimed 'destroyer of the worlds' recounted that all the witnesses to this alchemical event knew the world would never be the same? *How* did we change, exactly?

More to the point, how did we as a body politic respond psychosomatically to that traumatic cutting of the collective umbilical cord by which we had always been connected at some level to the natural world?

We fell asleep...

93

CHAPTER 7

EARTH'S LAMENT

"There is no grief like the grief that does not speak."

~ Henry Wadsworth Longfellow

WELCOME TO THE AMERICAN DREAM WORLD!

After World War II, there was a fundamental shift in the way we Americans lived our lives. Prior to the war, we had been a largely rural, mostly agricultural country populated by small family farms and farming communities, the backbone of our country. This landscape was dotted with a few big cities here and there, where all the commerce and industry was concentrated. There really wasn't much in between these two lifestyles. Once you drove out of the city, it wasn't long at all before you were in farm country. We would say there were two kinds of Americans up until this time: city folk and country folk.

Then came the successive traumas of the Great Depression, when it seemed like nature herself had turned on us, followed quickly by the Great War, fought by the 'Greatest Generation.' As we can see, 'great' wasn't always used in quite the same way then as it is now! Perhaps it would be more accurate today to say the "Immensely Widespread Depression" and the "Most Horrible War Round II."

When we look back on this tumultuous time, it really does seem like the country before WWII was a dramatically different one than the country we built after 'saving the world from evil.' Those boys went through hell in WWII. There was no such thing as 'tours of duty' - they were in it to win it or die, and millions died before it was won. What kept those young men going in the cold and damp mud of their fox holes were cigarettes and the dreams they shared about how great their lives would be when they could finally go home at war's end.

This created a tremendous psychological pressure to re-build America in a way that would somehow meet those lofty expectations and adequately reward our returning vets for what they had to endure - for what no one should ever have to endure. My own father had to drop out of high school at 16, during the height of the Great Depression, to help make ends meet in his family (he was the oldest boy), and then at the time when he should have been graduating high school, he was sent to the Philippines in 1941 to fight the first guerrilla war in the swamplands there, where he contracted malaria and had his leg sliced open by a bayonet in hand-to-hand combat. *Four years later* - 4 Years! - when the war finally ended, he and his mates were shipped out… to Nagasaki, to clean up the rubble and build bridges.

Nice reward!

As someone born in 1957, at the very height of the post-war 'baby boom' (how subconscious is that name?), I can attest to the obvious effects of this incredible pressure to create the perfect family life in the perfect neighborhoods with the perfect lawns, schools, parks, etc. One of the things that really stands out in my mind about my early life was the constant presence of hard liquor and cigarettes, especially when the adults gathered for regular parties, poker nights, or shared meals. Beer and wine were daytime drinks. Only the hardest drinks would suffice in the evening - Manhattans, rusty nails, martinis, Tom Collins… All very ritualized, nothing in moderation in those days. Even on a normal day, with no social events, my mom would have a pitcher of martinis in the freezer waiting for my dad's homecoming from work, which was a kind of ritualized form of the homecoming from war. This was not considered a sign of alcoholism, either - it was normal behavior in the vast post-war middle class. In retrospect, it almost seems like we were a nation of drunks and enablers. But really, we were just a traumatized people, trauma that reverberated right through our family living rooms and classrooms, with raucous arguments, violent whippings, constant fist-fighting outside the home (even among friends), and corporal punishment in schools.

While there was no such name for it at the time, and certainly no treatment, the fact of the matter is that the entire country was in the grips of a massive post-traumatic stress syndrome. And nobody talked about the way that war was ended - least of all those like my dad who had seen it with their own eyes. Instead, we lived with the fear that the same terrible hell might be visited upon us as well, courtesy of Nikita Krushchev - that big, bad Russian Bear pounding his shoe on the lectern. "We will bury you without firing a shot!"

As silly as it now seems, and likely it was either a form of societal manipulation or ritualized acting out, we regularly sounded sirens and hid under our desks. What was *that* about?

With remarkable pace, America was converted in the wake of the war into a largely urban/ suburban country sprawling out into the formerly rural areas. The largest cities were connected by metropolitan corridors created by the building of our expressway system (which was intended as a form of civil defense against nuclear attack), and small family farms were supplanted by agribusiness - large industrial mono-crop and 'factory' farms, heavily dependent upon chemicals for crops and drugs for livestock. *Supermarkets* replaced small 'mom and pop' grocers, butchers and bakeries. Who wouldn't want to shop at a *super*-market?!

We doubled our country's population in only *fifty years*, less than the span of a single life. *Think of it!* Today, over 70% of us live in one of nearly 500 urbanized areas. That's quite a radical transformation. The family farm is nearly dead, a relic of a bygone era when life was much simpler, people lived closer to nature (think Norman Rockwell, Jack London, Huck Finn, *A River Runs Through It,* Spanky & Our Gang), and we were in closer touch with the sources of our food. But the single most significant feature, the iconic symbol of the *American Dream* at the advent of the atomic age, was… the *suburb*.

We were not about to go back to the way life had been before the war, with the prospect of choosing between a dirty, congested city and a suddenly hostile farmland in order to raise a family. No, something 'new and improved' was called for, a whole new way of life. And we settled upon an artificial way of living - we called it 'modern' - in these artificial, man-made environments that were neither city nor country, places where nature itself was a direct product of our own design.

COLLECTIVE CLIMATE GRIEF

Stage One: Denying the Loss of our World Soul

The emergence of suburbia in the 1950s brought with it a preternatural obsession with manicured lawns of chemically preserved alien strains of grass.[66] This, in turn, rapidly gave rise to the communal ritual of gathering leaves every autumn for transport and disposal somewhere out of sight. A perfect expression of how we were beginning to deal with death and dying. We had no room in our formulated world for something as natural and timeless as leaves on the ground! Every neighborhood had access to a well-preened and pruned park, while forest preserves on the outskirts of civilized existence (with dead trees quickly removed, not realizing at the time that dead trees are the source of life in natural forests) were converted into picnic areas for family getaways (never mind the ants - *we sprayed 'em*). In the summertime, trucks would roll slowly through the streets at dusk trailing clouds of DDT to prevent any mosquitoes or other pesky insects from interfering with our barbecues. Who knew nature had a use for such things! As much as it pains me to say it now, one of my fondest memories as a child was chasing down fireflies in the gathering dark - and squeezing out their 'lights' into a glass jar. *Radium!*

It is safe to say that by the time Rachel Carson published *Silent Spring* in 1962, alerting us to the fact that songbirds were disappearing *en masse* due to the lack of insects to feed, along with their inability to successfully breed, due to all the poison in their systems, we Americans were becoming increasingly, if not painfully, aware of our growing alienation from the natural world. However, probably as a result of the continuing hangover from the war years - but also in no small part because of the advent of pervasive advertising - it was during this era that we also honed the fine art of denial. If you think about it, it was that kind of preternaturally cheery denial that most characterized fifties *Americana*. As long as the lawn got mowed, the weeds and leaves were removed, the houses got fresh coats of paint every few years, dinner was served every night, and water continued to come out of the faucets and hoses, we laughing suburbanites couldn't really be bothered about some vague notions of a more 'natural' lifestyle.

We were modern Americans! *Living the dream!* Life had never been better! Really!! *Ha Ha!!*

Theodore Roszak coined the term 'ecological unconscious' to indicate our deep connection to the world soul. And just as the special bond between a mother and her child gives rise to an intuitive sense of *dis-ease* when one or the other is imperiled, it is safe to say that *our ecological unconscious was deeply troubled* by the near total disconnection of humans from nature during this formative time in our emergent, post-war culture. Thanks to the miracle of the new plastics industry, we didn't even need wood anymore! People actually had tupperware parties!! *Neat!*

---

[66] Kentucky bluegrass is not even native to Kentucky! It's non-native to North America, brought over from Europe, presumably, by early settlers.

Americans became to the natural world what Scrooge was to Christmas.

This unease happened to coincide with the disturbing knowledge that we were now poised on the brink of nuclear annihilation. We had not only left our mother's natural embrace, but we were actively poisoning her with all the wonderful new chemicals that we were told were making our lives better, making our new life possible, replacing everything anything natural with plastic, and even threatening to do away with her altogether!

While it may be true that we were now only dropping nuclear bombs on nature, at an alarming pace once Russia (and later China) joined in, I've often wondered what unseen, unseeable effects such detonations have had. From the quantum worldview, physicist David Bohm postulates that there is a pervasive implicate order to the universe that undergirds the time/space continuum. I strongly suspect that a sustained nuclear fission reaction rips a hole in the fabric of that implicate order. We've ripped over 2000 such holes, which become open fissures in time and space, perhaps even explaining the common perception we have that time is speeding up. Certainly, we can all agree that the 'change' inaugurated by Trinity has transpired at an accelerated, 'modern' pace.

This post-war, post-natural 'nuclear' period when the *American Dream* took hold of our lives can be viewed in retrospect as the *Golden Age of Anxiety*, an anxious energy that surged through us for a couple of decades, abetted no doubt by the growing availability of Valium and other anti-anxiety medications from the booming new Pharmaceutical industry (not to mention the continuing omnipresence of hard liquor and loose availability of sleeping pills). Anxiety is really the first mental health trend we see as a result of living a life divorced from nature, and it makes perfect sense when you think about it.

As someone who had to deal with anxiety attacks in college after my father died, I can describe it very simply. You have a constant, nagging sense that something is wrong, there is something you should be doing or maybe forgot to do, but you can never really put your finger on what that something is. This can become cumulative, leading to the crushing insecurity of anxiety attacks, where your whole body shakes, unable any longer to hold the repressive energy. I can remember going to the health service not long after beginning my first job in the corporate world (environmental counsel to the City of Colorado Springs) to renew my own romance with valium. I asked my doctor what was missing from my physiology that valium seemed to supply? Why was it that when I took valium, I felt most like myself?? He said there was nothing missing from my physiology. Instead, he pointed out that I was wearing a suit and tie, and had to go every weekday to a place where I wasn't really allowed to *be* myself. All the valium did, he informed me, was to give me the permission that my workplace could not.

That's a perfect illustration of what anxiety is. You are painfully aware that you are no longer in touch with your own true nature, and that little blue pill allows you to place a person-to-person call to your mother. "Hi mom - where *are* you? I really miss you…"

That's where we were as a culture in the 1950s and well into the 1960s. We had lost something really important to us, something essential about us seemed to be missing, but we didn't know what it was in our conscious mind and there was tremendous social pressure to 'conform,' to pretend everything was *honky-dori* - just like in the uniformly popular TV shows *Ozzie & Harriet*[67] and *Father Knows Best*, or the insipid Doris Day & Rock Hudson movies - so we weren't able grieve that loss even if some part of us wanted to.

The 'beat' generation was the exception that proved the rule, thanks to free and indomitable spirits like Kerouac and Ginsberg (and Burroughs and Henry Miller long before them). They were our conscience, but only on the margins. However, if you really think about it they were just what happens to anxiety on steroids - as they were mostly inspired and fueled by readily available amphetamine (e.g., benzedrine from inside plastic 'Benzedrex Inhalers' you could purchase over the counter at any pharmacy back then for nasal decongestion - *whee!*). The beats were able to express and even transcend their 'high anxiety' in their writing, just as Charlie Parker - another big sufferer of nasal congestion - was able to with his saxophone.

The rest of us were more vaguely 'aware' at some level in our conscious being that something was wrong with the world - we could feel it in our soul - but we had no way of giving voice to that awareness, or even forming thoughts around it. We simply didn't have the language for that kind of unsettling feeling (unlike indigenous cultures), just as our fathers didn't have the advantage of knowing what 'post-traumatic stress syndrome' was when they came home from the war, and had no language for conveying to us what the war was like for them. Only Kerouac & Ginsberg really succeeded in putting words to it.

> *I saw the best minds of my generation destroyed by madness, starving hysterical naked...*
> — Ginsberg (opening line to Howl)

> *...the only people for me are the mad ones, the ones who are mad to live, mad to talk, mad to be saved, desirous of everything at the same time, the ones who never yawn or say a commonplace thing, but burn, burn, burn like fabulous yellow roman candles exploding like spiders across the stars.*

> *I realized these were all the snapshots which our children would look at someday with wonder, thinking their parents had lived smooth, well-ordered lives and got up in the morning to walk proudly on the sidewalks of life, never dreaming the raggedy madness and riot of our actual lives, our actual night, the hell of it, the senseless emptiness.*

> *"Sal, we gotta go and never stop going 'till we get there.'*
> *'Where we going, man?'*

---

[67] Ironically, this show was actually called *The Adventures of Ozzie & Harriet,* and ran from 1952-1966. *Father Knows Best* ran from 1954-1960, and was NOT called "The Adventures of Father Knows Best."

CLIMATE SENSE

'I don't know but we gotta go."
— Jack Kerouac, *On the Road*

Light up a cigarette. Have a drink. Try not to think about it. Certainly don't *talk* about it. There's a pill for that. Talk to your doctor… Or, better yet, just laugh it off. *Ha Ha!*

While mental health trends like anxiety surface in individuals, our cultural forms of expression provide us with another *collective* outlet for suppressed grief that is consistently revealed through every stage of our collective grieving. In the 1960s, with the anxiety reaching escape velocity levels, we created escapist entertainment in the form of silly situation comedies on T.V., Bond movies and musicals at the movies, and a growing fascination with the controlled violence of spectator sports (football came of age during this time when Americans discovered how perfect it was for that television in our 'living' rooms).

One thing that is really telling about all this is that many of the popular sitcoms of the 60's depicted fantasy realities that quite accurately reflected our conflicted feelings about living such an unnatural lifestyle. *The Beverly Hillbillies* made fun of people who actually lived their lives close to nature by placing them in a mansion in Beverly Hills. Ha Ha! *Green Acres* took the exact opposite tact, taking a couple who had no connection to the natural world at all, a tax lawyer and his high society wife from New York City, and plopped them down on a small family farm - making fun of how inept they were at anything natural (Oliver Wendell Douglass rode his tractor dressed in a tux). Of course, that didn't stop *them* from continually mocking the rubes who populated Hooterville. For intelligent viewers, however, it was clear that the real butt of all these jokes was us - the ridiculously pompous lawyer-farmer, so convinced in the superiority of reason, or the morally bankrupt and conniving banker and his anorexic secretary in Beverly Hills.

I Dream of Jeannie depicted a military lifer trying to conceal the fact that he had a genie at home, while the advertising executive in *Bewitched* hid the fact that he was married to a witch. Witches, of course, represent our connection to pagan cultures that worshipped nature, while genies harken back to a time when people entertained myths of creatures that could connect them to the unseen worlds they inhabited. Thus, the need to hide their true identities, these parts of ourselves that would subject us to ridicule in the confines of social structure.

My Favorite Martian, Get Smart, The Flying Nun, Addams Family, Mr. Ed (a man who talked to his horse!), *The Munsters, etc.* It is as if we were instinctively aware just how silly our life divorced from nature really was, and were compensating by presenting even more surreal worlds inhabited by even more clueless characters who we could take solace from laughing at. As we will see, this surrealistic silliness quickly dissipated at the next stage of collective grief.

So summing up, the first stage of collectively grieving the loss of our connection to the natural world was denial, and the primary mental health trend that resulted from repressing all this natural grief, from denying the denial itself, was chronic anxiety. The second stage of grieving is anger, and boy did we become an angry society by the end of the 1960s!

** It is important to footnote here that one thing we know about the psyche is that the longer we repress something, the bigger the associated problems become. At the level of an individual, we call this our "shadow self" - the self we do not want to think of ourselves as. A grotesque example of this is a serial killer, who usually is traumatized at some formative stage early in life, and over time creates a monstrous shadow self that completely overtakes them at regular intervals. But we all have shadow selves, because we all tend to suppress things we don't want to identify with. And even genetics now shows that trauma, if not processed, can be passed on to the next generation, only getting worse. So now watch how the symptoms of suppressing our collective grief over the loss of our true nature rather quickly grows in power and force with each successive stage we have moved through as a culture, until today it threatens our very existence.

Stage Two: Anger Over Unfulfilled Dreams

Gradually, from the mid-60s onward, our collective awareness of something being amiss shifted from our growing imbalance with nature, which was relatively easy to cheerfully suppress, to the increasing ecological devastation we were wreaking on our environment. Rivers caught fire and lakes began dying as foul smelling and multi-colored effluents poured forth into them from industrial sewage pipes. National forests were being liquidated with updated "bunch-felling" machinery (clear cutting), like mowing a big lawn, until only a small percentage remained in the old-growth condition so many species of owls and woodpeckers require to survive. The air in big cities started to become unbreathable, and rates of asthmatic children began rising. Breast cancer rates also began rising in the 1950s, coincident with the introduction of *better living through chemistry.*

Suddenly, the effects of our unnatural lifestyles were becoming alarmingly evident. We humans were now having quite a dramatic impact on our environment, and at an unprecedented scale as our population spread like wildfire across the land. Environmental illnesses were becoming more prevalent, and the idea of endless growth and prosperity that fueled the American Dream was now coming into question. While the seeds were being planted by radical youth throughout the late sixties, we can roughly mark this shift *culturally* (by which I mean the emergence of a consensus) from around the time of the first Earth Day in 1970 and into the early 1980s, when the awareness of human impacts began to shift even more dramatically - from devastation of our local environments to our impacts on the global climate and, eventually, the oceans.

Around this time (late '60s), too, anti-depression prescriptions had begun to supplant anti-anxiety drugs, with the combination of those two quickly doubling until, along with pervasive anxiety, nearly one in ten of us was being treated for depression -- from 16 million Americans in 1962 to roughly 31 million by 1975. This signaled the second stage of collectively suppressed grieving.

Depression is what happens when humans suppress anger. Though we were not yet fully aware of the *global* scope of our impacts, it was becoming quite clear that the planet was paying a steep price for our lovely, plastic-wrapped dream. We regressed from simply being apart from the natural world to actually being at war with it. The ultimate expression of this conflict between humankind and nature was our decision to wage *ecological warfare* on a country for the first time ever, dropping chemical defoliants (Napalm™) on Southeast Asia with devastating ecological impacts.[68]

At some base level of awareness, it was like we had this notion that our mother had mistreated us as children (e.g., perhaps the dustbowls of the Great Depression), and now we adolescents were exacting revenge on her. From the perspective of developmental trauma, however, one common symptom of unresolved trauma is to repeat the behavior over and over in varied symbolic ways, and in addition to over 2000 post-Nagasaki nuclear detonations, we certainly we do not seem able to stop ourselves from bombing civilian populations even up to this day.

Indeed, we were a very *angry* adolescent country during those turbulent years, waging unconscionable war over there, bringing it back over here into our streets and to our political conventions with police riots and even political commentator battles (Buckley & Vidal nearly coming to blows after trading invectives at the Democratic Convention in '68), expressing it with angry songs from groups like *The Doors, The Rolling Stones*, and Dylan, all climaxing with American soldiers actually shooting unarmed students dead on the campus lawn for the sin of exercising angry free speech - the ultimate form of suppression. While hippies certainly did not represent mainstream America at the time, more like an outgrowth of the beat generation's anxious discontent, it is no coincidence that these same rebellious youths advocated for a more natural lifestyle, starting the back-to-nature movement, or that they began equating the polluters with the warmongers -- all wrapped up into the *military-industrial complex*.

The tidal wave of angry rebellion that began on the Berkeley campus with a speech by Mario Savio in 1964[69] crested and then broke with the deposing of the paranoid establishment president in 1974 (note that '*the sixties*' generally refers to the decade from 1965-1974). Arguably there was a sea-change in our culture at that time as well, or at least a lull. We began in earnest to clean up our waterways and our air sheds, we abolished the draft, the human potential movement took hold, and we even elected a conscientious *farmer* as president!

---

[68] There was some precedent for this in our national psyche, as we drove bison to near extinction in the 19th Century in order to herd Native Indians onto reservations. While similar in concept, that biological warfare was much more targeted than wiping out whole ecosystems from above. Obviously, Hiroshima & Nagasaki had that effect, as well, but those were cities, not jungles.

[69] With these telling words: *"There is a time when the operation of the machine becomes so odious, makes you so sick at heart, that you can't take part; you can't even passively take part, and you've got to put your bodies upon the gears and upon the wheels, upon the levers, upon all the apparatus, and you've got to make it stop. And you've got to indicate to the people who run it, to the people who own it, that unless you're free, the machine will be prevented from working at all!"*

Jimmy Carter was a politician who was actually spiritual and cared about human rights. That was the first and, sadly, last time human rights became the focal point of our foreign policy. It's a significant point in this whole WWII traumatic development of modern culture arc, because it seems like there was a missed opportunity for us to wake up at that salient time. What we see here is a kind of national catharsis where even the older generation finally could see that something was rotten at the core of the American Dream, and we *very nearly* got in touch with our grieving process.

I came of age myself during that time, and remember the national mood during and after the Watergate hearings as being quite somber and pensive. President Carter even accurately diagnosed the country's psychological condition, characterizing it as a "national malaise" (def.: "a feeling of unease or depression" from Old French *mal* [bad] *aise* [ease]). He attempted to get us to face up to our oil addiction, and even installed solar panels in the White House.

Unfortunately, the country recoiled, shrank from its moral responsibility, and quickly resumed its more destructive path, as we will see shortly. Carter has gone on to become one of the few true statesmen from the ranks of our ex-presidents, and even a kind of conscience for our country. I often wonder what might have happened had we not allowed our national shadow-self to re-emerge so quickly after Nixon's shameful demise. We very well might have charted a course that averted the ecological catastrophe that we are facing now. Alas, it was not meant to be.

Culturally during this period of anger and sustained repression of anger, those ridiculous sit-coms and their silly fantasy realities were replaced by what could quite accurately be called 'angry sit-coms.' The one that most captured our collective imagination, and was therapeutic in a welcomed way, was *All in the Family,* which revolved around an angry old bigot by the name of Archie Bunker taking his frustration out on his angry liberal son-in-law. Not to be outdone, we had the angry liberal dame, *Maude,* and the angry social-climbing black dude, George Jefferson. There were also the disgruntled junk yard dealers, *Sanford & Son,* the perpetually angry sports writer Oscar on *The Odd Couple,* the interminably angry boss (Louie) in *Taxi,* and perhaps the angriest doctors ever - funniest, too - in *M*A*S*H. Note:* All of *these* shows were set in *ordinary* reality. [70] And even comedic variety shows flashed quite a bit of anger and hostility in between laughs: The Smothers Brothers, SNL, and Laugh-In.

The *Godfather* movies were wildly popular as well, which provided a fantasy outlet (all too real) for any deep-seated anger, with its vengeful plot lines and gruesome violence. Meanwhile, we become increasingly fascinated by aliens and outer space as forms of escapist entertainment, perhaps feeling that if there was nothing we could do to recover our lost paradise, maybe it was time to start looking elsewhere. These included *2001: A Space Odyssey* (1968), which begins with humans first discovering tools to shape our planet, and ends with a fetus in outer space; *Planet of the Apes* (1968), depicting a post-apocalyptic world where our natural selves,

---

[70] The only notable exception to reality-based sitcoms in the 70s was *Mork & Mindy,* which was a spin-off from the reality-based 50s show, *Happy Days,* and succeeded only because of the comedic genius of Robyn Williams.

symbolized by apes, control our so-called 'evolved' selves, symbolized by humans; and finally, climaxed with the cultural phenomenon that is *Star Wars* (1977). The 'force' in *Star Wars* is an apt metaphor for our lost connection to *unus mundus*.[71] The 1970s was also happens to be the time when the pornography industry took hold, which is in many respects its own genre of anger, suppressed and acted out in the subjugation of women.

Certainly, these kinds of juvenile/primal/sexual escapist fantasies are all consistent with the increasing need as a culture to release all the repressed anger and frustration we were feeling over the pervasive unsatisfactoriness of the experience of the *American Dream* (versus the promise). Looking to outer space can be seen as a suppressed fight or flight response to ecological plunder here on Earth; or, alternatively, as looking for mythical salvation from the heavens, an expression of the sense that we really need to be saved from ourselves. This may even explain the staying power of the *Star Wars* movies.

The associated mental health trend of depression has really never waned, either. Whatever anger we may justifiably feel in relation to the 'Lost Paradise' cost exacted by the *American Dream* is still there. It has never been allowed full expression. Instead, we were sold a rehashed version of the *American Dream* by an aging actor appointed by the power elite to squash that peanut farmer.

Yes, beginning in 1980, it was now… *Morning in America.*

Stage Three of Climate Grief: *Let's Make a Deal!*

Anxiety and depression have become endemic to American culture as the pharmaceutical industry has grown and sprouted tentacles reaching into every aspect of life - even the bedroom. Treating symptoms while ignoring underlying causes has the effect of freezing mental illness into place, making it a permanent part of our identity - since the symptoms are never allowed the freedom of full expression, the process by which causes can be rooted out. It's the difference between 'arresting' symptoms and 'processing' them. The former has proven to be much more profitable, and so the psychiatry industry has dominated western psychology since at least *The Bob Newhart Show* (angry psychologist!).

From an ecopsychological viewpoint, the underlying causes of our social neuroses have never been adequately addressed. In fact, there really hasn't even been an effort to bring them to the surface long enough to deal with them at a societal level. While ecotherapy[72] is still relatively obscure, our consumer lifestyle, lived within the ubiquitous structure of a corporate world and propped up by the incredibly narrow world view of the corporate media, continues to insulate us from the natural world and inoculate us against human nature. However, as we began to emerge

---

[71] In the most recent installment, *The Force Awakens,* it's described as being all pervasive, permeating all of us.

[72] 'Ecotherapy' is a general term for different ways of reconnecting people with nature, from something as simple as planting a garden to something as intensive as a wilderness vision quest.

from the tumults of the Viet Nam war, Watergate, the energy crisis brought on by the OPEC oil embargo, and the prolonged Iranian hostage crisis, things took a drastic turn right around 1980.

Collective denial of something fundamentally out of balance was powerfully resurrected and consecrated. In fact, it was practically enshrined in Reagan's campaign ad announcing it was now *"Morning in America."* Not coincidentally, our base level awareness of *anima mundi,* our relation with the world soul, entered an entirely new and previously inconceivable phase, a phase for which we have not been equipped by evolution. Our only preparation for it, in fact, was the sudden potential for nuclear annihilation which had dawned less than a generation earlier, but had since faded into the unreality of "MADD" (mutually assured death & destruction).

Suddenly, right around 1980, we were supposed to believe that our *hairspray* was opening a giant hole in the invisible shield that protects us from the sun's more harmful radiation! How could this be? Seriously, even in retrospect it has a preposterous ring to it. The unmistakable consequence, however, was observed as a gaping hole opening up in the thin bubble that encapsulates our home planet - a hole that is still as large as ever, by the way - allowing levels of ultraviolet radiation never before seen in geologic time through to the biosphere, suppressing the immune defense systems of all living beings in the process. In other words, beginning in the early 1980s we became aware, for the first time ever as a species, of an *existential* threat to life from our own mundane daily routines.

It wasn't long at all before diseases related to the weakening of our biological defenses began dramatically increasing - as had been predicted in earlier studies conducted for the National Academy of Sciences - including, for example, fibromyalgia, leukemia, Crohn's disease, chronic fatigue syndrome and, most notably, the AIDS epidemic (from a virus that has been with us forever). Rates of primary immunodeficiency diseases in the first decade of the new millennium were *five times* higher than they had been only three decades earlier.

Natural forest ecosystems started to sicken, too, with trees no longer able to fight off the pests that they had co-evolved with, leading to increasingly destructive wildfires. Frogs and other species who were the most sensitive to sun radiation began disappearing, too, or showing up with gross deformities. Kangaroo blindness became epidemic down under, and humans were warned to avoid direct sunlight.

Think about that for just a minute… *'Please avoid the source of all life on Earth.'* What kind of impact do you suppose *that* campaign might have had on our connection to the world soul?

Arguably, it seems we compensated for this attack on our *physiological* defense mechanisms by amplifying our *psychological* defense mechanisms - amping up our collective coping mechanisms in the process. Paradoxically, but tellingly, our elected leaders began to *roll back* environmental protections, even going so far as to ridicule concern for the environment as a sign of weakness. Al Gore became *'the Ozone Guy'* -- said with a snicker of dismissive superiority by a man famous for making movies with a chimp named *Bonzo*!

Gore, of course, went on to become closely associated with the climate crisis, and still is the subject of much derision in spite of (or perhaps because of) the fact that he is the only presidential candidate in recent history to have lost an election with more votes than his opponent. Very strange. Like Reagan himself, an Illinois boy who famously vacationed at *Rancho Mirage (!)*, American politics from 1980 on became all hat and no cowboy.

Now it is one thing to acknowledge that dumping sewage into rivers kills fish, and quite another thing altogether to acknowledge that the *consumer culture* -- our reward for enduring the Great Depression and the hell of WWII in quick succession -- could end up killing the planet! The natural psychological defense to this kind of existential fear is denial, something we as a culture already had so much experience with from our construction of the *American Dream* - and Reagan's handlers were shrewdly harkening back to this with their *Morning in America* propaganda. So while many environmentally awakened people responded to the new global threat paradigm with alarm, it seemed like our culture as a whole reverted back to the comfortable illusion of Ozzie & Harriet's America, going so far as to marginalize those 'environmentalists' as trouble makers and discontents. A very wide rift opened up between ideology and reality, one that our political system would never actually recover from.

Welcome to the bargaining stage of grief. At the individual level, the bargaining stage is often associated with unrealistic, magical thinking - along the lines, for example, that 'if only God will take my disease away I promise to devote my life to noble causes' or 'be a better husband and father.' At the cultural level of 1980's America, however, it manifested as a mad scramble for an elusive, though understandable, goal: *security.*

How to secure a future for oneself, one's family, and one's country in a world of ever-increasing threats?

This marked the beginning of a near-pathological hoarding of wealth, replete with conspicuous retreat into gated communities (while warehousing the demonized under-privileged class in an expanding, for-profit prison system), open warfare by corporate 'fat cats' on the labor force (which began with Reagan's symbolic attack on air traffic controllers), predatory corporate takeovers involving liquidation of assets (often *natural* assets, like the centuries-old California Redwoods) *with no concern for the future,* and brazen funneling of the newly created wealth up to pay obscene CEO salaries, in addition to 'derivative wealth' ponzi schemes and increasingly ostentatious displays of obscene wealth. Think Donald and Ivana Trump here, or better yet - Gordon Gecko in the popular movie *Wall Street*, which really captured the country's moody response to this brave new world perfectly: "Greed is good."

How telling is it that we developed a cultural fascination with *vampires* during these final decades of the twentieth century! Psychopaths who coldly suck the lifeblood out of their victims in order to support their own unnatural lives (and with an aversion to sunlight!). They weren't depicted as mysterious caped Transylvanians, either. Rather, they looked just like you and me, from Lestat in Ann Rice's *Interview with a Vampire*, to Bram Stoker's *Dracula*, *The Lost Boys*, and *Buffy the Vampire Slayer*. These vampires are an almost *too-perfect* metaphor for what our corporations had become in America and throughout the world - immortal and powerful beings that not only preyed on society, but actually have the power to assimilate those individuals who they seduce into their ranks, in order to prey on increasing others.

Welcome to America, Inc! It would not be long at all before American corporations would become 'transnational,' taking over other countries, too - even China - and persuading the highest court in the land to declare that corporations are people, too. How many of those creepy old ghouls in black robes had to be seduced in order for *that* to come about?

Subconsciously, this all makes so much sense. If the gig is up, 'I better git mine while the gittin's good!' Right? It's the American way, after all. If you can't pilfer a bunch of money from some get-rich-quick scheme or corporate schmooze, then a huge cache of guns and ammo and canned goods will do quite nicely, thank you, with which to retreat into the woods and await inevitable Armageddon. Ruby Ridge in Idaho and the Branch Davidians in the Waco siege (1992-93) were typical of this kind of lunacy, not to mention the Oklahoma City bombing a few years later, the 'unabomber,' the rise of militias, and the ascendency of the NRA, with the old actor who played Moses and God in *The Greatest Story Ever Told* telling us we'd have to pry his gun from his cold dead hands.

When it comes to bargaining, desperate times call for desperate measures...

Meanwhile, *Lifestyles of the Rich and Famous* enjoyed an extended (voyeuristic) run from 1984-1995 (Reagan-to-Clinton), state-run lotteries became the norm rather than the exception (monetizing the *American Dream*), with gaming spreading from a booming Las Vegas (the dark 'heart' of the *American Dream,* as per Hunter Thompson's cutting social commentary) to just about every state with an Indian tribe. And everyone started playing the stock market through their Individual Retirement Accounts, or else stockpiling gold coins or sports memorabilia (not just for kids anymore). For a while there, even our *vehicles* began to take on ridiculous proportions, stopping just short of becoming personal armored tanks. Don't even get me started on road rage...

Feeling secure yet, America?

Celebrity worship became so heightened (and ritualized) during this extended bargaining stage that it has become a regular feature on the once-staid evening news (which itself became a 24/7 affair during the Gulf War, since security requires instant access to information). We elected yet another celebrity president on the strength of a bumper sticker that informed everyone *"It's The ECONOMY, Stupid!"* and in spite of (because of?) his chronic infidelities. Even traditional sports like baseball became more about wealthy superstars than winning teams, while the teams themselves were suddenly all about winning *now*, dammit, without much regard for building future success. Win now! Get rich quick! Spend it as if there's no tomorrow!! Security, apparently, can only be found in the present moment, with gates and guns and oversized rigs.

In short, it seems that during this extended bargaining phase, our culture morphed into something that no longer just *reflects* our suppressed grief, but is instead the enabling *means* for that suppression. Do you get that? Suppression of grief over the loss of nature became a veritable art form, glamorized in the media and reinforced by corporate cubicles and marketing that now was targeted increasingly at individual tastes (rather than conformism). "You deserve a break today!" Security is an egg McMuffin, if it's marketed right. And the *American Dream* was reduced, for most, to a lottery ticket.

The dominant message that began to slowly emerge and take root culturally in America during this rather frantic span of time, as it became increasingly apparent that we are facing the gravest threat in our species' history, is that *'distraction cures all ills'* -- just stay distracted 24/7 and you will never have to be bothered with worrying about your future, let alone your children's and their children's. After all, as another bumper sticker popular during that era put it:

"He Who Dies With The Most Toys Wins."

You might be asking yourself how this bargaining stage was reflected in mental health trends. Good question! The incredible scale of greed and promotion of self-interest that was first celebrated during the Reagan era, and which subsequently ran rampant during the Clinton/Bush era, would certainly have been viewed by any *sane* society as symptomatic of severe neurosis - if not actual sociopathy. And, in fact, there is a name for such mental disease: 'narcissistic personality disorder.' Here's how the Mayo Clinic defines NPD:

> Narcissistic personality disorder is a mental disorder in which people have an inflated sense of their own importance, a deep need for admiration and a lack of empathy for others. But behind this mask of ultra-confidence lies a fragile self-esteem that's vulnerable to the slightest criticism.

Sound like anyone you know, or perhaps everyone you see in the media spotlight? Not according to mainstream psychology, which reports only 1% of the population suffering from this malady. Really? Do *they* watch TV?? Ever heard of 'American Exceptionalism?'

Curiously enough, the DSM ("Diagnostic and Statistic Manual," used for classifying mental disorders in America) did not even *include* narcissism as a mental disorder until... (drumroll, please)... 1980! Thank you Ronald Reagan! In modern American culture, narcissism not only flies largely under the radar,[73] it is actually *rewarded* with advancement in the corporate, political, and entertainment spheres. Indeed, unlike most mental disorders, in the U.S. narcissism

---

[73] Though in 2009, *Twenge and Campbell* conducted studies suggesting that the incidence of Narcissistic Personality Disorder had **more than doubled** in the U.S. in the prior 10 years, and that 1 in 16 of the general population had experienced NPD in their lifetime. See: *The Narcissistic Life*, Bergemeester, A. (2014).

is said to occur along a continuum from *"healthy" narcissism* (!) to psychopathic narcissism (this may have something to do with there not being any pharmaceutical profit potential for diagnosing people with NPD). As further support of its social tolerance/acceptability, recent studies have shown that narcissists not only don't hide from their personality disorder - they tend to *boast* about it. "Of *course* I'm a narcissist - wouldn't YOU be if you were ME?"

Finally - a mental disorder Americans can be proud of.

This foolish, insecure mask of pride is reflected in almost all segments of American culture - in our politics especially - and helps explain why the richest society in world history not only consumes a disproportionate share of the world's resources, but has become the largest obstacle to addressing the global climate crisis. We see this graphically displayed whenever some activists try to raise serious social issues at a political event, and the crowd responds with chants of "USA! USA!" As President Bush said in response to a question about America's nuclear legacy in Japan, "America will never apologize for anything we have done." Yow - a blanket non-apology! Because of this narcissistic strain of American exceptionalism, it is almost impossible to imagine our broken, polarized Congress ever ratifying a climate treaty that binds us to mandatory reductions of the same fossil fuels that their principal donors profit mightily from. Thus, we are presently saddled with a Climate 'Accord' that is more a shield against accountability than it is a plan for achieving its worthy goals.[74]

Obviously, the dysfunctional social strategy represented by the obsession with personal and national security that emerged during the bargaining stage of our repressed climate grief is not compatible with the well-being of the individual psyche. At the collective level, our awareness progressed from the simple *dawning* of an existential threat in the '80s - the idea that we as a species could actually somehow threaten the continued existence of life on this planet just by doing what we do - to actually *carrying out* that threat. This is yet another critical progression in the seriousness of this social psychosis, this 'great unraveling.' While we almost recovered our balance in the mid-70's, from the 80's on we have progressively lost touch with reality as a culture - the defining characteristic of psychosis.

It may seem harsh, but how could a society that is not troubled by the prospect of ecological suicide and mass extinction be described as anything *other* than gripped by a prolonged psychotic episode? Carl Jung defined dissociation simply as not being conscious of things we should be conscious of, which is what got us into, and is now prolonging, this crisis. This is a spiritual emergency, which is a way of characterizing psychotic episodes that recognizes their inherent value; that is, the potential for spiritual emergence from this crazy spell of narcissistic delusion and dissociation.

---

[74] While the accords properly set a goal of limiting the rise of average global temperatures to 1.5 degrees celsius, they set forth unenforceable commitments from signatory countries that would ensure 3-5 degrees rise before the century is out. It is believed that agriculture breaks down over 3.5 degrees. As we've seen, seafood also dies out. As leading climate scientist James Hansen pointed out, the Paris Accords are a 'fraud.'

So following two decades of fruitless bargaining, beginning right around the time of the new millennium we became increasingly aware of the following hard-to-swallow facts:

- the Sixth Great Extinction is underway, with wildlife populations already cut in half in just a few decades;
- the cumulative absorption of carbon by our oceans over the course of the entire Industrial Age has irreparably altered their chemistry, is breaking critical links in the food chain, and is triggering irreversible rising tides;
- extreme weather events are becoming the norm, with massive 'historic' floods plaguing a different part of the world every year,[75] while conflagrations burn out of control in other areas - including Alaska, Canada, Russia and rain forests - due to chronically prolonged fire seasons, the absence of deep freezes that normally kill beetles, and persistent drought;
- the Arctic and Greenland ice caps are melting, along with glaciers everywhere,[76] thanks to average temperature increases being double the global average in those critical areas; and,
- perhaps most troubling of all, it's all happening at an accelerating pace that consistently outstrips the climate scientists' predictive models, with regular revelations of unforeseen results (e.g., methane releases, oscillating jet stream, etc.).

On top of all this, as already alluded to, we have the awareness that our political leaders are either unwilling or incapable of addressing this rising tide of grave threats to life as we know it on planet Earth. Quite to the contrary, they seem to be throwing political gasoline on the global warming fire, with increasingly widespread and insane warfare that threatens the outbreak of WWIII (the ultimate distraction), as well as accelerating extraction of previously inaccessible or unprofitable fossil fuels (fracking, tar sands, deep sea drilling, exploration of newly accessible areas of the Arctic, etc.). Our President of the last eight years, who promised he would *reverse* the rising tides of climate change when he was running for office, now expresses eloquent concern for the climate out of one side of his mouth while bragging out the other about turning America into the world's leading exporter of fossil fuels with his 'all of the above' energy extraction policy - as if it matters to the climate whether our dirty coal is burned here or in China.

What's a mother to do? Are we cooked, or what!

Stage Four: It's *NOT* terminal!

So while the global-stakes bargaining escalates to unimaginable heights - with increasing resource wars, repressed rebellions, oppressive 'austerity' programs, mass surveillance, militarized police states, and plutocratic trade agreements - making it seem like our political leaders will forever be stuck in this hellfire downward spiral of aggressive haggling over the remaining energy chips on the corporate-sponsored world stage, the *rest* of us seem to have

---

[75] Pakistan, Thailand, India, UK, Bolivia, Burma, Argentina, etc.

[76] Note to National Park Service: Glacier National Park in Montana needs to be re-named 'Waterfall National Park'

mostly moved on from the bargaining stage of climate grief to the fourth stage of grieving our now long-forgotten connection to the world soul and our true nature - ***Depression.***

This one may be the most *repressed* stage of all.

It is quite understandable that the wretched, even scandalous situation which has developed over the course of this prolonged, dysfunctional bargaining stage has given rise to much dystopian pessimism about our collective future from the growing segment of our population that is *consciously* aware of the gravity of our world situation. It started with everyone deciding it was fashionable to wear black and pierce any and every body part. It didn't take long for suicide rates to start climbing, with the rate among baby-boomers - that generation which has witnessed this entire spectacle - surging by nearly *30 percent* in the first decade of the new millennium.[77]

Mass killings happen with chilling regularity now, with the overall incidence of mass shootings *tripling* in just the five year period between 2008 and 2013.[78] As I write this, mass shootings rate in the U.S. have become an almost daily occurrence. Really, America? A mass shooting every day?! We now 'escape' to movies about apocalypse and dystopian futures, which are legion. That in itself shows just how aware we are at the deepest level about our poor relations with our host planet. But those are actually rather explicit, more in the nature of cautionary tales than acting out suppressed grief. What is even more revealing is that we've progressed from the previous widespread cultural fascination with modern-day, blood-sucking vampires to today's morbid fascination with the *walking dead.*

Yes, *zombies* are all the rage now, and a more appropriate symbol of our collectively repressed depression over the dismal state of affairs on planet Earth could hardly be imagined. Given the tone deafness of politicians (also acting like zombies!) to the hue and cry of the scientific community, let alone the cries of the Earth herself, many scientists are now starting to conclude that the human race *itself* is tantamount to a 'dead man walking.'

That's pretty damned depressing... *Pass the popcorn!*

The depression stage of grief kicks in as death draws near and one realizes that no amount of bargaining is going to avoid the inevitable conclusion of a terminal diagnosis. Of all the stages of grieving over our lost connection to mother Earth, this is far and away the stage we are least equipped to deal with. It is becoming increasingly more plausible that the 6th Great Extinction, which is human caused, may well end up turning into another 'Great Dying,' swallowing the human species in its terrible toll.

***Nobody* wants to think about that!!** In fact, there has never before in the history of planet Earth been a species that was forced to consider its own demise. The collective psychological defense

---

[77] NYT, *Suicide Rate Rises Sharply in U.S.* (5.02.13)

[78] RT.com, *Average number of mass shootings per year in US has tripled - AG Holder* (10.21.13)

mechanism to those scientists, such as Guy McPherson or the *Arctic News Group*, who have concluded that near term human extinction is not just a possibility, but is now inevitable, is to reactively dismiss them as lacking credibility, relegating them to the margins of science and society. They are treated with the same disdain usually reserved for the climate denier scientists, the difference of course being that the latter are almost exclusively bought-and-paid-for by vested interests, and don't really believe their own pseudo-science, while people like McPherson seem to be genuinely acting out of humanitarian concern and scientific conviction.

If it is true that we as a culture are simply not prepared to even entertain the *prospect* of near term human extinction - or a vast ocean graveyard devoid of life, or the tragic loss of iconic species like elephants, rhinos, bears, and tigers - *in spite* of mounting evidence that these losses are at least imminent, though clearly not inevitable, and if as a consequence we actually *feel* the insipid depression bubbling up from the depths of our collective psyche, like a plaintive wail from a bereft Mother Earth, how is it that most of us (the ones who do *not* commit suicide) somehow manage to avoid being overtaken by such a powerful, primal emotions?

Indeed… just what *is* our 'strategy' for fending off (repressing) these natural feelings of depression?

Look around you… Think about it… wait - don't check your smart phone just now. That was not an invitation for you to log onto Facebook!

Have we ever been more distracted as a people? Has anyone, at any time, ever?!?

Observe people on the streets or in the subways of any major city. Either they are obsessed with their smart phones or they have earbuds in. We go home to satellite televisions and internet and on-line gaming or X-box or Play Station or porn or 'fantasy football' (because *we even need distractions from our distractions!*) -- FaceBook, selfies, iPads, tweeting, instagrams -- you name it. What am I missing? I'm sure by the time this book comes out, there will be at least nine new forms of mass distraction.

We can probably all agree on this point - we have become a culture of distraction. And its a perfect strategy, really. As long as I never actually have to think about things, I can keep depression at bay in perpetuity, like a shadow that is always there but never overtakes me as long as I continue walking into the light.

As might be expected, there has been yet another dramatic shift in mental health trends associated with this, the most troubled of all stages of grieving. How much psychological pain are we in as a nation? Well, *opioids* have now become the most prescribed class of medications in America![79] *OPIOIDS!*

> "Opioids are a class of controlled pain-management drugs that contain natural or synthetic chemicals based on morphine... effectively mimic[ing] the pain-relieving chemicals that the body produces naturally." (from *Psychology Today*)

In 2011 alone, there were over *238 million* prescriptions for these narcotic analgesics, prompting the National Institute of Health to declare it an epidemic. Opioids (addiction to which often leads to heroin, the champagne of opioids) are now responsible for more deaths than suicide or motor vehicle crashes, more deaths than from cocaine and heroin combined. Heroin has made a big comeback due to the fact that it has become more affordable than opioids, and easier to obtain thanks to a government campaign to restrict opioid prescriptions.

Now it should be just as clear that there is *not* an epidemic of chronic *physical* pain in this country that might explain the explosion in use of opioids. Just as we use anti-depressants to stave off symptomatic depression, we are using opioids to mask *non*-symptomatic depression; that is, *psychological* pain. We are not just *medicating* ourselves as a culture anymore, we are actually becoming our own palliative care providers!

Why???

Because mainstream psychology and psychiatry insists on treating symptoms without ever directly addressing the dis-ease we are all feeling!

That's why. And the massively profitable pharmaceutical industry would have it no other way.

Whether opioids have actually passed anti-depressants as the drug of choice in America depends on which study you consult - they are actually close to even. Think about *that* for a minute - the *combination* of opioid and anti-depressant prescriptions annually in the U.S. (over 500 million Rx) far exceeds the number of Americans living here. And, of course, we still have free access to alcohol, we have increasingly free access to potent strains of marijuana, and let's not even talk about cheap meth - the drug of choice among zombies everywhere (but especially in rural America, due to the ease of manufacturing it, as compared to the cheap accessibility of purer drugs in metropolitan areas).[80]

---

[79] Nora D. Volkow, Thomas A. Mclellan, Jessica H. Cotto, Meena Karithanom, Susan R. B. Weiss. "Characteristics of Opioid Prescriptions in 2009." *JAMA*, 2011; 305 (13): 1299-1301; Nora D. Volkow, Thomas A. Mclellan. "Curtailing Diversion and Abuse of Opioid Analgesics Without Jeopardizing Pain Treatment." *JAMA*, 2011; 305 (13): 1346-1347.

[80] More than 12 million Americans have tried methamphetamine and 1.5 million are regular users, according to federal estimates.

We're kind of a *mess*, aren't we? It seems, culturally speaking, we have a choice between endlessly distracting ourselves, numbing ourselves out, alternating between the two, or numbing ourselves out at the same time as engaging in distractions. Ask the average American consumer why they don't keep up on the news that matters most, or follow the political discourse, and what is the response you are almost certain to hear?

"It's too depressing." Which is kind of true, isn't it?

Of course, there is another way. A way free from the compulsive need to distract and numb ourselves until we die. And if you've really been paying attention up until this point, you may have already anticipated it...

ACCEPTANCE: *IT'S NOT THE SAME AS RESIGNATION!*

> *Clinging to how we think things should be*
> *brings confusion and despair.*
> *Seeing things as they are brings clarity.*
> *Clarity leads to effective action.*

> ~ Wm. & Nancy Martin, *The Caregiver's Tao Te Ching*

Is all of this gloom and doom really as oppressive as it seems?

Or are we maybe just missing the big picture due to our own inability to fully acknowledge and effectively process our deepest fears, our anxieties, and our depression? This is a question everyone who looks closely at this issue needs to ask themselves if they start to feel a sense of panicky despair creeping in.

Remember what we observed about unacknowledged fear? *Acknowledged* fear is a form of intelligence, as it counsels us to avoid dangerous situations. The same can be said for every stage of the grieving process. Problems only arise to the extent we suppress our feelings (fear being a feeling as well), and we've been collectively suppressing them at every stage thus far. The thing to understand about suppression is that it is a psychological defense mechanism that kicks in automatically, without conscious awareness. Once the suppressed feeling is identified and acknowledged, however, then it can be processed and released. Then problems are transformed into active energy that can be utilized in constructive endeavors.[81]

So to the extent that you have resonated with the discussion of the various stages of suppressed collective grieving up to this point, and especially to the extent that you can identify with the symptoms of suppressed depression, since that is where we find ourselves right now as a culture,

---

[81] This is one of the key focal points in Buddhism; that is, plowing adversity into the path of liberation.

to that same extent you are ready to begin processing and *releasing* that baseline depression through some form of active grieving. Also, to the extent you are able to process that accumulated grief, which we will get to, you will release yourself into the *constructive stage of acceptance*, at which point you can consider yourself a *Planetary Caregiver* capable and qualified to assist others in your own unique way.

Unprocessed depression, on the other hand, will eventually lead one into the dark, sticky tar pit of despair. That is the kind of chronic nagging from psyche that leads one willingly into a world of opioid numbness, mindless distraction, where one can even find oneself pulling the voting lever for a narcissistic demagogue like Donald Trump. Despair, like guilt, is a rather pointless, and largely unnecessary, emotional response in any context. It's just like the Dalai Lama says about worrying: if something can be done, then worrying is pointless, and if nothing can be done, then worrying is even *more* pointless!

The healthy alternative to guilt is always regret, which differs from guilt because it focuses on the action and doesn't come with all the self-judgment. Regret doesn't support the blame game. Healthy alternatives to despair are *resolve,* the intellectual determination to re-solve a problem that suddenly appears more vexing to us, and at the feeling level, learning to value and tap into our broken-heartedness. In other words, despair is nothing more than unresolved (repressed/unprocessed) grief, and unresolved grief is rooted in the unacknowledged fear of letting go of our losses (and/or facing the potential of future loss). Accordingly, when we find ourselves in despair, it is a strong indication that we simply have some more work to do.

It's kind of like you find yourself in a dark underground cavern, and you find a pathway you think will lead you out, but suddenly you reach a dead-end. If we are really attached to the idea that *this* path was going to lead us into the light, then when that expectation is defeated, there is a tendency to think there is no way out. The most counterproductive thing we can do is to dwell in despair, because if we dwell in any powerful emotion long enough, we begin to identify with it. And tragically, people who identify with despair end up seeing suicide (or the slow suicide of opioids) as the only way out.

Resolve means we reach that same dead-end in the same dark cavern, and rather than piling self-pity on top of disappointment, we simply *acknowledge* our disappointment ("oh well"), turn around (immediately), and look for another way. Maybe we're a little hungrier, maybe our thirst is greater, and perhaps even the air seems to be running out. But we don't panic, and we don't give up. We don't just collapse right there and start banging our fists against the wall and sobbing. What's the point of that?

In our present situation, *we can actually take HEART* and find realistic *HOPE* in our current state of affairs. Do not be distracted by all the chaotic dysfunction we are witnessing right now, or even by all the disruption and dislocation that is surely to come. Instead, **look at where we are** in the grieving process as a culture. Look at which stage you might have to work on yourself, and focus your efforts on joining those who are already at the liberating acceptance stage. We're so close!

Cuddling Up With *Chaos*!

What is important before going on with this processing of our accumulated grief is some perspective. It's necessary to keep things in proper perspective in order to work through difficult emotions. So there is a really amazing spiritual container for our grieving process that comes from an Italian physicist named Ilya Prigogene, who won a Nobel Prize for his elegant theory of how systems change according to the laws of nature. This theory has a fancy name, which you can impress people with at your next social function: *Prigogene's Theory of Dissipative Structures.* But fortunately, the theory itself is not as complicated as its name makes it sound.

Prigogene's theory of dissipative structures holds that any dynamic system becomes more disordered and chaotic with time, *but this is actually how systems reach higher orders.* In fact, a system needs to reach its highest tolerable degree of chaotic disorder before making a sudden, *quantum leap* - to a new and *unprecedented* level of order. Think about how water turns to ice at 32 degrees. Viewed at the microscopic level, the fluidic, random molecules suddenly stop banging around and come instead into a perfectly ordered, crystalline alignment. Or at the other end of the temperature spectrum, they reach a frenzied disorder in water before suddenly reaching escape velocity into the air, as steam.

And this systems theory is observed to apply to pretty much any dynamic system in nature that you can think of, whether organic or inorganic compounds, on macro or micro scales, involving ants or ecosystems. In fact, this is true all the way down to the most basic level of reality we can observe, where electrons somehow manage to gain energy and suddenly appear at the next outer orbit without ever having appeared for even an instant in the space between those two shells of orbiting frenzy. We inhabit a rather magical world, don't we?

So now let's apply this theory, which has never been disproved, to the world we are living in: *Things are really messed up...* GREAT! *The old order is breaking down and everything seems so chaotic...* WONDERFUL!! *I think I'm experiencing a breakdown.* SUPERB! WHAT A GOLDEN OPPORTUNITY FOR YOU!! *Everywhere we look there is confusion and tumult...* HOW HOPEFUL!!!

The truth of the matter is that, collectively, we are experiencing a very dark night of the human soul, one that will eventually rival the Dark Ages. *Isn't that great?!* I don't mean to sound facetious here at all, nor am I trying to downplay all the suffering this entails. I'm simply trying to decondition our conditioned thinking by pointing out that *dis*-integration and discord necessarily precedes (*re*)integration and accord. And we surely need to re-integrate our lives and social orders at every level we can think of. Isn't *that* the real point of all this? The Pope certainly seems to think so. And as anyone who has ever experienced such a crisis can tell you, (yes, obviously, present company included), if treated with the respect it demands, if met with the love and compassion of an appropriate support network, these kinds of breakdowns inevitably lead to spiritual rebirth and into a dramatically more meaningful, rich life.

I want to mention here what I consider to be the most accurate, insightful, and helpful model of human development I've ever come across, from a book on transpersonal theory - by a philosopher of all people! His name is Michael Washburn, a philosopher who integrates both psychology and religion into his academic discipline, and the book is entitled *The Ego and the Dynamic Ground* (SUNY 1995). In essence, the 'dynamic ground' is the transcendent ground of spirit, and Washburn's theory can be very briefly summarized (with apologies) as follows.

We are basically bipolar beings, with one pole being the ego of the isolated individual and the other the spiritual pole that makes life meaningful.[82] In the beginning, we are immersed in the spiritual realm (from infancy into childhood), but especially by the time we reach adolescence, all our conditioning from the sociocultural sphere is aimed at suppressing our spiritual inclinations in favor of developing our egoic pole in order that we may better compete in the adult world. This "primal repression" of our true spiritual selves mirrors the repression of our true nature that we act out at both the individual and collective level, and that keeps us separate from the natural world. If we're very good at it, we are rewarded with the material and egoic boons that society has to offer. If not, we probably become artists or Ecopsychologists!

Now here's the main point of Washburn's insightful model. It takes a lot of energy and effort to keep our spiritual pole suppressed. *Naturally*, according to this model, were it not for the overweening influence of our family, culture, and social structures (e.g., peer pressure), we would probably spiral between one pole and the other. But in repressing our spiritual pole, a lot of potential energy builds up there. As Washburn puts it, *if we are lucky* we end up having a spiritual breakdown/emergency, or a mid-life crisis. We 'get' that we've been forced to play a game where there are no real winners, and that all the boons bestowed upon us for playing well turn out to be unsatisfactory. We enter a dark night of the soul in our own lives, and in that dark place all that potential spiritual energy gets unleashed. It overwhelms our ego, because ultimately it's a much more powerful force. We label this a 'breakdown.' It's very much like the unraveling we are seeing collectively right now.

But that breakdown, as Washburn points out, is the greatest blessing we could have ever hoped for. Though we may never actually wish it upon ourselves, eventually we come to find that our ego is being "regenerated in spirit." As Washburn puts it, our "ego is given a new lease on life and a healing reconciliation between the ego and [spiritual] life commences," which is a period of "healing reconstruction" that we undergo for many years, since natural progress is a spiraling between the two poles (upward), and not a linear or 'either/or' proposition.

---

[82] As the groundbreaking astrologer Dane Rudhyar said, "Life is a cyclic interplay of bi-polar forces."

In the end, as regeneration culminates in integration, the sense of blessedness assumes its final form: glowing gratitude, the sense of being divinely favored... True bliss belongs only to [this] integrated stage of life.
***
The reawakening of [spiritual] life and its breakthrough into consciousness can be abrupt, but the ensuing transformation... is typically a long-term process... away from suffering and toward joy... Integration is not something that appears suddenly at the end of the regeneration process; it is rather the final realization of that process.

* * *

Collectively, if we are lucky, the climate crisis is our mid-life breakdown. We are each being called upon to act out this 'myth' (mythic in the original sense of ultimate spiritual truth) in our own unique ways, which will eventually translate into a *collective* regeneration in spirit.

We'll finally be cured of our national narcissism! We'll be free to renounce American Exceptionalism, and we'll finally awaken from the stupor of the *American Dream*.

This is the kind of perspective we need to contain our unprocessed grief over the climate crisis we are just beginning to experience. It is the safe harbor we can return to again and again in our psyche after getting battered around a bit by the breaking open of our wounded hearts. There are plenty of wonderful books about the 'dark night of the soul,' my personal favorite being Thomas Moore's, and it doesn't hurt to have one of these on your nightstand as you begin to process whatever kinds of grieving happen to be holding you back from loving more deeply.

Things may seem awfully dark now. They appear to be getting darker all the time, and will assuredly continue to darken for some time on the world stage. But we should not fear the dark. Just as love is the other side of grief, light is the flip side of darkness. In fact, darkness is not even a really existent phenomena. It is simply the absence of light, and as the old saying goes, it is always darkest before the dawn.

Let us embrace the darkness and welcome in new light.

CHAPTER 8
HEALING OUR BROKEN HEARTS

*The Cure for Pain
is in the Pain.*

~ Rumi

From Repression to Release

So what does the acceptance stage of grief look like at the individual level? We're straight on our world view, we've got this courageous perspective that not only can accommodate breakdown, but can view it as break*through* to an elevated spiritual dimension, a more meaningful life, and a higher social order. We're no longer afraid of acknowledging that we're more than a little depressed by the state of the planet. And we're beginning to comprehend how that barely repressed depression is shaping so much of what we see in others and in our culture.

We're ready for acceptance - *bring it on!*

Psychological processes are so mysterious, aren't they? Which is just a way of saying that we are not always consciously aware of what we're really feeling deep down, what we know to be true in our hearts, and yet we are not necessarily even conscious of what we're aware of or what we are feeling! Especially here in the West, thanks to our old French pal Rene, there is this vexing disconnect between our heads and hearts.

But here's the key to the kind of psycho-spiritual growth that reconnects our heart with our head: it follows a 3-step process of *recognition, acceptance,* and *understanding.* In that order, too. We can not accept something we have yet to recognize, and we can not understand something until we have accepted it - often referenced by the distinction between an open and a closed mind. So first we open our minds, and then that opening leads into our hearts. Someone we perceive as in denial refuses to *accept* an idea even after its validity has been acknowledged, and thus they can never get to the necessary understanding of that concept (which is exactly what they're trying to avoid with their psychological defenses, as it threatens their sense of separate identity, lifestyle, or more likely, both).

So if you are still reading at this point, then it is safe to say that you've recognized some special insights associated with the successive stages of collective, repressed grieving presented in the last chapter. If those ideas do not *at least* resonate with you at the level of intuition, then you are free to just stop here and pass this book on. But assuming you're on board with all this up to this point of our passage through Psyche into the Heart, then the acceptance stage of climate grief is *already* growing in you, fueled by your recognition of our discussion of the repressed stages and their disguised expressions in our psyche and in our culture. As you followed along, your mind stayed open and your heart started opening in response to these insights. You are now holding emotional reactions in direct relation to the relevance of these stages to your personal experience.

Now we need to begin processing all this at a more intentional, conscious level in our heart. As our collective *zeitgeist* is presently enmeshed with repressed depression, stage four, not much can really be gained by going back to the earlier stages (though personal grief does cycle through these stages, and there is no reason *not* to go back if you feel so inclined). Denial is a special case, since we are all in denial to some extent, but that is not the same as the kind of programmed denial we were at collectively back in the early days of the *American Dream.* At this point, we are finally beginning to appreciate at a cultural level that human nature is inextricably bound up with nature itself, and that our soul and the world soul are made up of the same 'stuff.' That is enough to work with for our purposes here.

To the extent that we still are harboring repressed anger and rage at the way things are, or at the way we perceive others to be (same thing, only projected), then our depression is not of the suppressed variety -- it is right there in our view of our life in the world.[83] The prescription for that kind of repressed anger, however, is not either to mask the symptoms or give ourselves permission to rage against the machine and denigrate others. Those emotionally reactive, defensive responses only tend to deepen the hole we are standing in. Instead, we must really work on our worldview at a very fundamental level - the level of the implicit story we are always telling ourselves *about* ourselves and our world.

I can tell you that I am speaking from experience here. This is where I was stuck myself in the late 1990s and early 2000s, defining my world view in this way: "It is an unjust world, and it is *particularly* unjust to me!" I built up a wall between myself and others constructed of *cynicism*, which is psychologically defensive (protecting a wounded heart), *and judgment*, which is a more offensive psychological strategy (seeking to inflict the wound on others).

Fortunately, I happened upon a well qualified dharma teacher right around that time, and she prompted me to start working on my worldview while following the tried and true path of Mahayana ('Great Vehicle' of compassion) Buddhism. The reason that worked for me, the intellectual skeptic still trapped in ego, is that Buddhism lays out a rather infallible system of viewing everything through the lens of cause and effect. I learned to accept responsibility for my life by broadening the perspective out to all the causes I had created myself in this and previous lifetimes (which are evidenced by their effects we are conditioned to view as happenstance). At the same time, this world view empowers us to shape future circumstance by practicing ethical behavior in relation to present circumstance - reacting in appropriate (rational) ways rather than habitually emotional (unthinking) ways. Responding rather than reacting. It is simply not feasible to maintain a victim mentality on the Buddhist path. This turns out to be a great antidote for those like myself (at that time in my life) who obsessively think things should be other than they are, and feel perpetually frustrated as a result.

The point of sharing this personal story is not to recommend my spiritual path to you, as I have a deep respect for any and all spiritual paths, but rather to point out that if you suffer from chronic depression or cynicism, perhaps a way out is to begin exploring how you feel about your relationship to the natural world and the world soul, and then following the roots of any rage, anger or hurt that comes up in that exploration.

I happen to know of at least one example of a particularly brilliant (and successful) individual who was *clinically* depressed from high school on, requiring anti-depression medication,

---

[83] I tend to differentiate between repression and suppression in this way. Repression is what we keep right below the surface of our conscious waves, barely and not without sustained effort, while suppression lies at a much deeper level in the sub-conscious, rarely surfacing, and it finds expression only through patterns of dysfunctional behavior (i.e., as with developmental trauma).

psychotherapy, and special schools after dropping out of public schools, but was able to drop her meds in her early 30s when she started practicing simple mindfulness meditation. It was incredibly difficult for her to sit there on the cushion in silence, as she seethed with anger and wanted nothing more than to run from the zendo screaming, but the payoff of being free from meds and their side effects kept her glued to the cushion - because it *worked*. In time, she calmed down and found refuge in exploring the Buddhist worldview through dharma texts and commentaries, in spite of all the resistance from her meticulously rational mind. A decade later, she can see no reason to ever return to a life of managing her symptoms with meds. She changed her worldview instead (though she never fully embraced the Buddhist worldview). And remember, this is someone who was *clinically* depressed, which is very different than the kind of natural, culturally induced depression I have identified as stage four of climate grief.

Even if you feel like you are stuck at the anger stage of climate grief, which probably manifests as extreme emotional reactivity towards captialism, politics, and the consumer culture we are immersed in, in no way does that mean you shouldn't deal with the successive stages. In fact, it probably saves you the trouble of going through the bargaining stage, as you can now see how pointless that would be, and you may find that processing grief at the level of climate depression is therapeutic in processing your anger and rage as well. The anger and depression stages have anger in common, after all - as depression is a form of repressed anger. From a Buddhist perspective, both are forms of aversion to not getting what we want or losing what we are attached to.

It may be helpful at this point to repeat that while it appears we are following a fairly linear progression through the stages of climate grief *collectively*, at the individual level we can go back and forth from one stage to another, or cycle through them repeatedly, or even follow a more spiraling path. It's a very individual process, and we should always let our own intuition be our guide once we learn to recognize the landscape and markers. In Buddhism, that intuitive sense is developed and referred to as our 'inner guru' - and a well-qualified teacher will always advise us to follow our inner guru, even when it's in conflict with our external guru. In other words, develop our open-heartedness and then learn to trust it's inherent wisdom - human nature.

From Our Head To Our Heart: Recovering Our Human Nature

The process of nourishing the seeds of acceptance that have been planted in our heart by the wisdom of recognizing collective losses in our mind will lead us into a deeper understanding of climate grieving. *Recognition->Acceptance->Understanding.* That deepening, active level of understanding is what the acceptance stage 'looks' like. At the affective, feeling-level, this acceptance manifests as *awakening*. Since collectively we are at stage four of climate grief, the process of nourishing the seeds of acceptance necessarily involves immersing ourselves in what we need to think of as our own '*healthy depression*' in relation to climate disruption.

To most of us, that probably sounds like a contradiction in terms. *How can depression be healthy?* Doesn't it seem, instead, like the one feeling we have come to fear above all others in this culture? After all, we have a drug to treat every mental deviation from the accepted norm. Of course - that's a big part of the problem. We are ruled by the things we most fear. We are ruled by *grief*, because we have denied it a respected place at the table, and we are ruled by depression, because to admit to depression in this culture is to admit to being a failure in life.

We know on some level that grieving is a healthy response to loss. We get that. Once we progress past the denial that has prevented us from acknowledging our own and our society's loss of an intimate connection with the natural world, with the world soul, and once we begin to really see what has resulted from this unnatural state of affairs, it is *naturally* depressing.

How can we possibly avoid actively grieving that loss? Why would we want to??

It is only through the grieving process that we will be able to release these feelings of depression that come to the surface once we have acknowledged our need for a much closer relationship with the natural world. In turn, it is this release that then opens the psychological and heart space necessary for us to *restore* a proper relationship - to recover our own human nature.

The Prodigal Child Comes Home

An exercise in climate grieving:

> *Imagine if you had run away from home at 5 years of age and never looked back. In the beginning, you scramble just to get by from one day to the next, living on the streets of one of our biggest cities, and eventually you adapt to the way of life that you found yourself immersed in. Imagine in this story that, due to the traumatic nature of your separation, you completely forgot that you had a mother in the world that loved you and nurtured you until you were big enough to survive apart from her, a mother who was distraught and falling apart more and more every day, month, and year you were lost to her. Imagine further that you grow up, you lead a functional life, but are plagued by psychological problems that eventually force you into therapy. In the course of that therapy you suddenly recover memories of your loving mother and remember your sudden, inexplicable departure. When you track her down, you learn that her health has deteriorated significantly in recent years, and she may actually be dying.*

This is not too far removed from the psychological situation we find ourselves in today. If you can actually put yourself in that imaginary situation, you will see that it is not just a matter of showing up at her bedside and saying "Hi mom, I'm home!" Instead, the recovered memory itself would likely trigger deep sadness and depression, and you'd need to find a way to contain your grief (likely to be experienced initially as anger) over the loss you will be feeling from not having had that source of unconditional love that only a mother can provide all those years when you were growing up fast on the streets and scrambling to survive, all those years of acting out in anger against all the injustices of the world.

CLIMATE SENSE

* * *

We are each that prodigal child finding our way home now. One way of processing our grief over our lost connection to *Anima Mundi* is to learn to really listen to her with all of our hearts. We're going to do that right here in this next exercise, which will take the form of reaching way back in time to a sacred text from a day and age when people were still in close touch with the world soul, who they related to in the form of a goddess. When seeking to restore the sacred in our lives, it is a good idea to look back to the spiritual roots in our own culture or lineage, and that is the idea behind this exercise. You may even find yourself startled by how much resonance you feel here.

Now let me just say that, from an ecopsychological perspective, it is not necessary at all for us to believe in a goddess for this exercise to work on our hearts. While I deeply appreciate Pope Francis telling his flock that they need to pray to a feminine deity in the form of the ascended Mary for wisdom at this time of crisis, my point in this next exercise is not to convince anyone that there is a goddess watching over us, or even that Mother Earth herself is a goddess. There is a vast difference between symbolism, which is therapeutic and effective by being affective, and reification, which is more dogmatic and can be problematic. Instead, I'm simply asking you to accept for the purpose of this exercise that *this is the way we are wired.*

We are trying to drop down to the feeling level of our heart here, to get out of the intellectual maze in our head. So when I inform you that early Christians believed in the Goddess Sophia, and share with you a transmission from Sophia set forth in an ancient sacred text, one of the early pre-Canon gospels, *it doesn't matter* if you believe in gods and goddesses or not. *Really!* It is enough that we 'suspend disbelief' and perhaps share a little awe in the mystery of the spirit, in the psychological power of archetypal imagery and myths. It seems that the only 'real' way we have of finding spiritual meaning in this world is through the symbols we conjure up, as when we are in dreams awake. This is called 'depth' psychology, and we practice it ourselves every night in our own dream worlds.

Spiritual energies take shape in the world of form through symbols, just as our ideas find symbolic form in language. Once we recognize that consciousness is unbounded in the same way light is not confined to a lightbulb, and once we accept that we are connected by and through awareness at the deepest level of psyche, then we can appreciate Carl Jung's (and Joseph Campbell's) observation that mythical figures emerge from spiritual awareness *of their own force*, quite apart from our own personal imagination. They find expression in symbols and words because that's the only way we really have of sharing these powerful energies with one another in meaningful and lasting ways. Words may be inexact tools for expressing feelings, but feelings are no less real because of that clumsiness, and our deepest feelings are filled with meaning in ways that language can never adequately contain.

Myths are the way we earthlings encode meaningful, eternal truths for the purpose of passing them down through generational time. It is almost as if myths create us rather than humans creating myths, seemingly emerging fully formed from the depths of our collective unconscious.

124

Unfortunately, we've been conditioned in our scientific, materialistic culture to think of 'myths' as lies and 'history' as truth. That is a superficial and biased misunderstanding that denies spiritual meaning in defense of scientific certainty. It also happens to be the same kind of literal superficiality applied by fundamentalists to sacred texts. Let's just agree that both myths and histories have one thing in common - they're stories! And it's left to us to determine what rings true and what does not.

So with that as context, we are ready to receive this beautiful and timeless heartening message from *Anima Mundi*, the feminine creative energy of the world, speaking to us from a place of "perfect primal intelligence" - our own intrinsic awareness. Early Gnostic Christians attributed this pure awareness to both *Pistis Sophia*, the goddess of wisdom whose light sparks our spiritual intelligence, and Eve, whose name means 'life.'[84]

Here we find Sophia calling out to Adam in the darkness of his dungeon. Adam is symbolic of the limitations of our own material existence (think 'atom' and 'mater'), and thus has special relevance to us today, raised and indoctrinated as we have been into a materialistic worldview in which we are limited by the impoverished ideals of a consumer culture -- always lacking, never complete. That is *our* dark dungeon.

So then here, Sophia is really calling each of us back to our true home, the 'clear light nature' that is our divine inheritance, but which we have somehow forgotten. Just as in Buddhism, the notion is that we've fallen asleep, and Sophia is here to awaken us from that long slumber. When you read these words, really take them into your heart and *feel* their healing energy penetrating your soul, comforting your own inner child, your true nature, rather than allowing yourself to get caught up in the intellectual labyrinth of your religious or non-religious mind.

This evocative, haunting poem comes from the *Secret Book of John* (ca. 200 A.D.). It strikes me as the fully embodied, mysterious voice of *Anima Mundi,* our Mother Earth speaking right to our hearts, through eternal time and boundless space, and is entitled:

Thunder: Perfect Mind

I am the first and the last.
I am the honored one and scorned.
I am the holy one and the whore.

---

[84] These same early Christians did not share the patriarchal view that Eve of Genesis was a sinful temptress. It was because of her intuitive intervention that we obtained the fruit from the *tree of knowledge*, which from a psychological perspective means we became self-conscious in a way that animals are not. For more on this and related points, the reader is referred to Elaine Pagels' inspiring book *Adam, Eve, and the Serpent* (Penguin Books, 1988). Pagels, the long-time religion chair of Princeton University, was the first scholar from the West allowed to examine and translate the Gnostic gospels held in the vault of the Egyptian king since their discovery during WWII.

I am the virgin and the wife.
I am the mother and the daughter.[85]
I am the members of my mother.[86]

I am the barren one
    and many are my sons.[87]
I am she whose wedding is great,
    and I have not taken a husband.
I am the midwife and she who does not bear.
I am the solace of my labor pains.
I am the bride and the bridegroom,
    and it is my husband who begot me.
I am knowledge and ignorance...

I am the silence that is incomprehensible
    and the idea whose remembrance is frequent.[88]
I am the voice whose sound is manifold
    and the WORD whose appearance is multiple.

I am the utterance of my name...

In my weakness, do not forsake me,
    and do not be afraid of my power.
For why do you despise my fear
    and curse my pride?

But I am she who exists in all fears
    and strength in trembling.

---

[85] Just like in Pope Francis' encyclical!

[86] Species? That is, all Earth's inhabitants?

[87] She is our mother, even though she did not bring us into the world.

[88] Or at least *used* to be.

126

I am she who is weak,
   and I am well in a pleasant place.
I am senseless and I am wise.

Why have you hated me in your counsels?
For I shall be silent among those who are silent,
   and I shall appear and speak,
Why have you hated me?

I am the one whom they call life [Eve]
   and you have called Death...

I am the one whom you have pursued,
   and I am the one whom you have seized.
I am the one whom you have scattered,
   and you have gathered me together.
I am the one before whom you have been ashamed,
   and you have been shameless to me...

I, I am godless,
   and I am the one whose God is great.
I am the one whom you have reflected upon,
   and you have scorned me.
I am unlearned,
   and they learn from me.
I am the one that you have despised,
   and you reflect upon me.
I am the one whom you have hidden from,
   and you appear to me.
But whenever you hide yourselves,
   I myself will appear.
For whenever you appear,
   I myself will hide from you...

I entered into the midst of their prison,
*   which is the prison of the body.[89]*
And I said, "Whoever hears, let them arise from the deep sleep."

And [Adam] wept, and shed bitter tears.
Bitter tears he wiped from himself, and he said,
"Who is it who calls my name,
*   and whence has this hope come to me while I am in the chains*
*   of this prison?"*

And I said, "I am the intelligence of the pure life;
I am the thinking of the virginal spirit...
Arise and remember... and follow your root, which is I...
*   and beware of the deep sleep."*

As Llewellyn Vaughan-Lee so beautifully puts it, "The mystery of the divine feminine speaks to us from within her creation… We have forgotten her, just as we have forgotten so much of what is sacred, and yet she is always part of us."[90]

Early Christians, who embodied the living church of Christ in their lives, prayed in a way that we would call 'meditation' today. They took to heart the revelation from Jesus that the kingdom was within, and they communed with the spirit of Christ in silent, contemplative awareness. As you can appreciate from this inspirational psalm, they had a lot to reflect on.

According to the Jesuit philosopher Thomas Sheehan, the Aramaic word Jesus used to exhort his followers - '*Metanoia*' - originally was understood to mean 'change your *heart* or *mind*' with a very radical connotation (that is, to radically alter your perception of what is real and what is meaningful). This exhortation was in perfect harmony with Jesus' central message that the kingdom of God is within us - not something the Pharisees held the keys to. Subsequently, however, this same term was misappropriated and twisted to mean 'repent' (that is, change your *ways*).[91] We can see how the original intention was to encourage people to work with their mind *internally*, while the more modern connotation is to conform our conduct to some externally imposed code of conduct out of fear of judgment. This critical distinction reflects nothing less than the difference between a *living* church, with no authoritarian middle man between us and

---

[89] Material existence (materialism, dualistic thought).

[90] *Return of the Feminine and the World Soul* (2009).

[91] See: *The First Coming: How the Kingdom of God Became Christianity* (NY: Random House, 1986)

our creator, church as a place of worship within us by which we take responsibility for our own salvation, and the institutionalized church that developed over time, a place of external power that we visit on Sundays and holy days, an authority which we charge with our salvation as our intercessor and ministerial representative.

This is the great secret Sophia is revealing when she says *"whenever you hide yourselves, I myself will appear... whenever you appear, I myself will hide from you..."* as well as assuring us that she will speak to *"those who are silent."* She is our own primal intelligence, the virginal spirit of the pure, unconditioned mind. In that space of non-conceptual, intrinsic awareness, which we all have access to beneath the waves of incessant internal chatter, there is no *ego* (the "you" Sophia is speaking of), no thought of self, only 'nature' - our true nature. There is higher conscience there, which is ignored in 'counsels' (e.g., political bodies).

So 'hiding' ourself here means quieting ego's internal voice in silent, contemplative awareness, and she appears in that light as impersonal (collective) 'perfect, primal intelligence' or *gnosis* (direct knowledge). *That* is the 'living church' Jesus founded. Then, as soon as ego arises into that space ('whenever *you* appear'), she hides from us. The awareness of perfect, primal intelligence, or spirit, recedes back into the depths of our subtle consciousness, becomes 'unconscious' once again - forgotten. Any experienced meditator, Christian mystic, or serious contemplative can attest to this phenomenon. I like to think of it as the axiom "if you use it, you will lose it," meaning as soon as ego rises up to 'own' the experience of the profound, the profound is no longer present.

The *'deep sleep'* is not referring to the mere absence of primal intelligence when our ego is prominent, as it is most of the time. That is more like *light* sleep, or the 'hypnogogic trance' that overtakes us just before we drift off to sleep at night. Rather, when Sophia warns us to beware of the deep sleep, she is referring to the danger of living in sustained ignorance of our innate ability to access that spiritual realm at any time, to check in with our true nature. Even when are not conscious of it, and no matter how long we've been asleep (like Adam chained in his dungeon), we remain connected to it at all times.

Even splitting the atom could not sever that connection.

This is the same 'deep sleep' that made possible the ascendance to power and all-pervasive influence and dominion of the *American Dream* - this idea that happiness lies outside of us in the material world, the world of senses and 'resources' (which even include other living beings, even *humans*), and we are meant to pursue it as sensory experience. The focus of someone who is asleep to his or her own nature, to the umbilical chord that connects us to our true mother, is on seeking rewards for their *conduct* in the world, like a good worker bee, rather than on being connected to the world and to others, or on knowing our own true nature as a state of exalted mind and open-heartedness. We come to believe that the mythical goddess is not 'real' - and does not even refer to anything that *is* real.

That is a profound and tragic misunderstanding of 'myth.' We learn to denigrate our internal, spiritual experiences (and scoff at those of others), and we become unwilling to take dominion over our own spiritual life and well-being. We accept the dogma of scientific materialism: the world is not ensouled. It is just there for the taking.

This is the road to perdition. We've been living in a purgatory of our own atrophied imagination. As Sophia says in her own inimitable way, it is time to awaken from this broken dream, to 'remember our root' - which is Her, our own true nature, the 'virginal spirit' within every one and all of us. In Buddhism, we say that we all have this same, pure nature, and that no matter how defiled human minds may become, that clear light nature is never so much as stained. It's like a mirror that is covered in soot - it never stops being a mirror capable of reflecting. This sounds to me like the same idea as virginal spirit. No matter how lost we've become in the morass of dualistic thinking, the non-dual spirit of human nature remains pure - waiting for the mirror to be wiped clean. Vaughan-Lee again:

> *And life is waiting for us to listen: it just needs us to be present and attentive. It is trying to communicate to us the secrets of creation so that we can participate in the wonder that is being born. We have been exiled from our own home, sold a barren landscape full of soulless fantasies. It is time to return home, to claim what belongs to us, the sacred life of which we are a part... She can help us to remember our true nature.*

Eliminating the Middle Man

So the first step in forging the kind of spiritual cauldron that we will each require to contain, process, and release the grief we have accumulated while we've been asleep as a culture - and to thereby transform ourselves into cultural healers - is to make room for the sacred… in our hearts and in our homes. We need to lovingly carve out a place for ourselves where we can quietly work with our own precious minds for the purpose of reconnecting with something we've lost touch with, or forgotten, but which has never really gone away, hiding in plain sight - our true nature. The simplest and most proven way of asserting this kind of dominion over our spiritual lives and our relation to the divine is to establish a simple meditation practice.

Please note here I use the term 'meditation' in the universal sense practiced by all religions, and not just Asian religions. So if you happen to be Christian like most Americans, or a lapsed whatever, there is never a reason not to meditate! In fact, Christians do meditate, but call it *prayer*. But here's the thing they never told us in church growing up - a deep contemplative practice like praying is not of much use if equal time is not devoted in that place of prayer to *listening*. By this I do not mean listening for an answer to your prayers, either. Rather, *deep* listening in the original spiritual sense of *honoring noble silence - Sophia, 'wisdom'* - and opening our *hearts* up to receive inspiration and grace.

This is actually the living church that the early Gnostic and Coptic Christians of the first few centuries A.D. practiced. It's been conditioned out of us by the idea that we can get by with magical formulas - such as going to church on Sundays, accepting Christ as our savior and lord, not questioning the trinity, getting final absolution before we die, etc. - all examples of charging the Church with responsibility for our salvation.

As soon as we are done 'talking' in prayer - from the Buddhist perspective, getting clear on our intentions and motivations - one then drops down into the sacred feeling and healing (non-conceptual) space of *heartfulness*. Clear seeing. This is where the real 'work' gets done - and it requires no effort - at play in the fields of the Lord, or in Buddhism the play of display.

Of course, there is a real *trick* to non-effort, especially for achievement-oriented Westerners. Really, though, what it comes down to is having faith in your intentions being heard and in some way responded to. It's like planting seeds in a garden. There is some effort in preparing the soil and choosing the seeds. But once they are in the fertile soil, we don't 'make' them grow. We simply tend the garden, returning to it daily, perhaps watering it if it seems dry, and we allow the seeds to sprout, take root, grow, and bear fruit. This is much the same way we cultivate the spiritual field in our heart. We water our garden with the golden silence of deep contemplative prayer - or what some call 'meditation.'

Establishing a meditation practice is especially useful because of the culture that we happen to be immersed in at this critical time in our social history. Modern American culture (which is quickly becoming global) actively works to undermine spiritual contentment, since contentment is not favorable to the sense of needy inadequacy our consumer culture demands. It accomplishes this very effectively by seducing us with myriad worlds of distraction. It is up to us to break free.

It doesn't really matter in the beginning how we choose to think of *anima mundi,* our Universal Mother - Sophia, Tara, Athena, Madonna, Scarlett Johansson's voice - because given the right amount of sacred space she will reveal herself to us in the due time. What *does* matter is that we each find a way to honor the spirit of Earth, carving sacred space out of our home environment as an outward manifestation of honoring the sacred within. There is mysterious reciprocity in that intentional action, properly motivated. We've all heard the phrase 'as above, so below.' I think it is much more accurate to say 'as without, so within.' What we arrange on our shrine or altar is a sacred reflection of what we intuitively feel within, and we come to see how that grows and changes over time with daily attendance - even if only for five minutes at a sitting.

For those who have not already done so, find a quiet corner of your home - or better yet a dedicated wall or even a room - where you can establish an 'altar' upon which to place whatever will serve to remind you of our shared, relational human nature, and will serve to foster and honor your spiritual connection to all of life. Flowers certainly work, especially if you find them in nature and keep replacing them. Plants are really nice, as they supply us with the air we breathe. Water bowls remind us how sacred water is, and how we couldn't survive without it.

When filling your water bowls, think about how hydrogen atoms are produced by birthing stars, and oxygen by dying stars, so water is two parts birthing and one part dying.

Pictures of loved ones, including those who have departed (or grown up!) are nice reminders of our interdependence and inter-penetration with all who are other. Representations of precious holy beings like Jesus, Buddha, St. Francis, Mother Theresa, the Pope, the Dalai Lama, Desmond Tutu, Ghandi, or Martin Luther King serve to inspire our better angels. I like to include realistic figurines of endangered animals, like Bengal tigers, elephants, and polar bears, to remind me not just of impermanence, but of my motivation to alleviate suffering. Beautiful landscape pictures serve as a nice, relaxing backdrop, especially of a place in the world that we have a strong spiritual connection to. Or sea shells, or really whatever puts us in that tranquil, natural state of mind that permits quiet reflection and expansive awareness.

Arranging a shrine is a highly individualistic endeavor, and there is no right or wrong way to go about it. Allow the child that still resides within you to play in the field of sacred imagination. Energetically, we are self-manifesting a field of morphic resonance. Candles and other lights are welcome aids, as is incense - anything that lends sensual beauty to sacred space. This is, after all, a place of *refuge* and retreat, and we want to make it so that we are drawn to it again and again. Not in a distracting way, of course, but in a welcoming, familiar way. We can put a cushion down, or a chair if sitting on the floor is too uncomfortable, in that place we make a promise to ourselves to return to again and again - at least daily, but preferably at the beginning and ending of each day. This kind of 'bookending' our time keeps it real.

Now I know from experience already there are many reading this who have gone right along with everything I've said so far, but are now feeling some resistance, due to preconceived notions we might have about meditation and prayer. So please allow me the courtesy of making one more persuasive case for the need to create this sacred space in our lives without turning this into a guide book on contemplative practices. In a way, this is the most important point of the book, so please bear with me…

Remember what we have said about developmental trauma. The first thing to acknowledge is that, as Dr. Epstein observes, "almost no one is exempt from [psychological] trauma. While some people have it in a much more pronounced way than others, *the unpredictable and unstable nature of things makes life inherently traumatic…*" Fortunately, "the mind, by its very nature, is capable of holding trauma much the way a mother naturally relates to a baby." That's the kind of way we hold our meditation space - like holding a fragile new little life.

Epstein, who is a life-long meditator in addition to being a psychiatrist, points out that "traumas are encoded in implicit memory" in a way that allows them to surface and become objects of our meditation when we are able to quiet the chatter of our monkey minds, much in the way images can be seen on the bottom of a pool once the surface waves subside. By creating an internal environment through quiet contemplation that "mimics the early infant-mother relationship… implicit memories are given opportunities to reveal themselves." This kind of mental process of 're-membering' memories that are carried in our bodies "creates a bridge between implicit and narrative memory."

When we least expect it, in the safe place of refuge, stories (trauma dramas) reveal themselves to us. Ready for processing. Quite… naturally.

Seen in this context, it is perhaps understandable why so many people have an aversion to meditation! The practice often begins by taking us to the places that scare us inside. However, as with my friend who was 'cured' of her clinical depression by repeatedly resisting the urge to run from the meditation hall screaming, it is important to trust the sacred nature of the refuge we've carved out, and to have faith in these natural processes unfolding within. As Epstein goes on to point out: *"The troubling aspects of self are a lot less troubling when held in the forgiving arms of one's own awareness."* This is a beautiful way of saying that our practice of compassion for the suffering of the world begins with compassion for ourselves on the cushion.

Dr. Epstein is an adept of the famous child psychologist D.W. Winnicott. You might be feeling some trepidation over all this talk of allowing implicit memories to surface, fearful of undergoing some kind of emotional/spiritual/psychological 'breakdown.' But Winnicott has a brilliant answer to this hestitation. The breakdown that we fear may destroy our life has already happened - it's been *"carried [a]round hidden away in the unconscious…"* all this time we thought we were living our lives.[92] From a Jungian perspective, what we fear is our own fully developed shadow, which is controlling our actions anyway via this very fear and denial.

In other words, we *already are broken* by our implicit traumas, we simply haven't *experienced* that broken state yet in our conscious mind. Instead, we carry it around in our body and project it into our relationships through habitual, unconscious patterns of behavior by which we secretly hope to recreate the trauma. But then, when our heart are finally broke open, we tend to recoil and go into a hardened shell, shielding ourselves from life. Until we experience this brokenness consciously, willingly, with an open (even bleeding) heart, there can be no hope for healing. We go to our graves as broken, unfulfilled promises, filled with dull regret and numb spirit.

If the key to healing the latent suffering and psychological blockage of developmental trauma is to experience it, and if we cannot afford the kind of psychotherapy that creates a safe container[93] for spiritual emergence, the way to experience this kind of healing is by allowing the sacred space for such implicit memories to surface in our minds. The payoff is not just freeing up these

---

[92] Quoted by Epstein at p. 156, from "Fear of Breakdown," in *Psycho-Analytic Explorations* (Cambridge, MA: Harvard Univ Press, 1989).

[93] Make no mistake from the analogies I draw between individual traumatic experiences and individually held collective trauma. Professional help is certainly necessary for severe forms of trauma, such as sexual abuse or PTSD. What I am addressing here is just the *collective* implicit trauma that has given rise to the climate crisis, though this processing of shared cultural trauma is likely to bring up less severe individual traumatic experiences as well, such as our original emotional wounding, since these kinds of traumas are related. As we've learned, when we are faced with traumatic experiences, all past traumas become present. See, e.g., *Trauma & Recovery,* by Judith Herman, M.D.

blockages to relational experience and loving, but just as significantly, getting in touch with our own true nature, described by psychoanalyst Michael Eigen as follows:

> *If you penetrate to the core of your aloneness you will not only find yourself, there will also be this [previously] unknown, boundless presence... at the core of your aloneness. No matter how deep you go, you'll find it there.*

That is our true nature, which is neither self nor other, nor is it not-self or something *other* than other! I like to think of it as the transcendent ground of all being, very similar to Jung's *Unus Mundus* or Buddhism's *clear light nature*. It is on this transcendent ground that we come into a kind of pure awareness that puts us in true relationship with ourselves and with all that is other (not just 'others'), with human nature and with sentient nature herself - the soul of the world.

In order to arrive at this, our true home, we first have to work through these developmental traumas we all carry around in our psychosomatic being, which from the perspective of our current crisis just happens to include this collective rupture in our relationship with nature that began with the chain-reactive (i.e., multiplying) trauma of splitting the atom in the Trinity Test. Remo Roth, Ph.D., who is perhaps the foremost expert today on the shared ideas of Carl Jung and Wolfgang Pauli, postulates from his research into their respective works that when we split the atom in the Trinity Test, the *unus mundus* (he calls it the 'psycho-physical' reality) may have become contaminated, with the results being multiplied in the form of contamination spreading like a mushroom cloud in our own collective unconscious. Pauli, in particular, grasped this potential unintended consequence of our hubris, viewing Trinity as the culmination of the alchemical quest for transmuting matter, and appreciating the inextricable connections between matter, energy, and psyche. As he saw it, *"the unconscious is in both man and nature..."* That is the 'nature' of psycho-physical reality.

Can you see why it would be so difficult to get to the experience of our own true nature without first dealing with this abrupt social departure from the natural world? *We have been pervasively conditioned by it our whole lives.* Charles Eisenstein calls it the "story of separation" that perpetuates the feeling of alienation that is endemic to our society. As a 'baby boomer' I was even raised in what sociologists call a 'nuclear family.' Nothing implicit about that!

The Final Solution to the banality of climate change

Being an ecopsychologist and life-long eco-activist, I have become firmly convinced that this psycho-physical reconnection, through both individual and mass meditation and prayer, this re-sacralization of our daily lives, is the only lasting 'solution' to the *existential moral* crisis that is being reflected back at us by our rapidly changing climate. It may seem counterintuitive to think that the solution to this external crisis is contained within contemplative practices, but please remember the lessons of quantum physics discussed earlier, and consider the possibility that only those who have healed this crisis within themselves will have the internal resources to weather the storms we are now just beginning to face. And we will do this not by sitting on our cushions while all those around us lose their minds, but rather by becoming wounded healers ourselves for all those they come into contact with, and by forming new communities with like-hearted individuals that will prove resilient enough to face into the storm and adapt to shifting ecological, cultural, and societal realities.

As we can hear in Sophia's wise counsel, it isn't really necessary to pray - though prayer may come spontaneously and may be necessary to quiet the mind. It isn't necessary for us to become Buddhist or to adopt any other religion we are uncomfortable with. All that we are being called upon to do in these sacred practices is to rest in open, spacious awareness. To 'remember our root' by acknowledging, accepting and coming to understand our spiritual selves. Depending on the circumstances of our daily life, this sense of rest may not come quickly, but it will come naturally to all who wait with open hearts and minds.

Metanoite! Change your mind!! (This is our 'come to Jesus' moment, though I prefer 'come to Sophia' or, as Pope Francis would have it, 'come to Mary.')

[There will be a short intermission now while those who have not yet done so go create a sacred space in their home, and consecrate it with a short inaugural meditation session]

* * *

It can be shocking at first to see how much mental chatter there is on the surface of our oceanic mind, and how difficult it is to calm those churning waters. Remain calm. Just be still. This is not rocket science - we do not have to re-invent the wheel here. We are connected to the awareness we seek by our very own breath, or '*pranna*' (Sanskrit word for "life force" or vital principle), and we access this portal by relaxing into a deeper, slower breathing pattern than we habitually use in our busy, scattered lives. Breath is a key portal into altered states of consciousness. We can lower our eyelids to limit the amount of light entering, and focus our attention on the rise and fall of the abdomen, which has the welcome effect of taking us out of our monkey mind by placing our awareness in our body, where those implicit memories happen to be stored. If we find ourselves getting drowsy during meditation, the opposite of monkey mind, we can experiment with gently retaining a breath every so often - not every breath, more like every 7th or 8th breath - and raising the shades on our eyes to let more light in, as well as focusing our attention on the point where air enters and leaves the nose.

There - that's it! It's just that simple, really. No need to over-complicate matters. *If it was overly complicated, it wouldn't be natural!* We need to trust our mind, and listen to our intuitions (in Buddhism, this is often referred to as listening to our 'inner guru'). Our intention is everything. Allow me to repeat that.

Intention is everything!

Once we establish a spiritual practice like meditation, prayer or, if you prefer generics, 'quiet contemplation,' the entire universe will conspire in our favor over time. *Really*. We're not the first to walk this path, and we never walk alone. We just need to be patient with ourselves, and have faith in our own true nature, our good hearts. For it is in this sacred space, on our cushions or seated upright with good intention and pure motivation, that eventually something quite marvelous happens - *conscious awareness drops from our head into our heart.*

(Now there's a big secret for you, at no extra charge.)

Then we are in touch with our feelings. *Then* we can access the depths of our psyche, through awareness, appreciate the scars on our heart, and feel the limitless, boundary-less and non-local nature of our relational mind... the self that is other... the otherness that is none other than our true selves. And once our spiritual container becomes strong enough, through the simple repetitive exercise of showing up, we can begin going deeper into the things we fear the most. We develop real courage in sacred space.

It is important that we recognize, accept, and learn to understand the basic premise underlying this spiritual program of awakening awareness: *Human nature is a beautiful thing.* We seem to have forgotten the inherent beauty of human nature. As my spiritual guide in Thailand always said to me, with a sparkle in his heart and a twinkle in his eye:

Don't forget to remember!

CHAPTER 9

OVERCOMING OUR FEARS

Pain has a purpose. The problem, therefore, lies not with our pain for the world, but in our repression of it. We need a different way of relating to the challenging uncertainties of our time.

~ Joanna Macy

Climate Psychology 101

The central premise of this book is that we have lost touch with nature and with our true nature due to rupture, developmental trauma, and repressed grieving; and that we can restore an appropriate, healthy balance with the natural world through acknowledging our losses, both past and prospective, confronting our fears, and processing our grief. As we've just explored, we can create a kind of 'alchemical container,' or spiritual cauldron, for this transformative process by establishing contemplative practices in the privacy of our homes - apart from the distractions of our daily lives, family and friends (though inviting others to share noble silence in sacred space is also quite powerful).

It's understandable why most people would have an aversion to this kind of spiritual exploration. The first thing we learn when we sit down to examine our mind is that it is a lot more unsettled and uncontrollable than we like to think - already our ego is in defensive posture. "I don't need to do this - this is silly! What will people *think*?" That's the very first barrier, and for most in this heavily conditioned, socially engineered culture, the last! Most never even get past this self-conscious fear of social approbation. Which is so sad, really. These people have no idea what they're missing out on in life.

At the next level of resistance, what seems like a normal, internal narrative thread in the hustle and bustle of daily life appears more like the ravings of a lunatic in the quietude of sacred space! By applying the simple tether of deepening our breathing, and by being patient with the universe and compassionate with ourselves, eventually the chattering of our monkey mind subsides. Granted this sacred space of noble silence, our feelings begin to surface from the depths of expansive awareness. Because of our strong intention, backed by a more accommodating worldview, rather than being swept away by these feelings, we find ourselves able to take them on as objects of our contemplative practice, managing all the while to sustain the perspective of someone who is just slightly detached from the process, both experiencing it and observing it. As one of my main lineage gurus used to say: we become our own therapist. Like a mother cradling her baby in her arms. The ability to do this is one of the unique traits that makes us human.[94]

Alas, dear reader, if your experience bears out everything put forward in this book so far, then you can expect that at some point in your practice, once the surface waves of the mind become rippling patterns that allow images just below the surface to start emerging, you will find yourself awash in that very natural state of depression that we expend so much energy distracting ourselves from. Obviously, this is something to be prepared for, a psychological experience for which we need to have a strategic plan in place. And so, before we go any deeper into our exploration of the kind of climate grief that awakens us into the final stage of acceptance, it is necessary to gain a competent understanding of the 3 D's and their antidotes - the 3 A's. Some of

---

[94] Remember, Pope Francis says that the climate crisis is calling on us to remember what it means to be human. This is one central example: contemplative awareness.

this may seem repetitive, but it's important enough that it bears repeating, so it really sinks into our psyche in such a way that we can readily retrieve it when needed.

Denial. The first 'D' is not climate science denialism, but rather the healthy kind of denial by which we consciously manage our emotions so as not to get carried away by the gravity of the situation we are confronted by. It is this trait that allows us to keep ourselves up to date on the information that is spiraling out there in the "great unravelling."

One of the hallmarks of suffering is proliferating thoughts - the kind of conceptual avalanche that we humans are prone to, where one thought leads to another, that to another, until we are firmly in the grip of whatever emotional affect (e.g., seething anger, panic, lust, despair, etc.) happens to have conjured up that particular thread. While practicing forbearance, bearing witness to difficult feelings, sometimes we just need to *cut* the thread of proliferating thoughts and emotions. Yes, in order to have appropriate compassion for our own induced suffering, sometimes we *distract* ourselves for respite. That is a healthy kind of denial. The first person a wise caregiver takes care of is themselves, which often means some kind of removal from a situation.

Related to this, we also have to be conscientious, in this day and age of endless social media and 24-hour news cycles, about what we are feeding our senses. Just as our physical health is directly related to the quality of our food and drink, so our mental health is directly related to the quality of sensory inputs. Or, to put it bluntly, 'garbage-in, garbage-out.' It's why so many spiritually oriented people in today's crazy, mixed up world have killed their TVs, so to speak. Especially with the advent of viewer-controlled, commercial-free programming on the internet, who really needs satellite or cable TV feeding commercial garbage and cultural pablum into their homes?

I remember about a week after the terror attacks of 9/11 visiting a friend of mine who had a framing studio in back of his house. Michael is a very sensitive, artistic soul. He had a television in his work studio that sat up high on a wall, and which he liked to keep on as background noise while he worked. During that particular time, he had CNN on 24/7, and they were showing the video of the planes flying into the towers incessantly, almost on a loop. By the time I found him, Michael was drowning in a sea of despair, having seen the video by his own estimate hundreds and hundreds of times, each time imagining in a different way what it must've been like for the people inside the buildings, in the planes themselves, on the ground, etc. Not only was he distressed, he had actually suffered some kind of nervous breakdown, and we ended up taking him to the psychiatric ward of a local hospital for recovery. This may seem like an extreme example to you, but it speaks to the power of sensory inputs - especially to empathic beings.

The climate crisis, quite simply, is the most serious crisis we have ever faced as a species. If we were to give it the kind of attention it really merits, we would be much like my friend Michael. We'd be walking around in between our media surfing sessions bereft, tempted to make a sign about the end being near - THE WORLD IS ON FIRE! THE POLAR CAPS ARE MELTING! THE OCEANS ARE DYING! REPENT!! CHANGE YOUR WAYS!!! - and walking up and down a busy sidewalk of working clones to alert all our fellow citizens of just how serious the situation really is. We would, in other words, be a mess! Totally justified when you really think about it, but of course everyone would tune us out - and who could blame *them*? Shaming and blaming our the worst strategies for changing human behavior.

We won't be doing anyone any good by losing our minds, either. No more than we will do anyone any good by living in complete denial that something really terrible is going wrong. These are the two extreme ends of the spectrum of psychological behavior, both ends marked by a dysfunctional kind of emotional reactivity. We have to cultivate healthy individual psyches if the real solutions to the climate crisis are going to emerge from our collective psyche, and that means maintaining a healthy perspective - a spiritually balanced perspective.

Here's one way I like to think of this kind of perspective. If I learned tomorrow that I had approximately three years to live, I wouldn't go around all the time bemoaning the fact that I have only this limited time, would I? At the same time, three years is long enough that I wouldn't necessarily drop out of my life and go on some mad cruise or dangerous adventure, as in the classic Tom Hanks/Meg Ryan movie, *Joe Versus the Volcano*. Nor could I put it completely out of my mind and go on as if nothing was wrong. Instead, it would just put my life into a different perspective, one that would actually make me appreciate the simple beauty of life and nature all the more - knowing that my time was limited. For those already at the acceptance stage of climate grief, this is the kind of perspective we can see being actively cultivated. Life is precious, and it is a limited time offer.

Life *as we know it* may well be ending - but it hasn't ended yet. From a historical perspective, all things considered, this may be as good as it has ever been or will ever be again. Look how close we are in the sciences to seeing things as they really are. Gaze upon those amazing photos of distant galaxies from the Hubble space station, or the pictures from spacecrafts flying by Saturn, Pluto and Ceres. Look at all the amazing things we have at our fingertips on the internet! As a Buddhist, I can watch live streaming video of just about any teachings His Holiness the Dalai Lama gives anywhere in the world, and I can access all my own teachers' dharma talks anytime I want. Not to mention watching great TV on Netflix with no commercials, or watching the 'real' news on Democracy Now! and listening to the music I love on Pandora - also with no commercials!

Consider the incredibly beautiful wilderness areas we are still able to get lost in, places we can still encounter grizzly bears, mountain lions, moose, hawk-owls, and hoary marmots! From a purely objective viewpoint, without projecting, what an amazing time this is to be alive in. The fact that it may all be very tenuous, that it may be unravelling and about to come tumbling down, that this may be as good as it gets, *only makes me appreciate it that much more*. If that sounds selfish, then fine - as long as I am doing everything I can to alleviate suffering in the world and avert ecotastrophe, I can live with a few selfish indulgences. No guilty conscience here!

That may not be a politically correct way of seeing things, and of course there are times when I am painfully aware of the connection between technology and suffering in the world. But by honestly acknowledging and managing our denial, we're able to enjoy the beauty of life and awe of nature and the cosmos (thank you Neil deGrasse Tyson!), and then balance it out by grieving the sobering reality that we are risking all this and have lost so much already, and future generations will probably not have these kinds of amazing privileges. In my mind, at least, I can offer these up to them. Remember, intention is everything.

This is not cognitive dissonance. There is no dissociation - it's just bittersweet, as life has always been. Or, as Walt Whitman would put it - "*I contain multitudes!*" By acknowledging my own healthy denial, you can see from this book that it doesn't mean I am precluded from being part of the solution. My goodness, we are *all* part of the problem. Acknowledging that doesn't prevent us from also becoming part of the solution. In fact, by acknowledging that we are both part of the problem *and* managing our denial, we actually make it *possible* to live a meaningful life filled with both joy and grief in equal measure, one informing the other.

As Epstein puts it: "*Destruction may continue, but [our] humanity shines through.*" Acknowledgment is therefore the antidote to denial: $A + D = D^h$ (healthy denial).

Depression. Healthy *depression* begins with simply acknowledging that, as a culture, we are depressed about the situation we find ourselves in. And then *owning* that feeling. And then taking responsibility for it - *doing* something about it. If we were *not* depressed about the impacts we are having on other species, future generations, and our dysfunctional relationship with the natural world, *that* would be unhealthy! Owning up to it on behalf of our society frees us up to be of service to society.

It's important that we agree about this now in a way that we were unable to when Jimmy Carter first tried to diagnose our national malaise. Let us consider a list of symptoms identified by the National Institute of Mental Health for diagnosing depression, and then let us objectively assess whether or not we cab see any evidence of this symptomalogy in our cultural *Zeitgeist*:

• *Persistent sad, anxious, or 'empty' mood.* I think we can sum this one up in one ubiquitous word - whatEV*er*! It is what it is… This is the affective disorder that we are chronically trying to distract ourselves from. In sampling people's general mood, walk down a busy street of any major city, where most of us happen to live (yes, me too), and look at the faces of those who do not happen to be distracted in the moment. What do you see? How would *you* describe that mood? I think empty is pretty accurate. Underlying those blank expressions is a deep sadness, and the anxiety of knowing something is not right, that our future is not so bright.

• *Feelings of hopelessness, pessimism.* Talk to anyone about the climate crisis, and this is usually the reason given for not really wanting to think about it. Actually, it is the *fear* of feeling hopeless more than hopelessness itself, as well as the fear of giving in to pessimism, which is what hardens into the psychological armor of cynicism.

- *Feelings of guilt and helplessness.* From suppressing the feelings of hopelessness and pessimism, while at the same time being haunted by feelings of complicity.

- *Loss of interest or pleasure in hobbies and activities.* This one we've turned on its head, as it is often the best strategy for keeping our unwelcome feelings at bay. We are, if anything, hobby-obsessed. It is by exaggerating our interest in sensual pleasure, hobbies, and a multitude of endlessly proliferating distractions and activities that we can pretend that we do not suffer from depression - even if, in our quieter moments when no one else is around, we know better. What we *have* lost interest in, however, is *meaningful* activities, *true* intimacy, and also *constructive* hobbies (e.g, arts and crafts).

- *Decreased energy and fatigue.* Perhaps the most common complaint we express in this culture is not having enough time or energy to keep up with all we need to be doing, or feel we should be doing. It's the sense of *overwhelm* - and it is endemic.

- *Difficulty concentrating, remembering, making decisions.* Our political system is paralyzed with gridlock at the top, and as a society we follow the 24-hour news cycle of flitting from one issue to another, without ever focusing long enough on any single issue to arrive at a solution. Levels of dementia are at an all-time high, curiously enough, with one out of every three people over 83 years of age afflicted. What to do, what to do...

- *Difficulty sleeping, early-morning awakening, or oversleeping.* According to the Center for Disease Control & Prevention, insufficient sleep has now become a public health epidemic, with almost *50 million* Americans reporting difficulty concentrating on things as a result, and *40 million* reporting difficulty remembering things. Wait - did we cover this already?

- *Appetite and/or weight changes.* The obesity rate in America has increased dramatically in recent decades, with over one third of adults in the U.S. now considered obese (34.9% or 78.6 million).[95] We are literally eating the planet, as most of this voracious appetite is associated with the livestock industry - the leading cause of global temperature rise. We are what we eat, and too many of us look like bloated cows or slovenly pigs today.

- *Thoughts of death or suicide.* Suicide rates among baby-boomers - the generation spawned by the post-WWII *American Dreamers* - surged by nearly *30%* in the first decade of the new millennium. And that does not include all those who mask their deep psychological pain with opioids, get addicted, and die of "accidental" overdose. If we, as a culture, are actually in the process of committing ecocide, it would be shocking NOT to see people at the more sensitive end of the spectrum acting this out. Along with unreasonably risky behaviors.

- *Restlessness, irritability.* Come on - do I really have to talk about this!? Can't we just move on? Okay, seriously - when did we decide that the best way to air public issues was to have

---

[95] CDC (2014).

representatives of extreme views scream at, over, and past one another on television? Oh, one last update. DONALD TRUMP! *Are you kidding me, America?* From the standpoint of cultural denial, however, it kind of makes sense. From a middling actor spouting nonsense about 'morning in America' to a narcissistic reality-TV star telling us he can "Make America Great Again." Politics…

- *Persistent physical symptoms.* Like, oh I don't know, *mass killings?* Domestic violence? Drug abuse? Body piercing?? Drone warfare??? How about dressing in black?! How long have we been in mourning as a culture, exactly? Remember, this particular fashion obsession with shades of black *pre-dates* 9/11. It began in the 1990s, achieving almost cult-like status before the terrorist attacks in New York, and has not really waned much since - unlike almost every other fashion trend you can think of. Hmm…

Okay, so this discussion is pretty depressing. What would happen if we as a culture were to actually *acknowledge* that we are depressed over the current state of affairs, including but not limited to the most unfortunate coincidence of destroying the life support system for all complex species on the planet while having a system of governance that is completely incapable or unwilling to address any problem that seems to big?

Maybe, just maybe, acknowledging our depression would feel like that brilliant 1976 movie *Network*, where the life-long news anchor Howard Beale rises up against the consumer culture from which he emerged to declare "I'm mad as hell and NOT going to take it anymore!"[96] Yes, maybe it would feel really good to finally get this really bad feeling out of our system, into the open.

Because of the corruption of the mainstream psychology 'industry' in America by Big Pharma, as they've come to be called, we have been conditioned to respond to depression instead by *masking* the symptoms and *avoiding* the underlying issues. Ecopsychology maintains that the depression epidemic in this country, beginning in the mid-60's and escalating dramatically into the new millennium, is a natural response to losing our connection to the natural world.[97] This is not just speaking figuratively, either. It has actually been shown that dermal exposure to natural bacteria in top soil (i.e., from gardening with bare hands) can be just as effective at dealing with less severe forms of depression as the commonly prescribed anti-depressant medications.

Hint, hint!

With the repeated disclaimer that what we are talking about here is a culturally transmitted form of depression that's been welling up from our collective psyche for many decades now, the 'cure' begins with simple acknowledgment and, just as importantly, *awareness* of our share of the

---

[96] Let's add this gem to our list of angry cultural expressions from the 1970s!

[97] This is a generalization concerning climate grief, and not meant to deny that serious cases of clinical depression may have more to do with physiological imbalances in the brain and/or severe traumatization.

symptoms of that underlying dis-ease (mal-aise). Once we stop masking the symptoms with endless distractions (or worse - opioids, alcohol, and chronic marijuana use[98]) and get in touch with our true feelings about our place in the natural world and what is happening to it, then there are as many ways as there are individuals for processing that depression. It is the intention to own it and process it that is critical.

Meditation in nature is a magical elixir. The Buddha sat under a tree for a reason, just as Jesus did a 40-day meditation retreat in the desert after the Spirit of Christ descended on him at the River Jordan, Muhammed and Joseph Smith had their caves, and Thoreau his pond. Even in big cities we have access to endless blue skies, roof gardens, municipal parks, greenbelts, waterfronts and starry nights. Backpacking into the wilderness or along one of the two coastal trails, especially alone or as a couple, is an intensive form of ecotherapy, as can be renting a cabin on a lake or simply walking at length along a creek. Religious retreats are usually situated in lovely settings. And yes, mindful gardening is a wonderful and vital way of connecting to the Earth, natural beauty, and our food.

When we have an addiction - whether it is to opioids, distractions, food, or self-destructive thought patterns - one of the best ways of breaking that habit is to embrace a healthier habit in its place. Thus if, like millions of us, you've been chronically distracting yourself from an underlying sense of depression over our lost connection to the natural world, or the deplorable state of the planet we are leaving to our kids, and if you're determined to process through these feelings but are not sure how to break the chain-of-distractions habit, the best way is going to be to adopt a new habit for re-connecting to the natural world free from distraction. In addition to our new habit of sitting for at least 5 minutes in solitude in sacred space each day. This can mean daily nature bike-rides, walks in the park, meditations under a favorite tree, going up to the roof before bedtime every night just to gaze at the stars, gardening, or any other way of honoring nature that appeals to us.

Please understand, this is a really important part of processing our depression. There is a reciprocal relationship between our lost connection and depression, just as there is between our diet and human nature. In other words, we are depressed over the state of the natural world, and it is our lost connectivity with the natural world that feeds our depression. And while feeling concern for the natural world leads us to adopt a healthy, whole food diet, it is also true that adopting a healthy, whole food diet will increase our concern for the natural world. Nature is full of feedback loops like this, and so are we.

The other part we have touched on already - facing our worst fears. We will come back to that in the next chapter, on healthy grieving. But it is important nonetheless to mention it briefly here as part of an overall strategy for dealing with natural depression. As long as those deepest, darkest fears about the future - whether our own individual future, our children's future, or the future of

---

[98] I recognize from personal experience that marijuana in moderation, and especially used as a sacrament, can foster a deeper connection to nature. But chronic use of potent strains, like those available legally now in many states, deaden that connection - along with everything else.

life on planet Earth - remain hidden from our waking consciousness, as long as they continue to be unacknowledged, we will continue to be stuck in this state of mild, lingering depression - no matter how much processing we've done of the easy, more accessible feelings. And this, in turn, is the kind of deep work that is best done in sacred space, as part of our contemplative practice.

So all of this is connected. It's all about re-connecting. We are relational beings, right?

The biggest fear we have to deal with is the fear of grieving, the fear of falling apart on our cushion in a sobbing heap of emotional disintegration. However, that happens to be what catharsis (emotional release) *looks* like. That's when we *know* we are making real progress, and getting close to real breakthrough. That may well be considered the dark side of depression, but in this context at least it is more like a dark tunnel that leads us into the light. Nobody has ever said that a meaningful life is an easy life. Nothing worthwhile comes easy.

Do not be afraid of falling apart, especially in the safe place of spiritual refuge. Psychiatrist Kazimierz Dabrowski even refers to this process as *'positive disintegration,'* and Joanna Macy points out that it can often feel like dying. I myself can attest to this. But we *need* to die to our old selves in order to be reborn anew - an eternal spiritual truism - and that happens to be an accurate reflection of what needs to happen in the world at large, as well. To take it on individually, then, is not just a form of spiritual warriorship, it's actually the world itself transforming through each of us in turn. She cannot be reborn without and apart from our own personal transformation. Just as the word 'human' is derived from the same root as soil, our species is the fertile soil from which the soul of the world will spring forth and grow.

Awareness is the antidote to Depression: $D + A = D^h$ (healthy depression)

Despair. The danger of failing to process our depression is two-sided. If we're 'lucky' we go to an early grave having succeeded in keeping ourselves deliriously (or numbingly) distracted. The other side of unprocessed depression is called despair. The mistake people make is thinking that if they actually confront their depression and work with it, they will end up in despair.

What despair generally points to is the lack of an adequate spiritual container for processing our depression and grief, and so we stop short. This is why our world view is so critical and even salutary, and why the kind of quantum ecopsychological worldview discussed in chapter four is so critical. For example, as noted therein, the emotionally reactive response of despair says "it's all falling apart, near term human extinction is inevitable, all life is going to be wiped off of planet Earth -- there's no reason for hope!" But according to Prigogene's lovely theory of dissipative structures, as we saw, this climate and socio-economic chaos is actually *quite* hopeful. Let's not forget that little psychological trick. And according to James Hillman, it is the world soul stirring toward herself, reawakening us through the drastic measures made necessary by our own hardened, dualistic and materialistic world view. So it's GOOD for us! We can focus on the delicate and beautiful eggshell cracking up and falling apart, or we can have some curiosity about what kind of strange new bird is emerging.

I have often found that when people fall into despair, and cite the 'hopelessness' of the situation, what they are really experiencing is the shattering of their own false hopes arising from their attachment to particular outcomes. I saw this over and over during my years in environmental activism, and even began preaching the *Gospel of Hopelessness*[99] to young activists in whom I recognized the tell-tale signs that inevitably lead to burn-out. We all crave certainty, and in the context of the climate crisis this means we want to believe not just in a happy ending, but in a happy ending *in our lifetime*. That's quite human. The problem is, in the limited framework of the next 20-50 years or so, which happens to be the timeframe most of us can expect to die no matter what, there are no happy endings - just uncertain beginnings.

So despair brings up the issue of hope, and here again we can learn a really valuable lesson from the hospice model of confronting our own mortality. When someone enters hospice, which is to say when their normal expectations about life-span and overcoming illness have been dashed, one of the first and most important tasks they are asked to undertake is called "re-defining hope." We don't say "give it up, there is no hope!" In truth, none of us get out of this thing alive, right? Instead, we say "Okay, your doctors are not going to be surprised now if you die within the next six months. We're here to make you comfortable and alleviate any pain. So given all that, what do you hope for?" Which in a gentle way is getting at "what are you most afraid of about the dying process?"

We're all quite familiar with the idea of "quality of life," but very few of us ever stop to consider what our quality of death might look like. What would a good death look like for you? Most people would say they want their loved ones nearby, they'd prefer having laughter and joy in the room to sobbing and lamenting. Maybe a spiritual friend, some soft music. Like that. Personally, I want to be sitting in half-lotus with mantra recitations filling the air. But that's me. I'm weird.

Again, as I have found that I need to keep reminding people, the lesson here is not that *all* life on planet Earth is ending, or that we need to start preparing for Judgment Day! Judgment day has been here for some time now, and while we do not know what the world is going to be like a hundred years from now, we do know that we personally will not be around at that time. We know that life as we have always known it is ending right now, that this is just the beginning of that end. So we need to adjust our expectations, change our perspective, and re-define our hopes.

This, in turn, means getting in touch with and expressing our worst fears.

I really hope that the oceans don't die out. That's one of my biggest fears right now. Huge, actually. And I hope elephants and rhinos and tigers and polar bears don't disappear from the

---

[99] Briefly, I'd ask them to assume that the forces of darkness would prevail, and that the state of the Earth needed to get much worse before it could start getting much better. Then I'd ask them to reconsider their actions in this light. What would be their motivation? The end result was almost always that they would still take the same stand, and still engage in the same kinds of protest, because it was the "right thing" to do. By switching the focus from some uncertain end result to the integrity of 'right action,' a profound shift in perspective (and temperament) results.

face of the earth any time soon. I hate to admit this, but given the urgency of the situation and the cluelessness of the powers that be, I hope our economic system comes tumbling down very soon (other people's worst fear!). Of course, I realize that would only hasten the kind of dislocation and disruption that climate change is already bringing, and would increase human suffering in the short term. So while I fear how it may play out, my hope is that it would be the kind of strong medicine that would be best for us long term - just as the brief economic collapse of 2008 was followed by the first year of actual declines in CO_2 emissions, or just as people started to think much more deeply about America's role in the world for a brief, compassionate spell in the weeks after the towers came tumbling down.

Mostly, my hope is just that whatever calamities arrive on our doorstep in the next several decades, that it somehow brings out the best in us.[100] I hope that we come to our senses in time to avoid all the worst-case scenarios being circulated out there in science world, and in time to stem the tide of extinction before biodiversity itself is permanently lost. Fortunately, there is actually good reason supporting this kind of hope. Rebecca Solnit researched and wrote a book on the emotional resilience of the human species under extreme adversity. Titled *A Paradise Built in Hell*, this brief description on Amazon illustrates my own vision for a planetary hospice movement beautifully:

> *The most startling thing about disasters, according to award-winning author Rebecca Solnit, is not merely that so many people rise to the occasion, but that they do so with joy. That joy reveals an ordinarily unmet yearning for community, purposefulness, and meaningful work that disaster often provides.* A Paradise Built in Hell *is an investigation of the moments of altruism, resourcefulness, and generosity that arise amid disaster's grief and disruption and considers their implications for everyday life. It points to a new vision of what society could become - one that is less authoritarian and fearful, more collaborative and local.*

Isn't that comforting? Consistent with this vision of beauty blossoming in the soil of adversity, ecologist David Orr defines *practical hope* as that which "comes from doing the things before us that need to be done in the spirit of thankfulness and celebration - without worrying about whether we will win or lose."[101] This requires a measure of acceptance, specifically the acceptance of what is (one definition of desire is failing to accept things the way they are). Orr's concept of practical hope is a wonderful guide for us to use in re-defining our own hope in relation to the climate crisis.[102]

---

[100] You can easily gauge from this what my worst fear is.

[101] Orr, D.W. (2004) "Hope in Hard Times" *Conservation Biology*, 18:295-298, at 297.

[102] See, also, Joanna Macy & Chris Johnstone's book *Active Hope* (2012) from New World Library.

It isn't about hoping for a happy ending, really. That starts very quickly to feel like denial masquerading as false hope. It's more about hoping for spiritual growth and transformation out of unprecedented dislocation and dying.

Whenever we feel despair creeping in, the very first thing we need to do is to remind ourselves that it is not really necessary to *give in* to that feeling. We can pause here just a moment to remember what our worldview looks and feels like. Next, we need to drop down into that pool of healthy climate depression from which this feeling is welling up. We need to swim around in that water just long enough to get its flavor, to see other parts of us floating around in there, and then we need to take a deep breath and dive deep down below that into the shadow-filled repository of our coldest fears. There, we will be able to sense directly just what unrealistic hopes we are harboring that are causing us to crash up against the rocky shoreline of reality. That's what I mean by working deeply once we trust the sacredness of our refuge.

The last thing I want to say about despair is this: In the same way that denial is fear-based, the despair that arises out of depression is grief-based. It's a teacher, really, because it's telling us that we have not yet acknowledged and processed *all* of the grief that we're feeling over the losses we are already experiencing now, and those that seem inevitable in the future.

Probe beneath the psychological defenses of a cynical person and you will inevitably find despair. Cynicism is the despair of a broken heart - the heart of person who has never learned that a broken heart is an open heart, a person who does not have the kind of spiritual container (and worldview) that would enable them to *hold* that broken heart open to the world, with serene acceptance. So we should alway remember that the correct response to cynicism is compassion. Cynics are emotionally crippled by understandable suffering, in dire need of spiritual emergency.

Just to summarize our report card from Climate Psychology 101: We have turned the three D's back from fear of failure (F's) into the straight A's of engaged coping. Unhealthy denial is vanquished by acknowledgment, leaving us with a healthy relationship to managed denial. The depression that is endemic to our present culture, and that we mask with OCD (obsessive/ compulsive distraction), has its antidote in the cultivation of simple awareness in sacred space, where we allow it to surface in our psyche, where we honor it and begin processing it, really listening to what it has to teach us about healthy relationship with self and other and Earth, our mother. Finally, when we encounter despair, we view it as a teacher who points out the ways in which we have not yet arrived at acceptance, pointing us back home to do our grief work.

That's the idea. There's no time like the present, so...

CHAPTER 10
THE GREAT AWAKENING

Finding Redemption Through Natural Grieving

"Perhaps the most important reason for 'lamenting' is that it helps us to realize our oneness with all things, to know that all things are our relatives." ~ Black Elk

Befriending Grief

Grieving is the shadow side of loving. What would it mean to consciously take grieving onto our path as a constant companion? Would it make us gloomy and foreboding? That's certainly the fear - a general consensus of those who avoid grief except when it hits them like a train with the loss of a loved one, a job, or a small fortune. But the reality is that the more we get in touch with our grief, the more loving, joyous, and vitally aware we become - and the more we are able to appreciate life.

We see this all the time with cancer survivors, don't we? Their experience *blesses* them with a keen awareness of *just how close* death really is at all times. We don't have to wait to get cancer to awaken to this awareness. We never pause to consider how we are risking death each time we drive our cars, even though logic tells us what an unnatural act this is to be hurtling ourselves through space at such ridiculous speeds. And so, whenever someone actually does not make it back from a car trip, we are shocked. Stunned. It's 'not supposed to happen,' we tell ourselves. And yet it does, every day, with great regularity. Do you think it might make a difference if, instead, each time we got into a car and clicked that seat belt, we paused for just a moment to consider the fact that we are voluntarily courting grievous bodily injury and/or death? How might our awareness of the driving experience be altered by such a ritual?

I was once hit by a car while on my bike. Though the bike was totaled, I walked away unscathed. But it made an impression on me, and I got into the habit with my new bike to recite a little 'gatha' I learned from a Buddhist cancer survivor: "Death is real. Comes without warning. This body will be a corpse."[103] Picturing my body as a corpse made me a more cautious, defensive bike rider. It also made me appreciate the experience more. With active grieving as part of our life, we stop taking things for granted, and begin appreciating the miracle of our existence.

According to Stephen Jenkinson, the *Grief Walker*, in Western culture grief comes only belatedly to us when we realize we've been "on the take" our whole life, living with a sense of entitlement. Grief has a lot to do with appropriate gratitude, seeing things as they really are (versus how we'd like them to be), and Emerson's natural law of compensation. Everything we gain comes from loss, most of our successes are built on failure, and ultimately every gift we receive from this living universe 'leaves a hole' in its interpenetrating, interdependent, interconnected fabric somewhere else, as Jenkinson puts it. Embodying indigenous wisdom gained only after obtaining a divinity degree from Harvard, he warns us to honor that loss, to 'feed' that hole, even if it is just with a brief prayer, some reflection, or simple rituals (e.g., offering our food up before partaking of a meal, sprinkling tobacco on the earth when harvesting plants, etc.). It's the practice of cultivating an attitude of gratitude, a genuine appreciation in receiving the abundance of the natural world - which also turns out to be a key to lasting happiness.

---

[103] Rick Fields, Buddhist scholar, interpreter, and former editor of Yoga Journal, who passed in 1999 at the age of 57 after a five-year dance with lung cancer.

Once we adopt this balanced view of give-and-take between spirit and *mater*, this realistic view of impermanent gains and incremental losses, then the "*grief of being alive*" consummates our love of life and for others. Unit our appreciation of beauty is informed by an equal appreciation of impermanence - our present awareness that this beautiful flower will not always be there, and we ourselves will not remain forever young - we are not fully human, not fully alive, and not capable of a completely satisfying, deep and contented love.

"You have to learn to love somebody as if it is not going to last," Jenkinson says, "because it's not." Hard to argue with that logic! He even goes so far as to counsel that, upon falling in love with someone, we need to fall in love *with their dying* as well - not just to 'accept' the fact that they are going to die, which is only an intellectual construct, but really learn to appreciate it in our hearts as part of the whole cycle of living, loving, aging, and dying that defines us and our relations. It is all of a piece, different petals of the same flower, and it all informs and is informed by our heartfelt grieving as a daily practice of overcoming (and managing!) denial.

How is this striking you? Are you grappling with it in your head, with resistance, or feeling it as a pang in your heart, with knowing acceptance? This is such an important part of honoring Pope Francis' injunction to remember what it means to be human. We humans have not always been so oblivious to the closeness of death. That is a rather recent development, in fact. In the not-too-distant past, it was unusual for all of one's children to make it to adulthood. Life-expectancy on the frontier was not that long - living to 40 was considered an accomplishment. And death was real - people were born and died in the home.

So part of our forgetting how to grieve in general is wrapped up in our buying into some fairy tale that we will all live into our 90s, thanks to the miracles of modern medicine. Premature death is simply not supposed to happen. We really do believe that, don't we? I know I do. And at the same time, I wonder which is more tragic - premature death, or my conviction that it isn't supposed to happen to myself or those I love?

If our love of being alive is rooted in this comfortable illusion that everyone dies, but none of us are ever really close to death, then it's lacking that "grief of being alive:"

> The grief that is for real, the big one, comes from knowing the way life is, that it must be, because life requires death to continue, since death feeds all that lives. The fact that it includes you, that's easy, but to see it as including all that you love and don't want to end -- that's grief, and it's not personal. When you can learn to be grateful for the things that don't benefit you in the least, just for them being in the world, then you are getting somewhere.
> ***
> Grief is not a feeling. Grief is not how you feel, it is what you do. Grief is a skill...

Life requires death to continue, since death feeds all that lives... How hard is it to wrap our minds around that little nugget in this day and age?

The flip side of grief is our capacity for rejoicing and giving praise. Going through each day praising this miracle of life, appreciating all the causes and conditions that have to continually come together and fall apart just for us to continue living (e.g., being grateful for people working on road maintenance rather than cursing the inconvenience - that common sense of entitlement we all have), looking deeply at the suffering in the world by which we profit (e.g., those who make our clothes, harvest our food, built our homes, work in factories, etc.), and reminding ourselves that literally hundreds of species will go extinct today because of the burgeoning human population. *There's* a hole that's hard to fill, though it seems the least we can do is grieve their loss in some small way each and every day, with a promise or prayer perhaps.

Even just considering the human perspective, about 300,000 people will die across the globe today, thousands of them quite unexpectedly, many of them children dying preventable deaths. A day will surely come when we, too, shall pass. As the Buddhist proverb goes, "a tomorrow shall come that does not include you." I can tell you from experience, even people with terminal disease in hospice are invariably surprised when that day comes! All of this roots out the ingrained feelings of exceptionalism we have been conditioned with our whole lives here in the West (esp. America), replacing them with attitudes of gratitude, appreciation, awe, and wonder.

Can we begin to see grief in a more positive light now? Grief + Praise = Love of Life.

His Holiness the Dalai Lama has become a universally beloved public icon because of the effervescent joy, happiness, and loving kindness that he exudes. And yet not a day goes by that he is not grieving the loss of his home land, that he is not painfully aware of the terrible suffering of his people at the hands of the Chinese - the monks and nuns that are tortured in prisons for their basic beliefs, and the rest who are treated as outcasts now in their own ancient cities. His Holiness instructs those who follow his teachings that the essence of Buddhism is preparing for death, and he himself practices dying as part of every meditation session he does. While it is tempting to effectively dismiss this apparent (from the perspective of our conditioning) paradox by thinking "oh, he's enlightened," the fact of the matter is that his joy and good humor in the face of grief and suffering is typical of most, if not all, Tibetan lamas and other Buddhist teachers, regardless of their country of origin. And it is closely related to this daily practice of contemplating the certainty and unpredictability of one's own eventual demise.

Denial of our own mortality is a special case. It's like we all *know* we are going to die, in our heads, but we just don't *believe* it, in our hearts! *And isn't that similar to the way most of us feel about climate chaos now?* Our own mortality is an intellectual construct that, for most, has never dropped down into the heart, so we don't *feel* as if we could, right now, have an undiagnosed terminal disease, or could next week have a fatal accident. Or even that we might die three years from now. Ironically, this robs us of the full experience and joy of living our life today.

Remember the words of our Thai monastic friend? "This glass is already broken. Yet when I learn to appreciate this, every minute I spend with it is precious to me."

It's worth summarizing all this for emphasis: We defer grieving over the daily loss of life and love by avoiding ideas like: everything arises with the seed of its own destruction; death is real and comes without warning; and, we expire a little with every exhalation of breath. We're afraid to admit that this body will be a corpse - "Oh, *morbid*!" - as if we secretly believe that we are really our body. In hospice, I'm always reminding people that only the body dies, and in truth these bodies can be a bit of a nuisance, can't they? We ignore and try to cover up the fact of aging, which is a very slow form of (naturally) dying, a constant decay and sloughing off of dead skin cells, with a diminishing ability to replace them, along with the gradual giving in to gravity. We almost never pause to consider the fact that our bodies are 90% non-human. And we go on living in the fairy tale of this story we are telling ourselves until we are no longer given a choice, until we are face-to-face with death, either our own or the impending death of a loved one...

And by then, as Jenkinson notes, it's too late. We have *all this repressed grief* stored up in our body, the unbearable tension of implicit memory of slowly, but surely, losing our toehold in life, and so when it finally comes it hits us like a tsunami wave. We are overwhelmed by grief. Or, unable to grieve at all, we go into shock. The great Indian pandit Shantideva put it like this:

> *Don't you see how one by one*
> *Death comes to claim your fellow man?*
> *And yet you slumber on so soundly,*
> *Like a buffalo beside its butcher.*

Contrast this experience of living with that of the aforementioned cancer survivor. One of the most impactful meditations we do on week-long Buddhist retreats is imagining our own death - beginning with receiving that diagnosis, imagining the feeling walking back out into the light of day, thinking about who we would tell first, and then moving the story forward in time. Who will take care of us when we're bed-bound? What will it feel like when friends come to visit - and when they leave? And then we imagine the dying process itself. I can tell you, people are always subdued the rest of *that* day of retreat, walking around in sober reflection. But by the end of the retreat, we're all more fully alive than at any other time of the year. Not like buffaloes at all!

I continue to emphasize that the collective terminal diagnosis we are now facing is the end of life *as we know it*. Which, of course, is undeniable. But what if I'm wrong? What if it is more than that? What if Guy McPherson is right that what we're really facing is *near term human extinction* - and there's nothing that can be done about it? If we knew that, would it not serve to awaken our deep compassion for one another? Like New Yorkers in the weeks following the attack on the World Trade Center?

"I wish it need not have happened in my time," said Frodo.
"So do I," said Gandalf, "and so do all who live to see such times. But that

is not for them to decide. All we have to decide is what to do with the time
that is given to us."[104]

It isn't even a question of whether near term human extinction is true or not. Nothing is certain at this point, really. We have to learn to appreciate *all* the risks we are engendering in the world, we have to fathom the magnitude of those risks, and we need to notice and listen to how our hearts are moved by these kinds of thoughts. The thoughts may be just thoughts, but the feelings that arise are real and need to be cultivated if we are to make the best of this predicament.

> The soul of the world is asking
>   each one of us
> to wake up to her beauty and
>   her impermanence…
> And to our own.

Peacocks in the Poison Grove

> *"Grief is the awakening. Grief is the sign of life stirring towards itself."*
> *~ S. Jenkinson*

I think that's my favorite quote from the Grief Walker, because it is so mysterious and deep, like a Zen koan: "What is the sound of life stirring towards itself?" Now let's put this in the context of climate psychology, and processing our natural depression over climate chaos.

Life as we know it is ending. We are day-by-day losing the rich diversity of fish and animals and reptiles and birds and insects and plants that was our rich inheritance. *These are real and quite profound losses…* Just as real as airliners crashing into skyscrapers. In a different dimension of time, perhaps, but also on a much greater scale. Less jarring to our senses, but more permanent. If a person is not saddened by this ongoing unraveling of the web of life, then I tell you - they are as if already dead. We cannot run away from this psychologically anymore. There is no escape. Let us *own* it. There is *wisdom* in 'no escape.' Let us one and all begin grieving these losses today and everyday for the rest of our days on Earth.

We need to take these losses personally, as if they were our own children. Find some pictures of species that have recently gone extinct, like the beautiful Javan tiger, the silly Bubal Hartebeest, the adorable Baiji River Dolphin, and the lovely Ivory-billed Woodpecker. Let us gaze at them, taking them into our hearts until the tears begin to flow over the tragedy of their *permanent* loss. It's surprisingly easy to generate this inter-species compassion when we look into their eyes. When we do this, not only are we enriched by their presence in us, but just as we do with our deceased relatives, keeping them alive in our hearts actually benefits them in some mysterious,

---

[104] Tolkien, 2001:67.

shamanic way. Because just like us, they are not their bodies. Conscious energy does not just cease to exist. It's the law - energy is neither created nor destroyed, it just changes form. And from the quantum worldview, this conscious energy interconnects non-locally (without regard to apparent separation) and non-temporally, across time and space.

We can do the same with those species that are most threatened by climate change, the ones that cry out to us individually, listening intuitively. I visit a local toy store that has shelves filled with realistic figurine animals, and have at one time or another taken home a Polar Bear, a Siberian Tiger, an African Elephant and her baby, an Orangutan, a sea otter, and a seal. I place them on my altar for the purpose of taking them into my meditation practice, believing we're united in, by and through simple awareness. Maybe you're an aquarium lover - think of your fish tank as a proxy for the ocean itself. Designate some of the fish as stand-ins for the big ones that are disappearing. We might even enlist our kids in building a diorama.

These kinds of practices are not meant to be rational, or even *mindful* - they're meant to be emotional, *heartful*. We are sensual creatures, after all, but conditioned in ways that reduce beings to intellectual constructs. In this particular instance, however, 'objectifying' other creatures is fine, taking advantage of our conditioning as a doorway into our own subjective experience. When we look into the eyes of another creature, even in a photograph, there is a *felt sense* of shared awareness. When, while gazing, we consider their suffering, or the injustice of their predicaments - such as polar bears and penguins starving for lack of ice flows and orangutans watching helplessly as their primeval home forests are felled and burned for palm plantations - they become a part of our awareness. We become no longer apart from them.

It's okay to cry. It's what healing looks like. Crying is a form of cleansing - in the sense of releasing emotional blockages. Healing in the sense of expanding our hearts with a greater feeling of wholeness and connection (relations). Like cognitive-based therapy, these kinds of practices change the way we look at 'our' world. They change the way we relate to our loved ones. And yes, they will even begin to change the way we think about food.

Once we begin to open our hearts to the suffering of all sentient beings, not just humans and pets, once we begin to see the connections between our diet and the climate crisis, once we begin to appreciate the devastation that is happening beneath the ocean's waves, naturally we do what we can to alleviate suffering in the world. We may continue to eat meat, but certainly not if it is coming from factory farms. Once we realize that organic farming takes carbon out of the climate, while Agribusiness is creating huge dead zones in the oceans and threatening honey bees and Monarch butterflies, we are going to pay the little bit extra it costs for healthy produce, organic alternatives, and feel good about what we are putting into ours and our children's bodies.

It's much like when we first began learning that cigarettes caused cancer and heart disease. At first, we kept smoking, but it wasn't the same 'cool' experience. We began to see it as a death wish. Over time, we cut back, implored our loved ones to quit, and in a relatively short period of cultural history, smoking went from being glamorized to being tolerated. When I see young kids today smoking cigarettes, I no longer see kids trying to be cool. Instead, I see kids who are too painfully aware of the world they are inheriting, kids who have no spiritual container for that kind of pain, smoking as an "acting out" of our own sociocultural suicidal tendencies. Same with their zombie-emulating fashion sensibilities. Kids are so perceptive.

In all of this processing, we not only remember what it means to be human, we also begin to become lousy consumers, and citizens of the world again - 'active participants' rather than culturally conditioned clones waiting to be exploited by the omnivorous corporate media. We're no longer just thinking of ourselves, we're thinking *for* ourselves (and of others) - awakening to a more sentient existence than we ever thought possible. We are living and loving and grieving in the world, and the easy tears are balanced out by an increasing capacity for joy, an expanding sense of connection and meaning, and ever-widening spheres of compassion and forgiveness.

One of my wise Tibetan teachers once said that in the practice of '*tonglen*' - the counterintuitive meditation where we imagine giving our happiness away in exchange for the suffering of others - we should never be afraid of taking on the suffering of the world. Fo the heart, he said, has an *unlimited* capacity for expanding to accommodate such compassionate care giving. Just as we say that a mother's love knows no bounds. This unlimited open-heartedness, too, is part of the vast expansiveness of the emergent quantum worldview.

> There is nothing to fear…
> Breaking down is just a prelude to
>   breaking through.
> Spiritual emergencies contain the energy
>   of spiritual emergence.
> A broken heart
>   is a broke open heart.
> Grieving is just the other side of loving.

And depression over the end of life as we know it is a healthy response. A humane response. These are the pathways to healing that, if and when they spread like a virus, can lead us through the darkness into the light of a new day.

Has it not always been so? Are these not eternal truths??

Now, as was the case with my artist friend Michael in the wake of 9/11, there is always the risk of overdoing it - we're so achievement-oriented and competitive! We must never forget to remember to have compassion for ourselves as we grow our compassion for others with these kinds of rituals, practices, and spiritual exercises. We can think of this process as a kind of 'emotional homeopathy.' In medicine, homeopathy refers to a system for treating disease by administering minute amounts of a substance that in large amounts actually causes the very disease we are treating. In this case, to avoid the kind of grief and despair that can overtake us when we experience a great loss, we are voluntarily taking on a daily practice of grieving the major losses we are already experiencing in the world. We find we are able to exercising our psychological 'grieving muscles' in a way that not only helps alleviate the flabby dis-ease of despair, but gratefully increases our capacity for love and compassion as well.

Consider the Peacock. The Peacock is nature's vain homeopath. The beautiful colors he utilizes to win the affections of a Peahen are produced by ingesting poisonous plants. Hospice workers deal with grief every day - and not just the incremental kind, either. The longer they do it, the more beautiful they become. In becoming caregivers for Mother Earth, we can think of ourselves as Peacocks in the poison groves. Just as poison deepens the beautiful hue of the Peacock's tail feathers, let the suffering of others and the losses we are now sharing only deepen and strengthen the beauty in our hearts, our love for one another and for all of life, and even our 'love' for the process of death and dying. "Let it begin with me."

Human + Nature = *Human Nature! Surprise!!*

The other side of grieving is loving. The more we grow in our practice of grieving those aspects of the natural world we are rapidly losing, and appreciating the fleeting nature of life *itself*, let alone life as we have always known it, the greater our affinity becomes with the natural world we still have the good fortune to inhabit. That's kinda the payoff. This is why it's so important - and also a *natural byproduct* - to balance out our grieving these losses with practices of enjoying the bounty we have gained through processing our depression and owning our grief. Practices in natural living include gardening, regular nature walks, stargazing, or simply sitting on the earth (it's big!) under a particular tree in our immediate environment. These practices become meditative when we make the simple conscious effort of informing them with quantum worldview, extending our perspective out to include the cosmos, then back in to include our internal ecosystems, then breaking it all down to a whirling fathomless - but *felt* and *sensed* - mass and exchange of energy. These two kinds of practices go hand-in-hand, keep us in balance, and at the same time elevate our consciousness with expansive awareness. It's magical.

We are redeemed by grief, recovering our lost sense of what it means to be human. We cannot help but feel increasingly connected to the natural world once we begin actively grieving what is happening within it's complex web of interconnected life that penetrates right through us. And we find solace there. Surrendering to nature yields the warm embrace of our mother. She holds us close with the immensity of her girth, animates us with her breath, suckles us with her rivers and lakes, nourishes us with the growth from her flesh. The deeper our connection to our own true nature, the greater the affinity we feel with the holistic natural world - the more healing that affectionate, all-encompassing embrace becomes.

It's a relationship, after all. Nourished, it grows - rather like planting the seeds of our own psyche in the receptive Earth. We sink our roots deep down into her fertile soil, we reach way up into her sheltering sky, growing strong, flowering, and bearing fruit.

People who have a negative view of human nature simply haven't spent enough time in nature. I don't have any statistics to back this up, but I suspect that people who spend the most time in nature, or at least have done so at one time or another in their life, are the very people who are most concerned about the climate crisis. At the same time, since this existential spiritual crisis is first and foremost a matter of psyche, it is not necessary to arrange wilderness outbound excursions for 300 million Americans in order to collectively resurrect our true human nature. If it's all interconnected, then that wilderness is 'wild-in-us.' We can feel it stir in us just watching nature films. But if we base our impressions of the world on what we hear from news sources, and what we see falsely labeled as "reality TV," it would be understandable to think humans are, by nature, terrible creatures!

I actually spent a year backpacking overseas in 1991, the year of the first Gulf War. Americans were advised not to travel overseas that year. Even while traveling in the war zone of Kashmir, even encountering soldiers in remote mountain ranges, all I ever encountered was human kindness, concern, and consideration. *Not once* did I encounter hostility. We just don't make the evening news by being kind to one another, and there are literally billions (trillions?) of kind sentiments expressed every day in this world by our fellow human beings.

That is our true nature. Everyone knows this to be true in their heart. As we've pointed out, nobody is traumatized by acts of kindness. We are only traumatized by violence because it goes against our true nature. Let us *celebrate* that human nature in all that we do. Let us build monuments to it, write poetry about it, and create festivals in honor of it. Now more than ever, we need to anoint human nature. If humans are indeed created in the image of the divine, then in human nature we must trust. People have always fought wars over their image of God. I doubt people will fight wars over human nature. Instead, it will serve to unite us around a common cause. For the first time in our history, instead of thinking ourselves as separate - as Americans, Russians, Tibetans, Germans, etc. - by identifying first and foremost with our human nature, by celebrating that nature and our relationship to the natural world, we will finally start to think of ourselves as who and what we really are - natural *Earthlings*.

In a truly global world, as tens of millions of people are displaced from their homes and countries by the capriciousness of climate chaos, as national boundaries and cultural barriers begin to break down themselves, isn't it high time for that 'transnational' awareness to dawn on us?

> *"We are the light hidden within matter*
> *that is being awakened…"*
> *~ Llewellyn Vaughan-Lee*

Acknowledgment =>Awareness => Acceptance => => => *AWAKENING?*

Consistent with this generous view of human nature, we can and must re-establish this renewed connection between humans and our natural world through *cultural* transformation. And it has to happen sooner rather than later. That's the idea behind finding new and meaningful ways of celebrating resurrected human nature. Fortunately, there are real reasons for hope here.

The seeds for this cultural transformation were planted long ago, by the most forward thinkers in our society. The roots from these seeds have already spread far and wide, the crops are flowering, and their fruits are beginning to ripen. What really must happen is that ever more growing numbers of us must join in this redemptive natural feast and start manifesting its flowering fruit in our daily lives.

There is nothing wrong with being skeptical about what I am saying here, and I understand the need for persuasion. So please hear me out. Perhaps the question can be put this way: could it be that we Americans are actually not sinking, but rather *emerging* from this decades-long dysfunctional cultural paradigm of suppression and repression? Might we not be entering into the one stage of grieving that is not susceptible to repression? If this were the case, then what would the clear indications of that societal emergence be? How might we best nurture and advance it?

Consistent with this integral model of climate grief, another way of getting at this question is to ask ourselves *just what is it* that we would become *aware* of at the deepest level of collective consciousness in relation to this, the final stage of collectively grieving the end of life as we have always known it? What is the culmination of the progression in *base level, collective awareness* from: imbalance (ca. 50's and 60's), producing anxiety; to ecological destruction (60's and 70's), giving rise to anger; to existential threat (80's into the 90's), resulting in bargaining; to the carrying out that threat with the Great Dying and the losses associated mass extinction (90's to present), engendering depression? What is it that *acceptance* is giving rise to, or expressing, from the depths of our collective consciousness?

If we were prone to spiritual nihilism, we might be quite justified in concluding that an awareness of the inevitability of near term human extinction is dawning, and we could certainly find evidence for that. The other extreme - spiritual "eternalism" - would support the kind of narrow view associated with Christian prophesy; that is, 777,000 of God's chosen are about to be lifted up to the heavens while the other 7 billion or so (and, presumably, all other sentient beings) are left behind for a massive quake & bake. Neither of these extremes feels very convincing on careful reflection. The middle way, of course, is the much more *natural* (and sensible) conclusion that we are in the process of experiencing anthropocentric regeneration through widespread physical death and spiritual rebirth. Out of spiritual, even cosmic, necessity.

If that is true, then the kind of deep awareness associated with the acceptance stage should be... *awakening*. Not in the traditional Buddhist sense, mind you, but rather something beyond (*trans-*) personal, something *generative* that is capable of seeing us through the adversity we will be increasingly confronted with.

This happens to be consistent with Emerson's natural law of compensation:

> *Our strength grows out of our weakness. The indignation which arms itself with secret forces does not awaken until we are pricked and stung and sorely assailed.*[105]

Here is a modeled depiction of what we are talking about, what we're collectively experiencing, which arose from the depths of a 2014 paper I wrote called *Planetary Hospice*, and was subsequently presented to a very receptive audience of neuroscientists, ecopsychologists, deep ecologists, systems theorists, and educators at an international symposium sponsored by the *Mind & Life Institute* (graphic artwork by Lama AlejAndro Anastasio):

Such an awakening should be evidenced by something new and quite unprecedented dawning in the spectrum of human consciousness -- a new perspective, a different way of seeing ourselves in relation to all that is other. Like radically interpenetrating interconnectivity, perhaps? As part of a world wide web, every one of us like mirrors at the nodes of Indra's Net, reflecting all and one? The breaking down of age-old barriers between self and other, mind and matter? Rather than trying to channel primal awareness here, let us turn to our own cultural *milieu* for clues, since these kinds of new paradigms reliably emerge first in a few individuals or groups who are ahead

---

[105] Ralph Waldo Emerson, *Compensation* (1841).

of their time[106] -- harbingers of what only in retrospect comes to be acknowledged as quantum shifts in human consciousness.

Stanislov Grof is certainly one such extraordinary thinker who has always seemed to be ahead of his time, always seemingly in on the ground floor of seismic shifts in human society. One of the more colorful illustrations is his story about opening a box from Sandoz Laboratories in 1954, while doing his internship in psychiatry, with an enclosed note from Dr. Albert Hoffman that someone really needed to research the extraordinary properties and potential therapeutic applications of the enclosed capsules of LSD-25. Years later, when Grof's continuing research along those lines at John Hopkins in Maryland was shut down by Congress, he moved to an obscure hot springs resort near Big Sur, California called *Esalen,* and helped found the human potential movement of the late 60's. It was Grof who coined the term 'transpersonal psychology,' in conversation with Abraham Maslow and others, creating a new kind of psychology that honored the entire spectrum of human experience, in contrast to the accepted dogma that we are little more than preening egos driven around by our prurient ids.

And so it should come as no surprise that Grof himself, a close student of human nature as well as an early cartographer of altered states of consciousness, was one of the first to point out this new form of human awareness as it began to bubble up from the gnostic depths of our collective psyche. In his 1985 book *Beyond the Brain,* at a time when the existential threat of climate change had just started to appear on the radar screens of prominent scientists, Grof posits as his "central point" that we were just beginning to see "a paradigm shift of unprecedented proportions," a course alteration in human consciousness that was changing "our concepts of reality *and of human nature....*"

What does it mean to be human?

Other visionaries could surely be listed here, not the least of which would be Arne Ness: "The ecosophical outlook is developed through an identification so deep that one's own self is no longer adequately delimited by the personal ego or the organism. One experiences oneself to be a genuine part of all life…" The deep ecology movement also emerged around that same time, tapping into this dawning global awareness of impending threat. As the groundbreaking author Frijof Capra (1995) stated:

> *Deep Ecology is rooted in a perception of reality that goes beyond the scientific framework to an intuitive awareness of the oneness of all life, the interdependence of its multiple manifestations and its cycles of change and transformation. When the concept of the human spirit is understood in this sense, its mode of consciousness in*

---

[106] See, e.g., Bucke, R. 1901. *Cosmic Consciousness: A Study in the Evolution of the Human Mind.* Perhaps the first Western scientist to study this phenomenon, and himself a harbinger of the century to come. As Bucke concluded: "This consciousness shows the cosmos to consist not of dead matter governed by unconscious, rigid, and unintending law; it shows it on the contrary as entirely immaterial, entirely spiritual and entirely alive..." (p. 17).

161

which the individual feels connected to the cosmos as a whole, it becomes clear that ecological awareness is truly spiritual.

However, a watershed event that showed Grof's prediction of a paradigm shift was really starting to take hold was the publishing of Joanna Macy and Molly Young Brown's book *Coming Back to Life: Practices to Reconnect Our Lives, Our World* just before the turn of the new millennium. Macy and Brown for the first time proclaimed a *"silent revolution [in]the ways we see and think and relate."* This silent revolution has only grown in scope and influence ever since, with thousands of people learning to grieve (and love) in Macy's "The Work That Reconnects" workshops, and with a revised edition of that evocative book having recently been published. As Macy put it herself in the introduction to the first edition:

> I imagine that future generations will look back on this period and call it the time of the *'Great Turning.'* **It is the epochal shift from a self-destructive industrial growth society to a life-sustaining society.**

Coming Back to Life noted that the most basic dimension of this Great Turning that the authors were themselves witnessing, in their ongoing work at the cutting edge of this nascent movement, was *"a profound shift in our perception of reality... both as cognitive revolution and spiritual awakening."* In her earlier (1991) book *World as Lover, World as Self,* Macy recognized "the most fascinating and hopeful development of our time... the greening of the self" - or the emergence of a "wider ecological sense of self." A sense of self that emerges, seemingly in direct response to the global crisis, from the woof and warp of quantum physics, transcendental psychology, and deep ecology, and is now maturing into Ecopsychology - or what some have termed (perhaps more accurately) as "Transpersonal Ecosophy" loosely translated as "beyond the self (or ego) lies the wisdom of our home in the world."

This is nothing other than the most basic level of integral awareness welling up from the most subtle level of collective consciousness in response to our own acceptance of the end of life as we know it, thus clearing the way psycho-spiritually to give birth to something entirely new, according to the natural law of compensation. Jung insisted that these compensatory images of wholeness always emerge from the depths of our collective unconscious in response to intolerable states of imbalance and discord. Macy described her own deeply felt sense of this shift in the 1990's as an *'ongoing revelation'* - and indeed she has since carried that work forward into what fellow ecopsychologist Andy Fisher calls *'ever-widening spheres' of meaning and participation.* And it really is spreading across the globe like a virus, fast approaching the critical mass where it will suddenly and silently, without anyone hardly noticing, make that quantum leap from radical new paradigm to accepted world view.

This is the redemptive spirit of climate catharsis that can and must breathe life into the transmutation of the human species if we are to survive in the short term, the next several decades, and thrive in the long term. It is far from an isolated movement, either. For example, this same compensatory spirit gave rise to *The Earth Charter*, a principled expression of shared awakening that points the way forward to "a change of mind and heart... [and] a new sense of global interdependence and universal responsibility." It isn't that the internet is giving rise to this new sense of interconnection, either; instead, it is this new sense of interconnection that made the advent of the internet and all its connective tissues inevitable. The world wide web itself is a manifestation of our collective unconscious, which is why it arose during the exact period that visionaries like Grof and Macy were giving voice to this newly emergent paradigm.

From the world of systems thinking - *yet another* important movement whose seeds were planted in the late 60's - we can look to the prolific Hungarian philosopher of science, systems theorist, and classical pianist Ervin Laszlo, and in particular his prophetic book *The Whispering Pond:*[107]

> The paramount feature of the emerging quasi-total vision of cosmos, matter, life, and mind is subtle and constant interconnection... The current shift in science's concept of the world from a life-less rock to an interconnected and quasi-living universe has intense meaning and significance for our times. The concept of a subtly interconnected world, of a whispering pond in and through which we are intimately linked to each other and to the universe, assimilated by our intellect and embraced by our heart, is part of humanity's response to the challenges that we now face in common. *Our separation from each other and from nature is at the root of many of our problems; overcoming them calls for a recovery of our neglected, but never entirely forgotten, bonds and connections...* The insight that emerges is both meaningful and timely. It confirms psychologist-philosopher William James' image: we are like islands in the sea - separate on the surface, but connected in the deep.

Much more recently, Laszlo took to the virtual whispering pond, commenting in an essay for *The Huffington Post* on this paradigm shift with the following telling statement:

> *The breakout from the old has started already, but it is not yet committed to a breakdown or to a breakthrough... Choosing our future by consciously furthering and steering the burgeoning world shift is the greatest opportunity ever to have been granted a generation in history. It is up to us to seize it -- and ensure the future of humankind on the planet.*

Which sentiment was then echoed in Naomi Klein's important book, *This Changes Everything:"climate change isn't just a disaster. It's also our best chance to demand—and build —a better world."*

Continuing to follow this emergent thread, this global meme, the visionary NGO from Great Britain, *Share The World's Resources,* has proposed a realistic economic model for such a world:

------

[107] (1996) Rockport, MA: Element, pp. 217, 224-25.

If humanity is to survive the formidable challenges that define our generation – including climate change, diminishing fossil fuels and global conflict – it is necessary to forge new ethical understandings that embrace our collective values and global interdependence. We urgently need a new [economic] paradigm for human advancement, beginning with a fundamental reordering of world priorities: an immediate end to hunger, the securing of universal basic needs, and a rapid safeguarding of the environment and atmosphere. No longer can national self-interest, international competition and excessive commercialization form the foundation of our global economic framework.

The crucial first step towards creating an inclusive world system requires overhauling our outdated assumptions about human nature, reconnecting our public life with fundamental values, and rethinking the role of markets in achieving the common good. In line with what we now know about human behavior and psychology, integrating the principle of sharing into our economic system would reflect our global unity and have far-reaching implications for how we distribute and consume the planet's wealth and resources. Sharing the world's resources more equitably can allow us to build a more sustainable, cooperative and inclusive global economy – one that reflects and supports what it really means to be human.[108]

There it is again! The question of what it means to be human… like an echo on the whispering pond, rippling out in concentric waves no matter where you start from. Economists, religious leaders, scientists, systems theorists, ecopsychologists, ecophilosophers - all asking the same fundamental question. What is human nature?

Does all this not point to a profound awakening taking place in human consciousness?

This is precisely the kind of constructive energy that can be released when an individual has processed through their emotions to the point of accepting the reality of the situation we face, and reconnecting at a very personal level with the natural world - where we once again embody in heart and mind our true human nature. That's the payoff. Is this not the kind of ever-widening sphere of meaning and participation that we all long to be part of? It begins with the simple acknowledgment from quantum physics that Descartes and Freud could not have been more wrong - we are relations, not objects; referent points, not isolated egos; spiritual, not jumbled masses of instincts. Jung and Pauli were right, after all - we are part of a vast, meaning-filled collective continuum of unconscious inter-being, or *unus mundus;* and as the Nobel Laureate observed this *"unconscious is in both man and nature…"*

The growing solidarity movement between humans and animals is a more current example of this collective spiritual awakening -- we're not just awakening to a shared awareness amongst

---

[108] *Rethinking the Global Economy: The Case for Sharing* (Rajesh Makwana and Adam Parsons, 2010).

ourselves, but thanks to compassionate harbingers like Jane Goodall, Peter Singer, and Geshe Thubten Phelgye, founder of the Universal Compassion Movement, we're starting to relate to animals in a whole new way. One in every ten American's now consider themselves to be 'mostly vegetarian,' *one in eight* Brits are now vegetarians, and veganism is not just another fad with Sir Paul McCartney as its spokesperson - it's a fast-growing subculture, especially among the millennials who are probably the least in denial about the import of the climate crisis.

All of this, of course, relates back to the emerging consciousness of our deep interdependence. It's not just a meme. It's more like an emerging new world religion. A kind of religious thinking that unites people (and animals and nature) rather than dividing us. And it is taking root.

Calling All Quantum Activists!

So there is plenty of evidence to support this idea that we are starting to transition into the acceptance stage of grieving over the loss of life as we know it on planet Earth, and that a new, adaptive kind of awareness is emerging, one that will sustain us through what promises to be a most difficult era of mass mortality, migration, and dislocation - an uncommon era that is well underway now, though we are just beginning to recognize it. There is one other critical conscious shift that needs to be addressed to fortify us against the demons of despair, and it has to do with the complicated issue of *just how to re-organize ourselves* as a newly emerging sociocultural force in a time of incredible strife, chaos, and growing corporate/state oppression. After all, the Great Unraveling and the Great Turning are unfolding simultaneously - things are bound to get quite messy before a new order takes hold.

While it has not received nearly the attention and recognition that it deserves - a common feature of any idea that is slightly ahead of its time - Margaret Wheatley has hit on a really vital systems theory in her books *Leadership and the New Science: Learning about Organization from an Orderly Universe*, and *A Simpler Way* (co-authored with Myron Kellner-Rogers). This may seem kind of wonky for the present book, but I think it's important enough to risk a little reproof.

Wheatley sees our organizational thinking as still being stuck in the Newtonian mechanical world view of linear causes and effects, with all the associated spatial and temporal limitations. Anyone who has suffered in a corporate cubicle knows exactly what I'm talking about. But history reveals that compelling ideas and myths tend to emerge simultaneously, without such logical, hierarchal connections. By cleverly looking to quantum mechanics for clues about how change actually transpires at a human scale, similar to Prigogene's theory that we explored earlier, Wheatley has identified a non-linear, non-obstuctive organizing principle that she calls **'boundaryless' organization**:

> Acting locally allows us to work with the movement and flow of simultaneous events within [a] small system. We are more likely to become synchronized with that system, and thus to have an impact. *These changes in small places, however,*

create large-systems change, not because they build one upon the other, but because they share the unbroken wholeness that has united them all along.

[excuse me for interjecting here, but that is some radical thinking!]

Our activities in one part of the whole create non-local causes that emerge far from us. There is value in working with the system *any place it manifests* because unseen connections will create effects at a distance, in places we never thought. This model of change - of small starts, surprises, unseen connections, quantum leaps - matches our experience more closely than our favored models of incremental change.

That certainly seems increasingly characteristic of our times. As ecopsychologist Betsy Barnum concludes in reference to Wheatley's innovative thinking:

I see this as a description of how change within *even a single person* who adjusts her life and energy to the flow of the Universe, and begins to live according to and in sync with the Universe's inherent pattern of order, can have impact *way beyond* the incremental notion of influencing those directly in contact with her. And then when more people join together in connection with each other and with the connecting fields around them, the incremental increases in people working in sync with the flow of universal energy greatly increases the potential power of possible non-local impacts.

This is my inspiration for building a planetary hospice movement over time, as our situation becomes more dire. Apart from modeling collective climate grief, there's nothing really all that new in this book. In fact, your author here is a bit of a late-comer to this growing eco-spiritual movement. I do seem to have a different take on the psychology of the climate crisis that seems to have struck a chord that resonates with others around the world, others who happen to share my own sense of this same emergent, growing awareness. Awareness is the water of the whispering pond in which we are swimming, a relational awakening that transcends any one of the millions of individuals who have felt it growing in them. As Joseph Campbell would say, were he still around, it is both *immanent* and *transcendent*.

Carl Jung noted, toward the end of his own life, that in the end, "it is a moral question" whether a person applies what they have learned or not." Our moral imperative, our strongest intention, must be to do *whatever we can* to help alleviate the suffering that is going on int the world right now, and that will no doubt continue to be fomented by climate chaos. We can and will be inspired by others engaging in similarly constructive efforts, and we will continue to build virtual networks that inspire others to do their *own* part in their *own* creative ways, working within their *own* communities and social networks. I would suggest that anyone reading this book either start or join a *Climate Club* in their community to help support processing and coming together over the climate crisis. We can have faith that the "unbroken wholeness" revealed culturally by all these related, compassionate activities will crystallize one day into the kind of social catharsis that, even under the greatest adversities, will have the combined effect to transmute our species into an ever more caring, ever more cooperative, conscientious and loving community of survivors on this nurturing planet we hold so dear in our hearts.

That is the hopeful vision of the Anthropocene we must share. Especially given our privileged status relative to all the suffering that is being unleashed in the world, we are morally obliged to be optimists. And we have all the good reasoning we need to maintain that optimistic, long-term perspective. As the wise Indian pandit Satyananda Saraswat said:

> Transformation comes not from discussing our problems and looking for alleged culprits. ***Transformation is only possible if a critical mass of people make the leap from unconsciousness to awareness.*** If we – you and me – ask ourselves what part we are playing in any present problem.

What part will you play?

Made in the USA
San Bernardino, CA
26 September 2017